Keith Abnett served in the Fleet Air Arm (FAA) from 1961 until 1985, initially as an artificer apprentice reaching the rank of Aircraft Engineering Warrant Officer. He was predominately part of the 'fixed wing' element (Sea Vixens, Phantoms and Sea Harriers) maintaining and managing in a variety of engineering capacities. He led the team that maintained the helicopters flown by HRH Prince of Wales, now King Charles III, whilst in the RN. Keith served on five different aircraft carrier types: HMS Ark Royal, Bulwark, Hermes, Illustrious and the mighty 'Sara', the USS Saratoga. From a young age and following retirement from the FAA, he has keenly studied both the historical and future developments of the UK's Naval Air Service.

This Book is dedicated to…

To all those who have served in the Fleet Air Arm, both past and present.

To those who toiled resolutely without complaint, through blood, sweat and tears in the hangar, on the flight deck or ashore, in getting aircraft ready for flying.

I would like to pay my respect and admiration to all Royal Navy fliers, who repeatedly took off and landed on to a tossing and turning piece of metal, the size of a postage stamp. They did this in all weather conditions, day and night, war and peace.

This respect extends to all those fellow colleagues, who I have worked alongside throughout my career in the Fleet Air Arm.

Finally, I humbly salute all those who lost their lives whilst serving in the Fleet Air Arm in whatever capacity.

Keith Abnett

THE FLEET AIR ARM

The Cinderella Airforce with
the RAF as the Ugly Sisters

AUSTIN MACAULEY PUBLISHERS®
LONDON * CAMBRIDGE * NEW YORK * SHARJAH

Copyright © Keith Abnett 2024

The right of Keith Abnett to be identified as the author of this work has been asserted by the author in accordance with sections 77 and 78 of the Copyright, Designs and Patents Act 1988.

All rights reserved. No part of this publication may be reproduced, stored in a retrieval system, or transmitted in any form or by any means, electronic, mechanical, photocopying, recording, or otherwise, without the prior permission of the publishers.

Any person who commits any unauthorised act in relation to this publication may be liable to criminal prosecution and civil claims for damages.

The story, experiences, and words are the author's alone.

A CIP catalogue record for this title is available from the British Library.

ISBN 9781398488298 (Paperback)
ISBN 9781398498068 (ePub e-book)

www.austinmacauley.com

First Published 2024
Austin Macauley Publishers Ltd®
1 Canada Square
Canary Wharf
London
E14 5AA

To gather information, stories and advice on how to approach the subject matter of this book required contributions from many people. I am grateful for the recollections and the time given by many of my fellow compatriots with whom I served in the Fleet Air Arm. This includes several pilots and observers I knew back in the 1960s and '70s.

My specific thanks go to the following, 'Ed' Cole, 'Fritz' Heritier, Bob Mason, 'Al' Slater, 'Rob' Shadbolt and Stuart Wakefield, who gave details of experiences they encountered during their service careers. They also jogged my memory and corrected me on some of the facts.

I am indebted to Paul 'Wiggy' Bennett, who although started his naval career as a 'Tiffy' in 1961 with myself, eventually became a fixed wing pilot in the FAA followed by a distinguished career in civil aviation. His contribution in Chapter 14 is enlightening, as he aptly describes his flying of the Sea Vixen with a mixture of humour and a 'matter of fact' genre. His contribution reflects the stress and strains, which a Navy pilot undergoes, when operating from an aircraft carrier.

To help the book's content from a historical and somewhat proofreading angle, I have to thank Terry Bullingham, who again join up with me 1961. He was an ex-Electrical Artificer (Air) in the Fleet Air Arm. His feedback was especially invaluable because Terry is blind as a result of the Falklands War back in 1982.

He had the necessary technology to convert my written words into speech, which gave him the advantage of hearing whether my writing flowed or otherwise, and hopefully avoided any gobbledygook.

I spoke to many senior naval officers throughout my service career with the FAA and more recently during the research for this book. I have also kept up to date via many reunions, Taranto dinners, especially the guest speakers where they gave me their thoughts and suggestions, along with correcting some of my pre-conceived ideas.

These include Bill Covington, and Steve George. I commissioned the latter to draw on my behalf, several amusing cartoons, which can be seen in Chapter 14 entitled 'Different Animals'. I thank them all for their advice.

Lastly, a deep gratitude goes to my other half, Carol, who has shown enduring patience and given valuable help during the initial proof reads. She had to deal and straighten out some of my erratic English and thought processes. Carol is somewhat in awe of the FAA and what it achieved. Morecambe and Wise once joked that although the musical notes they played were right, they were not necessarily in the right order. The same analogy applies to my writing, they are the right words but not necessarily in the right order!

Finally, I must thank the author Steve Bond the author of the Fleet Air Arm series of books for his input, guidance and advice. It was greatly appreciated.

During my research for this book, there were many contradictions on some of the points I was basing my findings. On one occasion, there were five different accounts of a bravery award given for the same action. Matters were further confused when these awards were attributed to different recipients. Any shortcomings or omissions in this book are mine and mine alone. Also, the opinions and conclusions contained in the various chapters are again all mine. Should I ever be fortunate to get a revised follow-up version published, any errors or omissions will be duly corrected.

Table of Contents

Ex Quaestione Veritas	13
Preface	15
Chapter 1: Introduction	19
Chapter 2: The Interwar Years (1918–1939)	29
Chapter 3: Sinking of the Graf Spee and Bismarck, 1939	37
Chapter 4: FAA in the Mediterranean 1940–41	46
Chapter 5: FAA's Pacific War – January 1945 to August 1945	60
Chapter 6: Korean War 1950–1953	71
Chapter 7: SUEZ – 1956	80
Chapter 8: The Middle East – 1958 to 1960	87
Chapter 9: The 1960s – The Defining Decade for the FAA's Future	91
Chapter 10: Fleet Air Arm – Success May 1969 (With Help from the RAF)	103
Chapter 11: Falklands Naval Air War 1982	111
Chapter 12: The Joint Force Harrier Fiasco	124
Chapter 13: The Lockheed Lightning II F35B Saga	134
Chapter 14: The FAA's Unsung Helicopter Boys	154
Chapter 15: Very Different Animals – FAA vs RAF culture	174
Chapter 16: Brave Exploits, Service and Sacrifices	196
Chapter 17: Fleet Air Arm Squadrons – Numbering	220

Chapter 18: Fleet Air Arm's Timeline of Actions Since 1945   233

Chapter 19: Summary   257

Bibliography   271

Glossary   274

Fleet Air Arm Battle Honours

1939	River Plate	1941–45	Arctic
1939–45	English Channel	1942–45	Malaya
1939–45	North Sea	1942–43	North Africa
1939–45	Atlantic	1942	Diego Suarez
1939–45	Norway	1943	Sicily
1940	Dunkirk	1943	Salerno
1940	Narvik	1943–44	Aegean
1940–45	Dunkirk	1944	Normandy
1940–45	East Indies	1944	Sanbang
1940–45	Mediterranean	1944–45	Burma
1940	Calabria	1944	South France
1940–42	Libya	1945	Palembang
1940	Taranto	1945	Okinawa
1940–45	Biscay	1945	Japan
1940	Spartivento	1950–53	Korea
1941–42	Malta Convoys	1982	Falkland Islands
1941	Matapan	1991	Kuwait
1941	Bismarck	2003	Al Faw
1941	Crete		

Ex Quaestione Veritas

778 Naval Air Squadron's Motto:

"From examination, truth emerges"

Preface

I spent some 24 years happily serving in the Fleet Air Arm. My role centred on the fact that whilst naval aircrew tended to 'bend' the aircraft, my job was to 'mend' them and get them back into the air ASAP. Some may think this role was a passive one but nothing could be further from the truth. Even before joining, I was always attracted to the FAA and knew a fair amount about its history and also its place in the history of both the Royal Navy and the UK.

Perhaps I should blame an uncle because he was an avid FAA fan and owned loads of post-World War II magazines, which I duly read along with stories of FAA's exploits and 'derring-do'. As a teenager, he observed during the Second World War, the build-up of the FAA, especially the assembly of the Pacific Fleet in 1944–45.

During a career in the FAA and experiencing flying operations both ashore and afloat, I kept myself discretely in the background absorbing everything that was going on around me. This included reading extensively military and political articles, magazines about defence and where the FAA fitted into the scheme of things.

Being on squadrons both ashore and afloat one knew fairly well from 'Daily Orders', flying and ship's programmes etc. what was going on. I also had first-hand knowledge of the aircraft serviceability rates, sortie rates and in what roles the aircraft were being operated.

On the engineering side, one knew what weapons and types were being carried and if they were effective, just by the serviceability rates, plus feedback from aircrew. This naturally led to an understanding of the aircraft being operated and their plus and minus points, especially their limitations.

It was natural to observe what other squadrons were doing and getting a pretty good idea how they were operating. Without even consciously trying, you got a feel of the outfit you were on or the squadron working alongside both ashore and at sea. You could reasonably judge how effective they were.

This background understanding and experience, which one instinctively knew, applied to both fixed-wing and rotary wing squadrons ranging from Sea Vixens, Phantoms, Buccaneers, Sea Harriers, anti-submarine Sea Kings, Wasps, Wessex 3s and Lynxes, the 'Junglies' (Wessex 5 Commando helicopter squadrons).

This also included the humble, but important role carried out by the Gannet Airborne Early Warning (AEW 3). By default, as I served on many, I was able to compare how good the flight deck operations were across a number of ships. All this came about by just being there.

Throughout my career, I was equally able to judge pilots and aircrews, witness the pressures they were under, watch the stress and strains that flying put them under. This was much more pronounced when at sea and especially during night flying sorties.

This strain was frequently etched into their faces. Throughout my service, I did my utmost to alleviate the stress of pilots, no matter how good they were or otherwise, even when receiving and absorbing unnecessary rollickings!

The purpose of this book, originally, was to write about the FAA from a different angle and try to highlight little known achievements and its history, which normally does not get into print. The chapter on the FAA's timeline was an amalgamation of at least a dozen sources in an effort to hopefully make the general public more aware of the range and scope of what the FAA did.

Most of the contents of this particular chapter never made the press. As I delved with my research into the FAA's history on areas I knew little about, an awakening took place. Running in parallel with this background research, a sense of realisation began to appear, which is shared by many former colleagues I served with. We collectively thought the FAA always seemed to get the rough end of the stick in comparison with those who wore the light blue uniform i.e. the Royal Air Force.

I wish to state clearly at this stage, I have the utmost admiration for those who fly for the RAF ably supported by a cadre of highly professional technical and background personnel. The problem I unearthed is a cultural one, which has been historically nurtured by those at the highest echelons of that service.

The contents of this book and comments contained within it have been collected over the last 60 years or so, based on comments and opinions from many of my colleagues, memoirs/stories by numerous former pilots, defence papers and books by prominent military experts on naval aviation.

This collection also refers to the vast source of information available on the Internet. It also includes, of course, my direct involvement of having served in the Fleet Air Arm from 1961 until 1985. I was predominately part of the 'fixed wing' element of the FAA maintaining, and then managing technicians in a variety of engineering capacities, including a minor staff job on Flag Office Naval Air Command (FONAC).

This work and experience covered a variety of aircraft types and squadrons i.e. Sea Vixens, Phantoms and then the Sea Harrier. Along with these aircraft types, I also had the privilege of serving on five different aircraft carriers: HMS Ark Royal, Bulwark, Hermes, Illustrious and the mighty 'Sara', the USS Saratoga.

Although earmarked for a ship's flight operating a Wessex 3, this move was rapidly changed to bringing out of reserve, HMS Bulwark. The subsequent stint on HMS Bulwark was as part of the ship's company for over 2 years as the 'Chief Tiff' in charge of the ship's aircraft engineering workshops. This was when she was configured as an anti-submarine platform carrying Sea Kings – assisting NATO to plug the Iceland/Faroes/Greenland gap against the Soviet submarine threat in the 1970s.

Lastly, I had the privilege of also being the 'Chief Tiff' of Red Dragon Flight when HRH Prince of Wales, now King Charles III, who flew the Wessex Mk 5 with the FAA, flying under 'Royal Flight' safety rules. The Flight was to go on HMS Hermes in her commando role with NAS 845 in 1975, where an interesting Western Atlantic trip was undertaken airlifting 45 RM Commando around.

I became by default and therefore part of a cog (albeit a small one), in the diverse operation of both shore and seagoing naval activities. This participation ranged from serving on genuine 'strike carriers' with the hustle and bustle of 'cats and traps' on both HMS Ark Royal and the USS Saratoga, to the more relatively genteel use of STOVL aircraft with ski-jumps and recovery operations of HMS Illustrious.

A brief period was served on the 'Lusty' (HMS Illustrious) with 899 Naval Air Squadron operating Sea Harriers following her return to the UK after the Falklands conflict i.e. Operation Corporate. Incidentally, it was here that when compared to my early days experience of strike carrier operations, there was a noticeable reduction in flight deck 'tensions' with ski-jump operations e.g. with those experienced-on HMS Ark Royal et al. Pilots might not agree with that statement because operating from an aircraft carrier or small ship is a highly dangerous business.

Throughout that career, I was unaware until the later part of my service, of the perpetual and uneven battles being fought by the Royal Navy and its Naval Air Staff against the historic influence exerted by the RAF on the UK's defence policies and equipment procurements. On becoming an Engineering Warrant Officer, I became much more involved with Commanding Officers and included in some of 'behind closed door' briefings.

It was only then an appreciation developed on what battles the higher echelons of the FAA's Air Staff had to face with MOD in London and military politics. It recently dawned upon me how much the RAF appeared to have a sway over politicians and compliant MOD civil servants in the procurement of equipment i.e. aircraft that flew off aircraft carriers. There has been since then a revelation that this has not only occurred historically but continues to this very day.

Now, some 30 years later with the reading of many articles and keeping abreast on what has actually happened to the FAA since leaving in the mid '80s, this enlightenment has expanded. One area, which has been ignored over the last decade, is the introduction of the new Lockheed Lightning II F35B aircraft and the two new Queen Elizabeth class of aircraft carrier.

It has been painful to watch the subsuming and absorption of the UK's naval air arm into a predominately land-based force. No other country in the world has allowed this to happen. The writing is on the wall for fixed wing flying under the control of RN. Whether this is by stealth and/or subterfuge by the RAF remains to be seen.

Entering the Royal Navy's air arm some 60 years ago, I knew without a shadow of a doubt that I was joining an elite and effective force, who despite the setbacks it received, punched its way; well above its 'weight'. Being relatively small, it was also a very cost-*effective* force whether in monetary terms or the huge tasks it was asked to carry out with limited resources.

It was also subject to a lot of political/military chicanery. This book is my attempt to try and put the record straight and bring to the reader a wider appreciation of some of the achievements of the Fleet Air Arm over its 100-year plus history.

Chapter 1
Introduction

First and foremost, the Fleet Air Arm is the Royal Navy's maritime aviation air force, covering both its fixed and rotary wing elements.

Originally, it was my intention to start in the 1950s as this period was during my early formative teenage years; it was when I began to become reasonably familiar and interested in aircraft and aviation. However, my research over the last two years has revealed a creeping awareness of the disparity in influence, quality and type of aircraft flown by the Royal Air Force over those of the Fleet Air Arm (FAA).

This disparity was well established by the 1930s. Further investigation and delving into the reference books, I discovered that this trend went even further back. I, therefore, widened the scope and decided to go back further to the end of the First World War. It seems incredible now that the bulk transfer of the Royal Naval Air Service to establish the formation of the RAF in 1918 was to have repercussions for the FAA, which was to reverberate for many decades.

Development of naval aviation was to be curtailed for some 20 years or more from that date. From the end of WWI onwards, there were no real or serious thoughts directed towards the naval air warfare requirements at sea until 1940. It is well known that the FAA was appallingly equipped at the beginning of the WWII.

Whilst the Fairey Swordfish did sterling work and caused devastation to the Italian Fleet at Taranto, it could hardly be compared to Mitchell's Spitfire or Sidney Cam's Hurricane. It was pretty obvious where all the R and D money for British aviation was going, hence the use of the term 'Cinderella' in the book title. This aptly describes the treatment of the FAA throughout its long existence up to the present day.

During the latter part of the Second World War, the Fleet Air Arm, once it became re-equipped with specifically designed carrier borne aircraft (of predominately US design), only then did it became an increasing cost-effective potent force. This recovery was aided and abetted by the building of armoured flight decks on British aircraft carriers.

On the public relations front, during WWII it was cleverly orchestrated and then further honed following the Battle of Britain in which 'Johnny' Johnson, Eric Lock, Douglas Bader and its fighter pilots et el, became household names. Naturally, a myth was allowed to develop, which was also to include Guy Gibson (CO of Dambusters 617 squadron fame).

As part of WWII propaganda, the wartime Air Ministry PR machine was able to steer these aforementioned pilots towards being given film star status. Guy Gibson was to tour the American continent following the Dambuster raid. These exploits, which occurred over 80 years ago, continue to this very day to be repeatedly espoused at every opportunity to those, who attend annual air shows in the UK, can attest to.

The RAF is lucky to be able to visually promote its WWII history with the twin-prong approach of the Red Arrows, the aerobatic team of 10 aircraft and the Battle of Britain Memorial Flight consisting of 12 aircraft. At one stage this number exceeded the number of the new F35B Lightning II aircraft on the RAF books in 2022.

It is sad to note, but that the general public can't readily name the COs of the FAA squadrons on the successful Taranto raid and destruction of the potent Italian Mediterranean fleet in 1940? Or, what Naval Squadron torpedoed and crippled the Bismarck or the Victoria Cross awarded to the FAA pilot trying to stop the 'Channel dash' of the battlecruisers Scharnhorst and Gneisenau in 1942? Were the public aware that a FAA pilot was the last serviceman to be killed in WW II or that the FAA flew Lancasters with 780 NAS from March 1946?

Whilst it was understandable during the dark days of WWII for propaganda purposes, this myth of defending the homeland and then flattening Germany's civilian centre of population was part and parcel of the war effort in 1939–45. On the latter point regarding bombing, modern day analysts questioned the cost effectiveness of this policy when nearly 50,000 bomber crews sadly lost their lives on top of the thousands of civilians killed in those raids.

On the former, it is clearly recognised by eminent military historians that it was the Royal Navy that prevented the invasion of Britain from 1940 onwards.

In other words, the 'Battle of Britain' was not the 'Battle for Britain' as has been portrayed. Whilst recognising the bravery and sacrifice of the pilots who fought in that battle over the skies of Kent and SE England etc. Britain had all the advantages of fighting from its home base with respect to logistics, fuel, quick turn rounds and having the obvious benefit of playing at 'home'.

The RAF had the ability of being able to stay on combat stations for longer periods than the Luftwaffe. Rarely mentioned is the fact that the FAA provided some 56 pilots, manning two Navy squadrons, namely 804 and 808 Naval Air Squadrons. Many others were embedded into air force squadrons and all these Navy pilots flew alongside the RAF during the Battle of Britain.

Neither is it widely known that the British Pacific Fleet in January 1945 was the largest collection of Royal Navy ships put together by Great Britain since the battle of Trafalgar, some 140 years earlier. This Far East fleet was to consist of six aircraft carriers; battleships and escorts whereby 200 plus aircraft from this Carrier Air Group flattened two heavily defended oil refineries at Palembang in Sumatra.

It was a significant achievement by the FAA, especially as some 50 B-29s Superfortresses had failed to inflict any real damage in an earlier raid. I have formed the impression gathered from the many books written by former Navy pilots involved at the time that perhaps the raid on Palembang might have been the more appropriate battle honour to be celebrated annually rather than the Taranto raid in 1941.

Nearly every major air defence policy decision on aircraft procurements since the 1950s has been predominately dictated by inter-service rivalry. This rivalry has duly been accepted with relatively little questioning by politicians, or the higher echelons of MOD, Government and the Civil Service.

Politicians have also been guilty of aiding and abetting this rivalry, which has been on many occasions detrimental for the FAA. It is noticeable that nobody has ever been able to solve this competitive and destructive rivalry between all three services, which continues to this very day.

One early post-war example of this rivalry, despite having nearly identical requirements, was clash of the RAF's specifications of the Gloster Javelin over those requirements of the FAA with respect to the De-Havilland DH110 (Sea Vixen). The latter eventually proving to be a much better aircraft and achieved greater longevity (the Vixen was retired too early and even a Vixen Mk 3 supersonic version was on the drawing boards).

Also, the RAF did not consider use of the Blackburn Buccaneer in order to protect its Tactical Strike and Reconnaissance 2 aircraft – the TSR2 project. Incidentally, the first TSR1 was the designation for the Fairey Swordfish, albeit the letter 'T' stood for torpedo! Ironically, the RAF eventually were to get the Buccaneer after inheriting the FAA's Mk 2 versions following the demise of the strike carrier HMS Ark Royal in 1978.

Subsequently, this aircraft was to be successfully used in a combat role during the first Desert Storm operation. Initially, it was used as a laser target designator whereby Tornados could then drop their laser-guided pathway ordnance. On several occasions, the Buccaneers were not only able to do the laser designating, but also capable dropping their own bombs.

This aircraft became a firm favourite with all the RAF crews who flew it, who in turn wanted to develop it further. However, it should be remembered that it was specifically designed as a low level transonic Naval bomber and the Mk2 version probably became the most successful post-war aircraft for the FAA.

It is a pity the RAF did not have this aircraft right from the start when it entered service in the 1960s. This would have ensured a cost-effective production run for Blackburn and undoubtedly led to far greater export sales.

Copy of the air cover map in March 1969 – Courtesy of Air Pictorial

The RAF convinced the Government of the day in the mid-1960s by producing and presenting a map of the world, showing they could provide land base air cover for RN and British military assets anywhere in the world under their 'island base' hopping strategy. Inexplicably on this map, Australia was seen to be some 400 miles further west.

However, the map was fairly accurate enough in respect to showing how far the Falkland Islands were away from any land base island air cover. Even the map published by Air Pictorial-see the 'Spot the Gaps' map opposite, showed this was nigh on impossible.

This gap was to become a major headache for military planners in a conflict that was to occur some 20 years later. On the other hand, the conflict in 1982 covering such vast distances may have been the catalyst for the eventual consideration for the resurrection of large aircraft carriers to equip the RN a generation later.

The battle and outcomes for the UK's new strike aircraft carrier programme of the CVA class namely the CVA01 (plus another – CVA02) was once again based on classic inter service rivalry. The demise of the Britain's strike carrier capability was driven by the then Labour Defence Minister Dennis Healey, who may have inflamed this rivalry.

The RAF was desperate to protect their share of the ever-reducing defence budget of the 1960s and funding for the TSR2 aircraft in pursuance of their land-*based* air power island hopping theory. Ironically, this aircraft was subsequently to be cancelled and the air force switched its concentration to the procurement of a UK version of the American F-111. The General Dynamics F111 (K) swing wing aircraft never came to fruition either.

Once again, it should be noted here that during many of the Operation 'Herrick'(s), (the formal name of the operations that took place in Afghanistan), were at times predominately Naval executed operations i.e. the FAA's Harriers GR7/9s provided fixed wing strike cover with Naval helicopters transporting and giving logistical support to the Royal Marine Commandos against the Taliban and insurgents etc. (The Naval contingent of the Joint Harrier Force was made of elements from 800, 801 Naval Air Squadrons along with the Commandos helicopter squadrons made up of 845, 846 and 847 Naval Air Squadrons carrying the Royal Marines into combat with their Sea Kings and then subsequently resupplying them).

Following the withdrawal from Iraq and Afghanistan, coupled with the reduction and recall of RAF squadrons based in Germany plus the return to its UK bases en-masse, serious questions were being asked of the junior service. When the era of the austerity circa 2010 began to bite in the UK, the question being asked by many military experts saying, would it not be sensible at this point to review the role of the UK's air force?

There were some interesting articles and comments along with a thought-provoking programme by the Daily Mail's feature writer Quentin Letts, "*What is the purpose of the RAF?*" There was a feeling at the time that the RAF was very perturbed by the public's perception and perhaps realised it may have been under existential threat.

Coming forward, it is probably a safe bet that the general public were totally unaware of the long-term consequences of the decision to downgrade the new Queen Elizabeth class aircraft carriers from a genuine US style strike carrier to a humbler STOVL platform utilising a flight deck with a ski-jump. This decision suited the RAF as the QE carriers now have a totally different type of embarked aircraft from the one originally envisaged.

Instead of getting a true carrier strike version in the shape of the Lockheed Lightning II F35C designed for catapult launches and arrestor wire landings, the FAA got the STOVL version i.e. F35B, but they would be subsumed under RAF command control and bizarrely, ownership. MOD and the Government had agreed that the RAF were going to own and command these new 5th generation aircraft, thus ignoring history and having no maritime carrier expertise.

In order to facilitate this ownership, a multi-million-*pound* building and infrastructures upgrade was to be spent at an air force base in East Anglia, which has no historical or traditional links with the Royal Navy. Furthermore, a famous land base squadron of long standing was going to lead and be the first to operate from Britain's new large aircraft carrier(s). An exciting new venture for them, albeit a rather puzzling decision and potential dilemma, as no other government in the world has deemed it fit to replicate this arrangement.

However, this arrangement is not unique because the British Army also has a chunk of its air assets owned and operationally controlled by another service. This, of course, refers to the heavy lift helicopter squadrons in the guise of the Chinook now within the Joint Helicopter Force but still owned and operated by the RAF. One can only guess at the uproar had the US Navy and Marines allowed the USAF to dictate the introduction of a new carrier borne aircraft.

The UK's initial order for the F35 was 138, with the first batch of 48 manufactured as the F35B VSTOL type. As of early 2021, arguments continue to take place over how many more F35Bs are required to sustain two carriers, or just one on a war footing, temporary or otherwise. There was conjecture that the RAF was seeking to have the balance of the remaining order converted to the F35As, which is a slightly cheaper land base version, but cannot be used at sea.

However, the latest Integrated Defence Review March 2021, has led to speculation that UK's number of F35Bs will remain at 48. There may be an extra dozen procured above this figure to take in account any future losses via accidents etc.

Another driving force for this article is the question on whether the British taxpayer got (or gets) value for money or will do in the future? Throughout the building of the two Queen Elizabeth class aircraft carriers, there has been constant criticism of their cost. They represent approximately £6Bn of defence expenditure.

It should be noted, that these figures pale into insignificance when compared to the procurement and the money spent on the Tornado (£32Bn), Typhoon (£50Bn), the new Maritime aircraft P8-Poseidon (£9Bn) and now the Tempest project initially costing some £2Bn. The latter's costs, as history has repeatedly shown, will invariably rise exponentially.

All the above have, over the last 50 years, cost billions; the question to be asked – has this expenditure been worth the money? My opinion and research has revealed a glaring weakness i.e. the UK's MOD has no robust mechanism, or objective feedback on any 'checks and balances' for its defence spending. The latest example of the UK's shambolic procurement procedures, centres on the potential cancelling of the Army's £3.2Bn AJAX tank project.

Since the 1930s and before, nearly every air defence policy decision(s) aircraft procurement and their use have predominately leaned towards the requirements of the junior service i.e. the RAF. There have been virtually no serious challenges on the cost effectiveness of these decisions made right across the defence community, or feedback based on historical economic facts.

This includes all the higher echelons of the Government, Defence Ministers, MPs, MOD, the Armed Forces, and defence manufacturers. There is much evidence to show that a lot of these procurements were not best value for money and there are instances of wasted millions because of inter-service spats. Frequently, those in the military who, shouted the loudest, got the most.

Also, all three services have been guilty of generating 'porkies' in order to safeguard their own interests. Why? The Navy to its credit did try to untangle the ownership of its aircraft between 1918 and 1938 by appealing via a variety of committees on the subject regaining operation control and ownership of its air assets. It eventually succeeded under the Inskip Report of 1936.

This leads to the speculation on whether history is going to repeat itself in the 21st century over the ownership and operational control squabbles for the new F35B when it is embarked. It will be interesting to learn who took the lead in the investigation of the recent crash in November 2021 of an embarked F35B on the Queen Elizabeth? Does the RN take charge as it was under operational control from an aircraft carrier or does the RAF form and lead a board of inquiry, as it owns the aircraft?

There have been claims in aviation articles in circulation during the last few years where some senior air force officers, who should know better, have claimed that the RAF won the air war during the Falklands conflict in 1982. This is most surprising as one would think they would have kept a low profile on this claim in light of the questionable success rate on the actual bombing of the Port Stanley runway.

Some 66 bombs were dropped and only one actually hit the runway, which was rapidly refilled. Had this been the hit rate that had occurred under the auspices of the annual Red Flag, Green Flag exercises and bombing competitions held regularly in the US at the Nellis AFB, there would have been some very red faces indeed.

Also, not mentioned publicly at the time or widely known since, these Black Buck raids used colossal amounts of aviation fuel (100,000 plus gallons at a time) carried by the 15 Victor tankers (two were used as reserves on each mission), required to get just one Vulcan there and back from the Ascension Islands. A single Sea Harrier could carry five of these 1,000-pound bombs using only 500 gallons of fuel when operating from either HMS Hermes or Invincible.

On a straight 'cost analysis' basis and with aviation fuel costing around £4 a gallon at 1980s prices; the fuel cost alone, the Sea Harrier's was £400 per 1,000-pound bomb. The equivalent fuel cost for the Vulcan's was over £23,000 per bomb.

An area where the RN has an Achilles heel both past and present, is its Public Relations efforts. Through my years of service, we frequently were baffled why the junior service always seemed to grab the headlines whenever it was obvious the FAA were the instigators of many achievements. For example, the majority of the search and rescues around Cornwall were carried out by Naval Aircrews flying Sea Kings and Wessex helicopters from the Royal Naval Air Station at Culdrose, near Helston.

SAR operations were also occurred further along the south coast by FAA helicopters operating and based out of Portland and HMS Daedalus. Perhaps their PR organisation and the BBC had overlooked the fact that RAF Chivenor, St Mawgan and Thorney Island had closed many years previously? The same was also repeated in Scotland whereby a high percentage of the mountain rescues that took place there were made by Sea Kings from HMS Gannet based at Prestwick.

The public were generally none the wiser that a FAA squadron of Sea Kings operated out of there. Their principal role was to exercise with the nuclear submarines out of Faslane, but they also had a secondary role in many Air Sea and Mountain Rescues.

This book is an attempt to highlight and give some background information on the sheer number of operations and successful military achievements of the Fleet Air Arm throughout its history. A wide range of sources were sought and studied, these include memoirs, reference books, personal recollections, studies and military historical records. Also included are many Government and Defence Committee papers, including many parliamentary debates about the FAA duly recorded in Hansard.

The Internet also produced a whole plethora of interesting information, some which was irrelevant but many websites produced a mixture of interesting comments with general, political and military opinions. It has been like a dot-to-dot drawing, all this book does is join those dots up and enable me to refine my opinions.

I decided to put my thoughts to paper. In short, this is not an in-depth intellectual paper but one based on some historical facts, my personal experience during my service life, comments made by eminent defence experts along with many related articles/books written on the FAA. It also reflects the views of many experienced ex-FAA personnel, who served throughout the 1960s, 1970s and well beyond the 1980s.

Chapter 2
The Interwar Years (1918–1939)

Despite the name Royal Naval Air Service (RNAS), several Navy squadrons were active on the Western Front during World War I. The Naval pilots tended to be more experienced than their counterparts in the Royal Flying Corps (RFC) with many in the former becoming aces. Such was their experience that two of the top five air aces of World War I were Naval pilots.

Raymond Collishaw of Naval 3 and 10 Squadrons became the top ace with some 60 kills for the RNAS and earning a string of awards. Also, Robert Little of Naval 8 Squadron was attributed with 47 kills. They were in effect in company with the better and widely known WW I aces of Von Richtofen and RFC ace, Edward Mannock.

During this period, the then Brigadier General Trenchard was lobbying in Government circles including the Prime Minister Lloyd George and the Navy's 1st Sea Lord Winston Churchill, for the formation of an independent air force away from interference from the other two services i.e. the RN and the Army.

His proposals received very little opposition from these two services. On the RN front, the Sea Lords and Admirals knew very little about the use of airpower at sea as it was still in its infancy. Their mind-set was still in battleships, cruisers and destroyers mode.

At a stroke, the RN was able to rid itself of the irritation of these pioneers of naval aviation and enable it to concentrate on their battleships and the development of submarines. That was what the RN was all about, seamanship, navigation, manoeuvres on the high seas and of course showing the flag with all those lovely cocktail parties.

Then, on 1st April 1918 the decision was made for the RNAS to be merged with the RFC and transferred to a new force to be named as the Royal Air Force.

At the time of this merger, the Navy's air force had over 55,000 officers and men, nearly 3,000 aircraft, 103 airships and 126 coastal air stations.

It should be remembered that Trenchard, the instigator of this merger, was a great believer in the strategic bombing of rail and industrial centres, which were to feature prominently during WWII. This philosophy was to be endorsed by Stanley Baldwin, then the Conservative Leader in 1932, who said the bomber would always get through.

This decision undoubtedly killed all but a trickle of development and pursuance of British aircraft carriers and naval aircraft. At the time, Great Britain was level pegging with the US Navy on experimenting and adapting to what were going to be the new capital ships for the future i.e. aircraft carriers. This move was the main reason why the FAA took such a hit and it would take until the onset of World War II until the middle 1940s to recover.

Many future RN Captains, Naval Squadron Commanding Officers and Flight Leaders were now suddenly in the RAF, which now embraced an Army based philosophy and ranking system. At a stroke, all the experience learnt with the fledgling naval aircraft and prototype carriers, the rudiments of operating at sea were gone. The Royal Navy was to fall rapidly behind the US Navy for over twenty years. No wonder there was so much scepticism of the FAA's capability at the beginning of WWII.

Although there was some involvement of the RAF operating at sea during the 1920s and early 1930s, there were farcical occasions when there were clashes between RAF Commanders arguing with the RN Captains over where the aircraft carriers should operate at sea.

The RAF wanted the ship to be positioned close inshore, therefore reducing the range for land targets, whilst the RN Captains insisted they wanted to be further offshore giving them the flexibility of sea room for manoeuvring and safety reasons. There was also the ludicrous situation, where shore-*based* RAF Flight Lieutenants suddenly became Lieutenant Commanders RN when embarked.

The disparity in influence, quality and type of aircraft obtained by the RAF was well established in the 1930s, with no real thought being made for any naval air warfare requirements. It is well known that the FAA was appallingly equipped at the beginning of the WWII. At that time, the Navy flew Barracudas, Fulmars and avoided the badly thought-out Roc aircraft. The mainstay was the

Fairey Swordfish, which although was doing sterling work, it could hardly be compared to Mitchell's Spitfire or Sidney Cam's Hurricane.

The RAF thought that the requirements of operating at sea would severely hinder the development of land-based aircraft, thereby diverting the energy and priorities of the Air Ministry. The FAA only caught up with effective game changing aircraft during the middle part of the WWII with the introduction of American built aircraft like the Corsairs and Wildcats. It was pretty obvious where all the Research and Development on aviation was going pre- WWII.

To understand and get an inkling of the tensions that this period generated coupled with some historical perspectives on what happened, the resultant Inskip Report makes for very interesting reading. It relates to the period from the formation of the RAF in 1918 under the Air Force Act of 1917 until the eventual reinstatement of the FAA back under Admiralty control eventually in 1939.

This report was compiled in the late 1930s and published in July 1937 at the request of Mr Baldwin, the then Prime Minister to Sir Thomas Inskip. At that time, he was Minister for Co-ordination of Defence and was asked to prepare a report on the ongoing conflict that existed between the Admiralty and the Air Ministry with the Navy repeatedly wishing to regain control of its air assets since losing them following the formation of the RAF in 1919.

Within that report, the arguments put forward by the Admiralty to gain back control and management of its own aircraft and men, reflected the undoubted tensions and conflicts that existed through the 1930s between the two services. Until the publication of the said report and the implementation of its recommendations, the Air Ministry was repeatedly able to maintain the status quo despite the constant badgering by the Admiralty to regain power over its own naval air force.

The Air Ministry appeared to hold sway over many committees that had been convened with even Prime Minister Baldwin in 1926, dismissing the Admiralty's contention wanting to own the naval air assets and some RAF shore establishments.

At one stage in writing this book, there was a temptation to use the historic Inskip Report as a basis in the concluding chapter, as numerous points raised in it appear to lead to similar scenarios that were going to be repeated many years later in the shape of Joint Harrier Force. There also appears to be a sense of déjà vu as ownership operational and control is being reflected today with regard to the F35B aircraft on board the Queen Elizabeth class aircraft carriers.

Following general comments and some key opinions from several publications, it was thought appropriate to dedicate a few paragraphs to the Inskip report, as it does give a potted history and the circumstances of how and why the FAA came back under control of the Admiralty in 1939.

Aviation Pre-1918

In April 1912, the Committee of the Imperial Defence approved the formation of a Flying Corps operated jointly by the Army and Navy. The new Royal Flying Corps (RFC) comprised of separate Military and Naval Wings together with a Central Flying School. The Air Battalion of the Royal Engineers, formed in 1911 by the War Office, was then absorbed in the new Military Wing from which the Naval Wing was to diverge, becoming a separate Royal Naval Air Service (RNAS) on 1st July 1914.

This left the RFC as an entirely Army service. Airships and balloons, which had become the responsibility of the Admiralty's naval construction department in 1916, but remained an Admiralty responsibility until 1919 when this too passed to the Air Ministry. The Admiralty retained control of the aircraft carriers, operations at sea, with naval officers and ratings being seconded to the RAF for training and service.

Aviation Boards 1916–1918

In February 1916, a Joint War Air Committee was appointed in order to co-ordinate the design and procurement activities of the separate air services of the Admiralty and the War Office. In May 1916, an Air Board superseded this committee. Following the New Ministries and Secretaries Act 1916, the Air Board was reconstituted as a Ministry in January 1917. Its president was deemed to be a minister and it was given responsibility for aircraft design, requirements, and their allocation.

At the same time, the Ministry of Munitions took over from the service departments responsibility for the supply and inspection of aeroplanes, seaplanes, engines, and accessories. The Air Board was dissolved in January 1918, following the creation of an Air Ministry. Its function in regard to aircraft design, programme and policy passed to the Ministry of Munitions.

Aviation Ministry 1918-1941

This is the era when aviation policy became crucial and very interesting. On 3rd January 1918, the Air Ministry was set up under a Secretary of State for Air advised by an Air Council. The Ministry's first task was to plan for the amalgamation of the Royal Flying Corps and the Royal Naval Air Service, which was effected on 1st April 1918 when the Royal Air Force came into existence.

In February 1919, the ministry became responsible for civil aviation, which, before the outbreak of war in 1914, had been the responsibility of the Home Office. In January 1920, it took over responsibility for aircraft production from the Ministry of Munitions and between 1919 and in 1922 it took over, by stages, from the Treasury the Meteorological Office, into which its own meteorological service and those of the other service departments was absorbed.

From 1918 onwards, this new air force i.e. the RAF had to settle in and establish itself. Nevertheless, the records illustrate from time to time the dissatisfaction of the Admiralty of the use of aircraft, their control, administration and use of naval personnel. The RAF of course gave equally robust counter arguments. Inskip states:

"The two Services directly concerned are in sharp disagreement as to the principles on which a sound policy should be based with regard to the use of aircraft."

These disagreements were discussed and debated, when an announcement was made in March 1922 by Parliament that the RAF would be continued as before. This did not appease the Navy as it continued to badger for the return of its naval air units. As these two empires continued to lock horns, another committee was formed in 1923 and was known as the Balfour Committee whose remit was to investigate the two views being advanced by both the Navy and RAF.

On the question of personnel, there was a shortage of officers and pilots needed by the Admiralty. Inskip duly reported spats over the manning of the FAA regarding both officers and ratings with maximum and minimum percentage levels of RAF personnel on RN units. At one stage, the Admiralty stated that the proportion of Naval Officers borne in the FAA should be increased at the Admiralty's discretion to 70%.

The Balfour committee had previously recommended that the number of officers seconded from the Navy to the Air Force was to be left to the Admiralty to determine 'subject to the proviso that not less than 30% of air force officers should serve on board the carriers'.

Hawker Nimrod-802 Naval Air Squadron colour scheme – Author's image

Because of these shortages, there was an interesting period in 1928 when the Admiralty wanted naval ratings to be trained and employed as pilots for the FAA. It was referred to Lord Salisbury, who rejected it. The Air Ministry, by agreement, in 1932 had secured the right to train a limited number of RAF sergeants as pilots for the FAA.

No corresponding agreement could be reached concerning the use of naval ratings. At one stage, the Air Ministry's case was largely based on the contention that the petty officer in the Navy is not suitable for flying training as a sergeant in the RAF.

The conflict between the two services on the question of naval ratings pilots was to be renewed in 1934 and became one of the matters to be reviewed by Inskip at the direction Mr Baldwin in 1936.

The Balfour report contained some interesting statements e.g.

- *In their (the Admiralty) view, a Fleet Air Arm is now as necessary to a fleet as cruisers, destroyers or submarines. Aerial reconnaissance and aerial 'spotting' are strictly naval operations as gunnery, torpedo work and wireless telegraphy. It seems to them intolerable that, while they are responsible for the safety and success of our Battle Fleets, the air work that safety and that success in large measure depend should be performed by persons belonging to another Service, imbued by different traditions, and looking for support and promotion to a different department.*
- *The Admiralty are apprehensive lest in times of war or other emergency, the Air Ministry might withdraw from Navy units of the FAA and use them for other purposes. In respect of this, we recommend that it should be definitely laid down that personnel, material and reserves should not be withdrawn by the Air Ministry without consent of the Admiralty or a decision by the Cabinet.*
- *As expected, the Air Ministry objected to these demands stating, "It would lead to many administrative difficulties and much overlapping while in the region of supply and research, it would hamper progress and increase expense."*

The supply of aircraft for the Fleet Air Arm was then governed by the decisions of the Balfour Committee. It was decided that the Air Ministry must provide all the material required by the Admiralty and that the Air Ministry should carry out research experiment and design in consultation with the Admiralty.

The Navy was to put forward suggestions as to types for the Air Ministry to embody in designs and then obtain specifications and tenders from the trade. At all stages, the Admiralty was to be kept informed. This state of affairs was to continue until 1940, when the Ministry of Aircraft Production was instituted and played the same part in relation to the Admiralty that the Air Ministry had carried out previously.

Inskip's conclusion and therefore recommendations were that the employment of FAA aircraft be the responsibility of the Admiralty. He went on to say that the FAA not only co-operates with the Fleet, it is an integral part of that Fleet. Furthermore, an air unit on a carrier is a great deal more than a passenger in a convenient vehicle. It forms a part of the organisation of the ship and is a factor in the efficiency of the ship, its whole raison d'être being the employment of air power in naval operations.

Though the Royal Navy successfully regained aircraft assets in 1937 following the Inskip Report, the changeover took two time-consuming years to complete. There was a new charter drawn up between the Aircraft Ministry and the Fleet Air Arm at the time of Churchill, the Ministry was formed in 1940. Under that charter, the Fleet Air Arm had a full relationship with the Aircraft Ministry and was freed altogether from any responsibility to the Air Ministry.

It is disputed between those who say that the Admiralty did not get what it wanted for the FAA and those who say that the Admiralty was not very clever at explaining what it really wanted. Whatever may be the rights and wrongs of this controversy, there is certainly no doubt whatsoever, that the outbreak of WWII found the FAA equipped with extremely poor aircraft.

The Admirals of the time, who were trained in sails and yardarms, were the same leaders, who had also historically resisted the introduction of steam power and the submarine. The same was to occur when naval aviation appeared on the horizon.

The concept of aircraft and its weapons at sea caused great difficulties and the older generation of officers were slow to accept and not sufficiently flexible to appreciate the full impact of aviation upon sea warfare. However, whatever was going on in the background, the fact remains that the Fleet Air Arm was badly equipped when compared to the RAF on the outbreak of war in 1939.

Sources

Sources – globalsecurity.org

Chapter 3
Sinking of the Graf Spee and Bismarck, 1939

Graf Spee

This engagement, which became better known as the Battle of the River Plate, was fought in the South Atlantic on the 13th December 1939. It was the first naval battle of the Second World War. It was also one of the first actions where the FAA aircraft were to figure, via spotting and shadowing the German ship and assisted in the destruction of a 'Pocket Battleship', the Kriegsmarine heavy cruiser Admiral Graf Spee.

It was commanded by Captain Hans Langsdorff, who had engaged a Royal Navy squadron, commanded by Commodore Henry Harwood. The RN squadron consisted of the cruisers HMS Ajax, HMS Achilles (on loan to New Zealand) and HMS Exeter.

The Graf Spee had sailed into the South Atlantic in August 1939, before the war began, and had begun to commence raiding after receiving appropriate authorisation on 26th September 1939. Harwood's squadron was one of several search task forces sent in pursuit by the Admiralty. They sighted Graf Spee off the estuary of the River Plate, near the coasts of Argentina and Uruguay.

The British cruisers were outgunned by the Admiral Graf Spee and therefore were at a tactical disadvantage but the British did have the upper hand strategically, since any commerce raider returning to Germany would have to run the blockade of the North Sea and probable encounter with the Home Fleet.

For victory, the British only had to damage the raider enough so that she was either unable to make the journey or unable to fight a subsequent battle with the Home Fleet. Whilst having numerical superiority, that even the loss of all of the three cruisers would not have severely altered Britain's naval capabilities, whereas Admiral Graf Spee was one of the Kriegsmarine's few capital ships. The British could therefore afford to risk a tactical defeat if it brought strategic victory.

The brief summary of the action involving the action is as follows:

- HMS Exeter, carrying two Walruses of 700 NAS (Catapult Flight), was straddled by the third salvo from the Graf Spee. An 11-inch shell burst amidships, killed the starboard torpedo tube's crew, damaged communications equipment and riddled the two aircraft. The Walruses were being prepared for catapulting during this salvo, the explosion caused such damaged that both aircraft had to be ditched i.e. manhandled over the side.
- Meanwhile, HMS Ajax launched her two Fairey Seafoxes. Lt E.D.G. Lewin RN the pilot with Lt R.E.N. Kearny RN as observer, carried out their catapult launches with the two aft turrets X and Y firing forward. Following a delay in establishing WT communications, air spotting and reconnaissance was to be the order of the day. The aircraft were recovered under very difficult circumstances throughout the action, thus enabling the Graf Spee to be shadowed.
- The following day, HMS Ajax in company with HMS Cumberland and Achilles had made rendezvous off San Antonio. The RN Squadron closed towards the River Plate at dawn and HMS Ajax flew off her aircraft with orders not to fly over territorial waters. At 08:30, the aircraft returned having been unable to see anything because of bad visibility. They had been fired upon, which seem to indicate that the Graf Spee was sailing under the cover of fog and mist. However, a report shortly received afterwards from Montevideo was that she was still in harbour.
- On the 17th December, the Graf Spee slowly left harbour after 6 pm and proceeded to sail westward followed by the German cargo passenger ship, the Tacoma. Tacoma incidentally had taken on some 800 crewmembers off the pocket battleship. The RN squadron was brought to action stations.
- HMS Ajax aircraft sighted the Graf Spee in shallow waters, some six miles south west of Montevideo. At around 23:00, the aircrew reported that the Graf Spee had scuttled herself. The aircraft was recovered in near darkness.

Aftermath

This was the first time that FAA aircraft had been used in action and whilst they did not directly attack the Graf Spee in an offensive role, they did provide and assist with important aerial reconnaissance and intelligence. It is interesting to read what Commodore Harwood reported back to the Admiralty, in regard to the aircraft and their use.

1. The launching of HMS Ajax's aircraft with the aft turrets firing and pointing forward when the aircraft were waiting was gallant and resolute. He was impressed with handling of the ship and the aircraft in recovery of the Sea Foxes was well executed. He also praised the capabilities of this aircraft in rough weather conditions.
2. While HMS Exeter's Walruses had been refuelled before the engagement, it was fateful that shell shrapnel hit both before they could be launched. Harwood pointed out that the ship was extremely lucky. Even though petrol had been sprayed all over the aft end of the ship, it did not catch fire. He goes on to mention the need to empty the aircraft of fuel during the night in the anticipation of any pending action.
3. The method of catapulting needs to be speeded up.
4. Once airborne, they were very valuable but not entirely successful.

Note: the Graf Spee's aircraft was unserviceable and did not take part in the battle.

As a result of these 'hairy' launches and recovery of the Sea Fox from HMS Ajax, the pilot Lt Lewin RN was awarded the DFC, with his observer Lt Kearny RN being Mentioned in Dispatches. The London Gazette of 23rd February 1940 has a citation entry stating, "… who was catapulted after the action had started when the air-worthiness of his aircraft was in doubt."

It also reflects on the seamanship of Ajax's crew and flight crew's handling in launches and recoveries. Also, the sheer hard work and tenacity of the FAA maintenance crew in looking after these aircraft, which were simply latched on to the top of gun turrets. There is also the fact of the Sea Foxes and Walruses being constantly exposed to the harsh sea conditions. On the 21st January 1940, 718 NAS (Catapult Flight) lost its squadron status and eventually got absorbed into 700 NAS.

In summary, this was the first naval action by the Royal Navy and the use of naval aircraft. Remember, it was still 1939; the FAA had got back control from the RAF and was still finding its feet. The Sea Fox first flew in 1936, built by Fairey to an Air Ministry specification to serve aboard the RNs cruisers. Although not a spectacular aircraft and with some 66 being built, it was phased out by the FAA in 1943 by more modern aircraft.

The Bismarck

- Curiously HMS Hood, a battlecruiser with four twin turrets carrying 14" guns, was known as a 'wet' ship. This was due to additional armour being added during construction, which made her sit lower in the water. In heavy seas, water would enter via the quarterdeck into the mess decks and subsequently the living quarters. The constant dampness coupled with poor ventilation caused high incidences of tuberculosis.
- Following the blowing up of HMS Hood on the 24th May 1941 during its first salvo engagement with the German battleship Bismarck, the Royal Navy and the British people were in shock. When Winston Churchill heard of the sinking, he immediately gave orders that every effort be made to sink the Bismarck, come what may.
- Referring back to Taranto on the 11th November 1940 and subsequently, it has been reputedly reported that one reason the Swordfish was a successful torpedo aircraft, was its apparent ability to fly so low, that the anti-aircraft guns of the German Navy's pocket battleships and battlecruisers were unable to deflect downwards enough in order to hit it. Swordfish aircrews frequently reported that they flew so low that their undercarriage wheels skimmed the sea during their attacks; this lack of deflection was due to some very courageous low flying. Also, several aircrews have mentioned that German anti-aircraft guns fired incorrectly set proximity fused shells, which exploded way in front of the aircraft. This was certainly not true in the actions later on the Scharnhorst, Gneisenau and Prinz Eugene in what was known as the Channel Dash in 1941.
- Lt Cdr Esmonde RN was a survivor of the sinking of the aircraft carrier HMS Courageous on the 13th September 1939, a little less than two weeks after the official declaration of war with Germany on the 3rd in

the Western approaches. He was to serve at RNAS Lee-on-Solent (HMS Daedalus) and other air stations on the south coast. He was then appointed to HMS Victorious as CO of 825 NAS flying Swordfishes. These nine aircraft were brand new, with three of them fitted out with the latest attack technology fitted with the Anti-Surface-Vessel (ASV) radar. The 'Vic' having been just commissioned on the 15th May 1941 and was the newest carrier to join the fleet. There was no shakedown or workup cruise as this being wartime, shakedown was invariably the first operational mission!

The RN's newest aircraft carrier HMS Victorious sailed on the 20th May 1941 after having previously embarked 800Z Flight with six Fairey Fulmars II fighters, along with nine brand new Swordfishes of 825 NAS and also took on board RAF fighters with the view of ferrying these fighters to Malta.

As in war, plans turn on a sixpence and with the discovery of a potential breakout by the battleship Bismarck and the heavy cruiser Prinz Eugene on the 21st May, Victorious was ordered to unload the RAF fighters and proceed to Scapa Flow.

Here, she joined the Home Fleet. On arrival, Admiral Sir John Tovey personally interviewed Lt Cdr Esmonde to whether his 825 NAS Swordfish squadrons was up to scratch in delivering a torpedo attack. Only once Esmonde had convinced him that the squadron's training was satisfactory, did Admiral Tovey allow HMS Victorious to join the Home Fleet. Shades of doubt perhaps on the FAA's ability by a surface fleet Admiral?

HMS Victorious accompanying the battleship HMS Renown and was only 200 miles distant from the Bismarck following the original engagement. At 22:10 on the 24th May, nine Swordfishes of 825 NAS commanded by Lt E K Esmonde RN took off. Once airborne, they formed up into three sub-flights. At

23:00, three Fulmars of 800Z Flight also took off with orders to observe the attack and report back should another strike be required the following day.

On the dot of midnight (23.59), the first sub-flight led by Esmonde took the aircraft in a simultaneous attack. Because flak hit his starboard flying control, he abandoned attacking from the starboard side; so, he dropped to the port side as Bismarck presented a perfect silhouette against a setting sun. Both the second and third members of the sub-flight, flown by Sub-Lieutenant Thompson RN and Lieutenant Maclean RN respectively, attacked separately on the port side. Captain Lidemann and his crew skilfully dodged all three torpedoes with some terrific ship handling skills.

Meanwhile, the second sub-flight led by Lieutenant P Gick RN (who was later to become a Rear-Admiral in the FAA), pulled from attacking the starboard side of the ship and manoeuvred his way around to a better attacking position. Meanwhile, the other two Swordfishes of the sub-flight carried on Lt Garthwaite RN and Sub-Lieutenant Jackson dropped their torpedoes on the starboard bow and starboard quarter. Again, the Bismarck's Captain avoided these air-launched weapons.

Two Swordfishes of the third sub-flight appeared on the port side and dodging a hail of AA fire, Lieutenant Pollard RN and Sub-Lieutenant Lawson released their torpedoes. Although launched from a good attacking angle, they failed to hit the Bismarck. Suddenly and to the German's surprise, Lt Gick appeared on the port side and they were unable to avoid his torpedo, which hit the Bismarck amidships exploding right on the armour belt. The ship subsequently survived this torpedo attack and sailed on.

The single hit was observed by an accompanying Fulmar and reported back of dense smoke on the starboard side of the ship. There is a variance in all the follow up reports on why the ship slowed down. According to a documentary on a diving expedition made on the Bismarck by James Cameron entitled 'Expedition Bismarck' in 2002, two shells from HMS Prince of Wales hit the ship on the port forward side.

One went straight through and the other penetrated a water-tight compartment, which allowed 1,000s of tons of sea water to cascade into Bismarck causing her to list 9 degrees to port. This in turn caused Captain Linemann to reduce speed to approximately 20 knots and sail the ship towards France's west coast and apparent safety.

One interesting humanitarian fact emerged from this first strike; 825 NAS Swordfishes subsequently became part of the search for the Bismarck. Three aircraft were put up on the 25th May, but unfortunately one of the Swordfishes had to ditch. Just prior to their forced landing, fate and good luck took charge, when they spotted a lifeboat beneath them.

Once they had scrambled aboard, they found it fully stocked with emergency food and water. Victorious continued searching for its missing aircraft and when the ship came across it empty, the crew was assumed lost. However, lady luck still had a part to play when this lifeboat and crew were discovered and rescued eight days later on the 3rd June, by the Icelandic steamer Lagufoss.

Two days later, in weather and sea conditions that bordered upon the horrendous and at the extreme range of its aircraft, HMS Ark Royal launched a fifteen strong second Swordfish strike. This attack was carried out by 810, 818 and 820 NAS. They pressed home their attack from all quarters of the compass in driving rain, low cloud and winds gusting up to 50 mph.

Two torpedoes were to hit the ship on the port quarter and a third on the starboard. The latter torpedo exploded causing the Bismarck's twin rudders to jam and therefore, crippling her steering gear and leaving her to reel out of control in heavy seas and steer around in circles. At this point in time, the Bismarck's fate was sealed.

Admiral Tovey with HMS King George V and Rodney, the battleship/cruiser of Force H caught up with the Bismarck. They were able to illuminate Bismarck with searchlights and closed virtually to point-blank range, able to pound her to a wreck from both sides. It took torpedoes fired from HMS Dorsetshire to both sides of the German warship to apply the coup de grace with the ship eventually sinking at 10:36.

On who actually launched the one torpedo from the Swordfish that caused the critical damage to Bismarck's rudder, is subject to conflicting accounts across a wide range of sources. It is not the intention of this narrative to speculate or confirm either way, which aircrew inflicted the crucial damage.

Suffice to say in the fog and chaos of battle, with participants pumped up with adrenaline, it is difficult to get full and precise details given during debriefs after such a mission. This is even more so especially with the psychological relief of having got back and landed safely on board 'mother' i.e. HMS Ark Royal in atrocious weather conditions.

It seems incredible that only nine days after setting sail on the 18th May 1941, under guise of Operation Rheinübung that the mighty Bismarck was at the bottom of the Atlantic Ocean. Rheinübung was a follow up to the successful Operation Berlin to continue the sinking of British ships in the North Atlantic. These actions in the Atlantic following on from those in the Mediterranean during late 1940s, shows the FAA beginning to spread its wings and extend the reach of the Royal Navy's surface fleet.

It became clear from these engagements that the FAA's aircraft based on aircraft carriers was gradually becoming the offensive spearhead of the fleet. It was the beginning of the 'flat tops' time in becoming the capital ships of the RN. Although the obsolete biplane in the shape of the Swordfish did not have the clout in armament to sink a ship with 14" thick nickel-steel armour protection, it did deliver and land a fatal blow on Bismarck's Achilles heel i.e. its rudders, thus disabling the ship's ability to manoeuvre.

It goes without saying that the aircrew, who flew on these missions were cool, had an unrelenting determination and an abundance of sheer guts. To fly in a flimsy fabric covered piece of machinery into a withering cordon of anti-aircraft fire was beyond the call of duty. Also, they had to face appalling weather and visibility conditions and the certainty of not being rescued should they either ditch or be shot down. Some FAA thirteen aircrew were to lose their lives either by being shot down or being lost at sea on this attack.

This bravery was recognised in the London Gazette on the 14th September 1941 with four DSOs, eighteen DSCs and eighteen Mentioned in Dispatches, four DSMs and four DSMs. Battle Honours were awarded to the following FAA squadrons, 800, 808, 810, 818, 820 and 825.

Sources

https://navywings.org.uk/portfolio/sinking-of-the-Bismarck/
https://www.youtube.com/watch?v=MtZkBqlQYAc
ttps://ww2today.com/26th-may-1940-torpedo-attack-on-the-bismarck
https://fleetairarmoa.org/fleet-air-arm-battle-honours
'Congratulations to the Fleet'. The Times (48938). 29th May 1941. p. 4.
https://en.wikipedia.org/wiki/Eugene_Esmonde
https://www.kbismarck.com/article2.html
http://www.historyofwar.org/articles/battles_river_plate.html
https://www.thoughtco.com/battle-of-the-river-plate-2361437

https://www.britain-at-war.org.uk/WW2London_Gazette/river_plate/html/part_iii.html
https://www.militaryfactory.com/aircraft/detail.asp?aircraft_id=1386
https://winstonchurchill.org/resources/speeches/1939-in-the-wings/the-sinking-of-the-graf-spee/Bismarck
https://www.historyonthenet.com/bismarck-battle

Chapter 4
FAA in the Mediterranean 1940–41

The Swordfish

The naval aircraft, which bore the brunt of the operational workload and brought much success for the FAA during this period of the war, was the Fairey Swordfish. Its successor, the Fairey Albacore, which basically was a Swordfish with an enclosed cockpit, also saw action in the Mediterranean. The Swordfish was to outlast its successor, as the Albacore was withdrawn before the former's demise.

Surprisingly, although nearly 2,400 Swordfish were to be built, the majority were manufactured by Blackburn and not by Fairey. To be precise, some 1,699 were produced by Blackburn, which represented just over 70% of the total built. Visually, it was an ungainly and lumbering looking aircraft built on classic aerofoil frames, stringers, struts and tensioning wires, covered with a canvas fabric to form the skin.

It was given the affectionate name of 'Stringbag', not because it looked like a bag held together by string but because aircrews likened it to those domestic shopping bags made of string, which were in fashion during the 1940s. These string bags were able to contain any shape or size and the Swordfish, like the bag, could carry anything. These string bags can still be seen in use today and readily hold a variety of shapes and sizes of shopping goods, particularly fruit/vegetables.

The Swordfish first flew in April 1934 and by 1939, it was obsolete. However, although it was uncomfortable to fly, it provided sterling service in the Mediterranean and elsewhere. It was one of the few naval aircraft with such a low speed that it could land and take-off with no wind over the deck. There were occasions where if the wind was in the right direction, the Swordfish could take off when a carrier was at anchor.

Being a biplane, it had an unusually large wing area for its size, 607ft^2 (55.4 m^2), which could be folded inwards when embarked. With this high wing loading ratio (the Lancaster had only 1,297ft^2 and four engines), it could carry a phenomenal range of weapons:

- 18 inch – 1,670 lb torpedo.
- 1,500 lb mine.
- 1,500 lb of a variety of sized bombs under both the fuselage and wings.
- 8 x 60 lb rockets (fitted on later Mk II with a metal lower wing)
- 1 x fixed forward firing303 Vickers machine gun on the right upper fuselage.
- 1 x .303 Vickers (or Lewis) machine gun.
- Flares
- Large radar unit introduced in 1943.

The crew consisted of three members: pilot, observer and radio operator/rear gunner (known as TAGs). The observer's place could be and was frequently replaced with an auxiliary fuel tank for long-range missions.

There were 26 Naval Air Squadrons, operating the Swordfish, which was to include 705 NAS where they also had float equipped aircraft for service on the battlecruisers HMS Repulse and HMS Renown. A further 20 squadrons were to operate Swordfish in training, tuition and familiarisation roles.

One of the largest squadrons ever to be formed in the FAA's history was equipped with Swordfish, 836 NAS, which at one stage had some 91 aircraft on its books. This was because three to four of these aircraft, which invariably were the Mk II and III versions, were carried on twenty merchant aircraft carriers called 'MAC' ships, sailing as part of the Atlantic convoys.

Swordfish cockpit – Author's photo

The Fleet Air Arm was very active in the Mediterranean in the early 1940s and whilst the Taranto action was considered to be the most successful and celebrated of its operations in WWII. It was also involved along with many others. Attacks by FAA aircraft enabled British battleships to engage and then led to the sinking of three cruisers and two destroyers of the Italian Fleet off Cape Matapan.

Little known outside of the FAA was its involvement during the Western Desert campaign with naval squadrons based ashore. Finally, at the behest of the RAF, frequent use of RN aircraft carriers were utilised to ferry aircraft to Malta. The carriers HMS Ark Royal, Furious and Victorious made fifteen high-speed round trips to Malta in 1941. Unfortunately, HMS Ark Royal was hit and sunk by a torpedo from a U-boat on the 13th November 1941 when returning from one of these fast trips.

The Battle of Matapan

During late March 1941, the Royal Navy was to learn via Bletchley Park that an Italian battle fleet consisting of one battleship, six heavy cruisers plus a number of destroyers were sailing to intercept merchant convoys, which were supplying British Forces. This was the first time the Italian Enigma had been cracked and in order to protect the intelligence source from Bletchley, a plausible reason was made known to the Italians that the information had been collected via a reconnaissance plane.

To add to the deception, Admiral Cunningham made a clandestine exit from the golf club he had been visiting in Alexandria. He had arrived at the club in the afternoon with an overnight bag and pointedly spent time on the golf course making sure he could be seen from the Japanese consul. He knew somehow his presence would be fed back to the Italians and/or Germans. Also, his flagship, HMS Warspite had advertised a party for the night but it was never meant to take place.

The Italian battle fleet was sailing off Cape Matapan, which is west of Crete on the most south-westerly point of Greece. Under cover of darkness on the 27th March, the carrier HMS Formidable with only 14 aircraft available was ordered to carryout strikes against the modern Italian battleship Vittorio Veneto as part of this Italian battle fleet. The first of three attacks took place in the late morning of 28th March with six Albacores from 826 NAS. They scored no hits.

The Italian Admiral then realised a British carrier was in the area and having no land based friendly air cover, decided to turn northwards to relative safety at Taranto. A second strike on the battleship in mid-afternoon surprised the Italians. A torpedo dropped by an Albacore of 829 NAS hit the outer portside of the hull by the propeller causing 4,000 tons of sea water to flood the ship.

Unfortunately, the Commanding Officer of 826 NAS Lt Cdr J Dalyell-Stead RN and crew were shot down and killed by anti-aircraft fire from the ship. This stopped the Vittorio Veneto but after 1½ hours of repairs, she was able to get underway again.

Six Albacores of 826 NAS made a third attack and Swordfish of 828 NAS along with two further Swordfish of 815 NAS based in Crete took place in the early evening at 19:36. The Italian Admiral Iachino had deployed his fleet into three columns. Smoke, searchlights and a heavy protective defensive barrage were utilised to protect the battleship Vittorio Veneto.

These tactics worked and prevented further damage to the ship but a single torpedo hit the Zara class heavy cruiser Pola. It struck amidships, water entered five of her boilers and disabled the ship bringing her to a standstill. At this point, she was unable to use her guns. Unaware of Cunningham's battleships, HMS Barham, Valiant and his flagship Warspite, Iachino sent back a force made up of cruisers and destroyers in order to protect the Pola.

The allied forces detected the Italian ships on radar but being undetected themselves, they closed within 3,700 yards. In battleship terms, they were virtually at point blank range. They opened fire at shortly after 20:20 with searchlights of the British force illuminating the Italian ships.

Just before this engagement, the Italians had spotted the Allied force and thought these ships were theirs. Neither had they anticipated a night action nor was their main armament ready for action. The ensuing battle resulting in the loss of many Italian ships for the loss of only one FAA aircraft.

The result of this engagement is summarised in materiel and crew losses as follows:

Royal Navy	Italian Regia Marina
4 light cruisers damaged	2,300 killed
One Albacore with 3 killed	1,015 captured
	Three Heavy cruisers sunk
	Two destroyers sunk
	One Battleship damaged
	One Destroyer damaged

Taranto

Little known outside of the Fleet Air Arm at the time, that on the 11th November 1940, some 21 Fairey Swordfish flew from HMS Illustrious and attacked the Italian Navy in the harbour of Taranto. Planning had begun in 1938 for such a strike from the sea. This attack proved to be crucial because three battleships/cruisers were badly damaged requiring extensive repairs and widespread infrastructure work was required on repairing the harbour and seaplane facilities.

All this collateral damage resulted in the loss of only two aircraft. The Conti di Cavour required such wide-ranging repairs/salvage work to be undertaken, that she remained out of commission until Italy's surrender in 1943.

Planning for neutralising the Italian fleet based in the south eastern port of Taranto was part of an ongoing problem for British Naval planners during the early 1930s. There were plans to actually capture the port as early as 1935 during the Italian invasion of Abyssinia, which had occurred. Britain had a lengthy supply line in support of the British Army's North Africa campaign.

This logistics support stretched along the whole length of the Mediterranean from Gibraltar to Malta, skirting the coast of Sicily. Alternatively, it had to be shipped via the Cape of Good Hope up and through the Suez Canal. The Italians had no such supply problems and were ideally placed to intercept the British using supply routes, when sailing directly through the Mediterranean.

By the 1940s, the Italians had mustered a powerful fleet at Taranto consisting of 6 modern battleships/battle-cruisers, 9 cruisers/light-cruisers and 8 destroyers. The threat to British supplies and reinforcements became critical.

As far back to the Munich crisis of 1938, Admiral Sir Dudley Pound the commander of the Mediterranean Fleet was worried about the survival of the aircraft carrier HMS Glorious in any future conflict with the Italians. He gave instructions to his staff to investigate all options of attacking the Taranto port. Captain Lyster of HMS Glorious advised the Admiral that his embarked Fairey Swordfish torpedo bombers were capable of a night attack.

They were at the time, the only naval squadron with this capability. Pound took this advice and ordered training to begin. To ensure tight security, this was kept secret as no orders were issued. When the Munich crisis was apparently resolved, these plans were shelved. Pound also advised his replacement, Admiral Cunningham of the possible planned attack on Taranto, which was to be designated Operation Judgement.

In September 1940, Operation Judgement plans were reactivated and were to be part and parcel of a wider and complex operation called Operation MB8. Suffice to say that MB8 ran from the 4th–10th November 1940, consisting of a number of convoys both actual and decoys in preparation for Operation Judgement. These various forces and convoys deceived the Italians into thinking that only normal convoying was being undertaken.

The attack was originally due to take place on the 21st October 1940, which was Trafalgar Day. However, a fire in a 60-*gallon* auxiliary aircraft fuel tank caused a delay. This tank as fitted to the Swordfish in the observer's position, was to give the aircraft more range. This minor fire developed and became serious and caused the destruction of two other Swordfish.

By now, Rear Admiral Lyster, who had originally planned the attack on Taranto was in charge of the 'task force', which included the brand-*new* carrier HMS Illustrious. Because of HMS Eagle's breakdown in its fuel system, it was decided to transfer five Swordfish to 'Lusty' – the nickname for HMS Illustrious.

Days before the strike, several reconnaissance flights by the RAF's 431 Reconnaissance Flight based in Malta confirmed the location of the Italian Fleet and the intelligence team on HMS Illustrious, spotted extra and unknown barrage balloons in the harbour. The attack plan was altered to take these balloons into account. Over 100 anti-aircraft guns and only 27 barrage balloons defended the Taranto base.

Some 60 balloons had been blown away by high winds on the 6th November. The Italian ships were supposed to be protected by anti-torpedo nets but only one third were rigged. Also, these nets did not reach to the bottom of the harbour leaving a gap, thus allowing the British torpedoes to clear them by some two feet.

Author's illustration

The first wave of 12 aircraft of 815 NAS took off from HMS Illustrious led by Lt Cdr K Williamson RN at 21:00 hours on the 11th November 1940. Ninety minutes later, a second wave consisting of 8 aircraft (although 9 had been lined up) took-off from the flight deck. Number 8 and 9 had collided and although one took-off, it turned back due to a problem with its auxiliary fuel tank.

After minor repairs, the other was launched late. Three aircraft led by Williamson attacked and struck the battleship Conte di Cavour with a torpedo blasting a 27-*foot* (8.2 m) hole in the side below the waterline. Unfortunately, Williamson and his fellow crewman were shot down but the remaining two aircraft pressed on their attack unsuccessfully on the battleship Andrea Doria.

The next flight of three aircraft attacked from a northerly direction, attacking the battleship Littorio hitting her with two torpedoes. The Swordfish bomber element of the force led by Captain O Patch RM attacked next. Although they found the targets difficult to identify, they hit two moored cruisers with a single bomb on each.

The second wave of aircraft was led by Lt Cdr J Hale RN of 819 NAS, it also approached from a northerly direction. Just before midnight, flares were dropped and two aircraft aimed their torpedoes at Littorio, one eventually hitting her. Another Swordfish hit the battleship Caio Duilio with a torpedo splitting open her hull causing the two forward magazines to flood.

Lieutenant G Bayly RN was shot down by anti-aircraft fire from the cruiser Glorizia, which was the only aircraft lost from the second wave. The last of the aircraft arrived on scene only 15 minutes after the others had made an unsuccessful dive-bombing attack on one Italian cruiser before returning to HMS Illustrious at 02:39.

Although two aircraft were shot down, one during the first wave with the crew Lt Cdr Williamson and his observer Lieutenant N.J. Scarlett being captured. Sadly, Lieutenant G Bayly and his observer, Lieutenant H Slaughter were killed in action in the second wave.

The result of this action by the FAA caused the Italian Navy to lose half of its capital ships in just one night with the Italians moving their undamaged ships to Naples the very next day. The resultant battle damage required some four months of repairs for the Littorio, seven months for the Caio Duilio but the Conte di Cavour required extensive salvage work and repairs to her, which were still incomplete when Italy eventually surrendered in 1943.

There were several consequences arising from this successful aircraft carrier borne mission:

- The balance of power in the sea, for the time being, immediately swung towards Britain's Naval Mediterranean Fleet and reduced the pressure on convoy attacks in the Mediterranean.
- It provided an immediate morale boost for the country in 1940, when things were going badly militarily for Great Britain.
- This naval attack from aircraft carriers led to a fact-finding mission to Italy in May 1941 by the Imperial Japanese Navy (IJN) to investigate and study the raid with their Italian counterparts. From this, the IJN drew up plans, which formed the basis of the much larger attack on the US Navy at Pearl Harbour on the 7th December 1941. Unfortunately for the Americans, copying is a form of flattery.
- Secondly, there was an immediate impact on global naval tactics and strategy, which accelerated the demise of the large capital ship in favour of the use of air power at sea. As events a year later were to prove, it became the principal offensive weapon for fleets i.e. not only the Pearl Harbour attack but also the loss of HMS Prince of Wales and HMS Repulse by Japanese aircraft some three days later on the 10th December 1941 in the South China Sea. The battleship had become obsolete.
- Once again, the silent service reputation of the Royal Navy came to the fore, as very few awards were initially made for this successful 'decommissioning' and crippling blow to a very modern and ever threatening Italian Fleet. It was only after a public outcry, questions being asked in Parliament and astonishment by the ships companies and squadron personnel of the Mediterranean Fleet, that this oversight was rectified at a later date.

The Western Desert Operations

The FAA flew from numerous bases in the Western Desert like Dekhelia (to become HMS Grebe), Maaten Bagush, Fort Maddalena, Fuka, Abukir, Mersa Matruh and Sidi Berani, which were to become familiar to FAA personnel. They were part of Operation Crusader, which was a British military operation in North Africa during World War II that resulted in the liberation of Tobruk, Libya from Axis forces.

Tobruk had been under siege since April 1941. The Alexandria airport, known as Dekhelia was used in World War II as a shore base for aircraft of the Fleet Air Arm. The airfield was taken over by the Royal Egyptian Air Force on the outbreak of World War II and then subsequently loaned as a Naval Air Station on 16th September 1940.

It was commissioned as HMS Grebe, with a capacity of 72 aircraft. The airfield became the base for all FAA units in Egypt and the Western Desert, as well as acting as a fleet requirements unit.

Such deployments were often at short notice due to damage or losses to the aircraft carriers. The earliest forays into the desert involved 14 Swordfish from HMS Eagle and Illustrious base at one of the three airfields, namely Fuka in October 1940. This airfield changed hands during the course of the desert war, as the Long Range Desert Group (forerunners to the SAS) were to raid it later in 1942.

Operating away from their carrier bases ashore proved to be tricky, arduous and took a toll on both men and aircraft. Serious problems occurred for servicing and maintenance because of the environment i.e. heat and sand. Sand was to become a debilitating factor in Western Desert operations. It penetrated into everything, choking air filters, which were hardly adequate and required frequent changing and cleaning. It also readily contaminated fuels and oils.

In order to keep these aircraft airworthy, many veterans recall working under flimsy canvas shelters to keep out of the dust and continuous sand storms, with the bare minimum of tools and spares. Improvisation was the order of the day whereby welding was accomplished by assembling and connection of vehicle batteries to enable welding to take place. In many of the conversations from this period, the use of camels as transport was frequently mentioned.

Following the sinking of HMS Ark Royal on the 13th/14th November 1941, Aircraft of 805 NAS (Martlets), plus those of 815 NAS (Swordfish and Albacores) and 826 NAS (Swordfish and Albacores) were disembarked from HMS Illustrious. Also disembarked from HMS Formidable were 803 and 826 NAS.

At the height of operations in the summer of 1942, there were some 60 aircraft from five squadrons based there. Navy squadrons were used on a variety of tasks from bombing, dropping flares against shipping, landing grounds, ports and military transport. 821 NAS was to fly over 470 sorties, dropping over 200 ton and over 4,200 flares. Naval aircraft acted as Pathfinders for the RAF's

Wellington raids over a three-*week* period against the runways at Martuba and the adjacent airfield at Derna.

What was also noticeable was the number of aircraft types used in the desert by naval air squadrons. Take for example 805 NAS, which was first commissioned at Abukir Egypt in November 1940, operated Fulmars and Sea Gladiators on convoy protection duties. The squadron operated there until January 1941 when it was transferred to Crete.

The stay there was only a brief one when it moved back to HMS Grebe and re-equipped with Brewster Buffalo fighters. These were to be replaced by Grumman Martlett III's in June 1941. At one stage, it was also equipped with Hurricanes. Therefore, in a space of just six months, 805 NAS had to operate and maintain five different types of aircraft.

The same happened to 806 NAS of HMS Illustrious, who were embarked with a mixture of Fulmars and Gloster Sea Gladiators, when they were sent to the Mediterranean. Engaged in combat on numerous occasions, nine pilots flying Fulmars were to become aces. In November, the squadron received the Sea Gladiators, which had belonged to HMS Eagle.

806 NAS moved back to HMS Formidable after Crete but were disembarked to Aboukir in Egypt after the ship had been badly damaged by bombing in May 1941. Here, they fought in the Western Desert as part of the Royal Navy Fighter Squadron (RNFS) until February 1941 and then re-equipped with Hawker Hurricanes.

Upon the disbandment of the RNFS, 806 NAS reverted back to Fulmars. The squadron was moved to Ceylon. This once again was a headache for aircrew and engineers having to familiarise themselves with three different types of aircraft over a period of a year.

A back-and-forth series of battles for control of Libya and parts of Egypt followed, climaxing in the Second Battle of El Alamein when British Commonwealth forces delivered a decisive defeat to the Axis forces pushing them back to Tunisia. This ultimately led to their surrender.

By making the Axis powers fight on a second front in North Africa, the Western Allies provided some relief to the Soviet Union fighting the Axis on the Eastern Front. Squadrons from the Fleet Air Arm, RAF, and other Allied forces, together formed the composite 'Desert Air Force', which provided close air support to allied ground forces during the North African Campaign.

Fleet Air Arm Squadrons in the Western Desert

Squadron	Dates	Aircraft Types
803	1940–41	Fulmar I Hurricane I
805	1941–42	Fulmar I, Sea Gladiator, Buffalo I, Hurricane I, Martlet I
806	1940–41	Fulmar I, Sea Gladiator, Hurricane I, Fulmar II
813	1940–41	Swordfish I, Sea Gladiator, Buffalo I
815	1940–41	Swordfish I
819	1940	Swordfish I and II
821	1942	Swordfish I
826	1942–42	Albacore I, Swordfish

During this period, the FAA received very little acknowledgement of the successes in either communiqués back to parliament or in the British press of the number and wide range of operations, except perhaps the battle of Taranto. But even that was somewhat muted, especially on the awards until there was a clamour from the public.

Admiral Cunningham was one of the first admirals to recognise that the battleship was being eclipsed by naval airpower and he made good use of this new weapon of war. The Mediterranean showed that the FAA with its incremental success rate could be used in a variety of flexible roles ranging from defence to attack, operating without blinking from either ship to shore or vice versa.

When ashore, this flexibility was extended by support to the 8th Army in the Western Desert carrying out, fighter, bombing, flare dropping, spotting and in the later part of this phase of war in the Mediterranean, the use of airborne radar.

After the engagements resulting in the tonnage either badly damaged or sunk at Cape Matapan and Taranto, the Italian Regia Marina never ventured east of the area of the 'boot' of the Mediterranean. This therefore removed the threat to the British convoys.

Also, the actual use of aircraft carriers at sea was beginning to be recognised that in order to be effective, a minimum of two or more carriers operating together as an air group was the most effective and optimum way to deliver offensive power from the sea. Up and until 1942, Britain had only used its carriers as singletons i.e. alone. That was, of course, to change in the later part of the Pacific war.

Chapter 5
FAA's Pacific War –
January 1945 to August 1945

It was little known then and also relatively unknown until fairly recently, that the last British serviceman to be killed in combat during WWII, was a Fleet Air Arm fighter pilot, who was secretly executed after being shot down over Japan. This execution took place some 9 hours after Emperor Hirohito announced the unconditional surrender of Japan at midday on the 15th August 1945. See more later.

This period in the Pacific was undoubtedly the zenith of the Fleet Air Arm's operations during WWII, as it was part of the largest fleet ever assembled by Great Britain since the battle of Trafalgar under Lord Nelson. Once again, the British public and press paid little attention to some formidable battles conducted by the FAA, which were taking place against the Japanese in the Far East during the spring of 1945.

The FAA thus joined the same club as the 'Forgotten Army' in becoming the 'Forgotten Air force'. Even some Burma Star veterans to this day were unaware of the presence of this large Royal Navy Fleet operating in the same South Eastern corner of Asia.

One reason for this lack of awareness of these RN operations at the time or lack of press reports, was the fact that the war in Europe was coming to an end. The war-weary public were unaware of the presence of a very large British aircraft carrier task force in the Far East, which was still on a war footing. The same of course applied to the 'Forgotten Army' in Burma.

Following VE day on the 8th May 1945, Britain's population threw itself into rejoicing with church bells ringing, dancing and wild festivities in the towns and villages. The country was in 'relief' mode celebrating until dawn following the end of hostilities in Europe with Germany. However, for many hundreds of families these celebrations were rather muted as many of their loved ones still had to endure hostilities since January 1945 on the other side of the world i.e. the Pacific.

The reason for their continued worry and fretting was the presence of Britain's largest fleet in joining up with the US in pursuance of their island-*hopping* strategy. This RN fleet operating in the Pacific was entitled the 1st Aircraft Carrier Squadron and consisted of six British aircraft carriers, with 250 aircraft supported by 10,000 sailors and aircrew. This fleet included a battleship, cruisers and escorting destroyers under the command of Rear Admiral Fraser.

Author's photograph – Fleet Air Arm's Seafire Mk LFIII and Corsair FG-1G

Many books have been written by former FAA pilots of this era and it becomes obvious that these operations were without doubt, intense and bloody. There were high attrition rates in both materials and aircrew. Downed pilots on these missions also had the added nightmare that in the event of being captured, there was a high probability of being beheaded. 9 out of the total number of some 16-*aircrew* captured during the Palembang raids, were beheaded.

In late 1944, Churchill the Prime Minister and the British Chiefs of Staff Committee had discussed and argued that Great Britain should take part in the end-game operations against Japan so that it could maintain its close relationship with the US. They also wanted to ensure that once the war against Japan had concluded, British influence would still have some say in the region. This large carrier fleet would be offered to work alongside the Americans as they slowly crept, capturing island after island towards the mainland of Japan.

On the American side, there were factions opposed to Britain taking part, no doubt partly due to the US policy stance of anti-colonialism, which prevailed at the time. It did not want the pre-war status quo to be re-established once Japan had been defeated. President Roosevelt was also mindful of American public opinion, which would have been horrified to learn had the offer of British assistance been turned down. The idea that only their countrymen would face and die fighting a fanatical enemy all the way to Japan and beyond, through to a potential invasion of the Japanese homeland, was probably unthinkable.

While the Americans could have easily continued operating on their own and taken the Pacific war all the way to Japan, diplomacy prevailed and the British contribution was accepted. In late 1944, Churchill and his advisors were considering the formation of a large aircraft carrier fleet in the Pacific. Therefore, throughout 1944, many RN ships consisting of Fleet and Escort Aircraft Carriers, battleships, cruisers and destroyer flotillas were transferred from the European theatre to Ceylon to the British Pacific Fleet (BPF). They assembled in the huge harbour at Trincomalee.

Also at this time, Britain under the lend-lease scheme with the US, started to get large numbers of aircraft ferried to Ceylon. These were of course, the Avenger dive-bomber, Hellcat fighter and the superb fighter-bomber, the Corsair. The inadequate Barracuda was being phased out, much to the relief of FAA aircrew, but still the incompatible Seafire was being used in large numbers.

Here was another aircraft, which although the backbone of the RAF during the early 1940s, was totally unsuitable for use on carriers. It's somewhat delicate construction caused it frequently to crash whilst landing, had limited range and was invariably lethal if it had to be ditched in the sea. Although slight improvements were made with the fitting of drop tanks and raising the pilot's seat for better visibility, its operational use as a carrier aircraft was limited.

Throughout the operations in the Pacific, it was simply used for Carrier Air Patrols (CAP) because of its limited endurance. There was also the problem of there never being enough Seafire pilots and frequently the number of aircraft embarked exceeded the number of pilots. If it were not for these new US aircraft, the FAA could not have matched the operational capability of the US Navy as it did.

The BPF and its air groups spent from mid-1944 until January 1945, working up its aircraft carriers in unison with its battleships, cruisers and covering destroyers. The FAA learnt how best to use their new US designed aircraft in combat and how to quickly get into a large formation following the launch of some 120 plus aircraft in one go. It has to be noted that up until this time, the RN aircraft carriers had operated in the European theatre and only one carrier was generally allocated to a task force.

The RN was not used to the concept of a carrier air group forming up and operating together with aircraft from three to four other carriers. The British carriers were smaller, carried fewer aircraft and did not park them quite so compactly on the flight deck as the Americans. However, as events were to prove later on in the year, the British carriers had one ace up their sleeve i.e. armoured decks.

HMS Illustrious exercised with the USS Saratoga and therefore, learnt a lot from the Americans on how to operate a number of aircraft carriers in unison. The US after all, had several years of experience of capturing islands from the sea across the Pacific. This period was used partially in readiness for bigger 'fish to fry' and other combat opportunities. Therefore, on the basis of these preparations, regular attacks were carried out against a variety of Japanese held targets i.e. ports, airfields on the coast of Sumatra using a combination of BPF assets.

Meanwhile in the background, Admiral Fraser continued to seek approval from the Admiralty Board and through a good personal relationship with the US Admiral Nimitz, was able to get mutual agreement to use the BPF alongside the huge US 5th Fleet in the Pacific. It was agreed that the British would attack the oil refineries at Palembang in Sumatra.

Admiral Fraser was a far-sighted Naval leader who had confidence in the FAA to carry out this task. He was one of the first to recognise that the days of the large battlewagons was over and that naval airpower was the new main attack and defensive weapon for the navy. Thus, under the US designation, Task Force 63 was formed.

Author's Sketch – HMS Formidable and Corsair II of Naval Air Squadron 1842

The Palembang Raids – Operations Meridian 1 and 2

In January 1945, the FAA took part in the largest mission of its history whereby four aircraft carriers and some 240 aircraft were deployed in attacking the Japanese-held oil fields at Palembang in Sumatra. As a prelude to joining up with the huge American 5th Fleet, the Admiralty and US Navy agreed that these oil refineries at Palembang were to be attacked by the RN carrier force known as Task Force 63.

Palembang is a fairly large town on the eastern side of Sumatra linked by road, rail and river. Also importantly, it housed the headquarters of the Japanese Army based in Sumatra.

These two oil refineries were situated on the eastern side of Sumatra at Palembang just south of the town. They had been captured by the Japanese in 1942 and were sabotaged by the Royal Dutch Shell technicians before abandoning them. They were quickly repaired and started to produce petroleum products again.

The Americans considered them to be a major target as they produced some 75% of the aviation fuel and 22% of furnace fuel oil for ships required by the

Japanese in sustaining their war effort. The United States Army Air Force (USAAF) under Operation Boomerang using fifty-*four* B-29s despatched them to bomb the refineries.

The aircraft operated out of RAF China Bay in Ceylon. The results of this bombing raid at night were somewhat mixed, with little damage (only a single building was destroyed) to the actual refineries and no aircraft were lost to the defences. This strategic facility was therefore still intact as a refinery.

The main problem for this British Air Carrier Group was the extremely long supply/logistic trail. The Americans with their industrial power had by 1945 a fairly efficient and well executed logistic chain all the way back to the US Pacific west coast, which provided the vast majority of supplies, manpower, materials and equipment. The Chief of US Naval Operations, Admiral E King accepted the British Fleet but only under the proviso that it be self-sufficient.

However, some American officers in the Pacific war theatre largely ignored the burden of this requirement. It was considered to be inefficient in the overall context of the war effort and possibly unworkable. Supply requests that had to go via Washington were turned down. Senior American Officers told the Head of Britain's Fleet Supply, that he could have anything as long as Admiral King did not know!

However, Britain had built up its own supply train operation out of Trincomalee and appears to have used a mixture of both supply chains. Also joining this British task force was the addition of two escort aircraft carriers, which carried spare aircraft, aircrew, repair facilities and on occasions became a spare flight deck when the decks of the Fleet Carriers were put out of action.

Author's collection – Corsair F-1D FAA colour scheme

Operation Iceberg

Notwithstanding the supply problems, the RN Pacific Fleet saw combat operations in three separate periods with the first being from 21st March until 20th April 1945. The British Fleet then became Task Force 57 and operated as part of the American Fifth Fleet under US Admiral Spruance in readiness for the invasion of Okinawa.

The RN task force was positioned on the South Western flank, between Formosa and Okinawa and its mission was to neutralise the Japanese airfields in the Sakishima Islands. The RN task force was immediately faced with a kamikaze blitz. These suicide attacks turned Okinawa into the bloodiest onslaught the US Navy had ever experienced. The British Task Force was to experience the same onslaught.

Task Force 57 rapidly became a real asset to the US Pacific Fleet. It quickly became obvious to both the USN and RN Commands that the British carriers were able to absorb and stand up to these relentless suicide attacks far better than those of the US. The armoured flight decks of the British carriers were designed to operate in European waters and therefore able to take a heavy beating from land based enemy aircraft.

They were therefore better protected. A heavy toll caused by kamikaze aircraft on the lightly armoured US carriers led to a proportional increase in the use of the British carriers. The Americans were astounded how quickly the British carriers were able to recover back to a combat readiness state. This ability dispelled the concerns of logistic/repair requirements that Task Force 57 may have required.

The US liaison Officer on HMS Indefatigable was amazed at the resilience of the ship. When kamikazes hit a US carrier (the USS Franklin was turned into a blazing inferno), it invariably meant a trip back to Pearl Harbour, for a minimum of six months of repairs. He quipped that the "The Brits only had to get their brooms out, sweep up the mess and their aircraft carriers were soon back in business." For example, one British carrier, HMS Indefatigable, had her flight deck directly hit by a vertical diving kamikaze Zero.

The ship was operational again within one hour. This of course is rather simplistic and disguises the fact that many British sailors died during these kamikaze onslaughts but the armoured decks did save many, many lives. If a Zero had hit one of the US carriers with their wooden flight decks, it would have been immediately put out of action for months and many had to limp back to major repair facilities in the west of America. Another reason why British carriers carried fewer aircraft was because of the extra weight of the flight deck armour.

During researching and collecting information for this chapter, several disparaging comments and misleading analysis on the effectiveness of this Pacific campaign by the RN came to light. If placed into context, the predicament that the British fleet found itself in at the time, such comments are somewhat unjustified.

Firstly, Britain was broke, war-weary and was breathing a collective sigh of relief. Our main protagonist in Europe had been defeated and the majority of the British people were winding down from a war footing and facing a battle-*damaged* economy. They were simply fed up with war.

In 1945, the Americans had been making numerous amphibious advances across the Pacific for nearly four years from their west coast. By that time, albeit in much blood and sacrifice, they had got the experience, operational knowledge and efficient supply lines to keep large fleets at sea. Secondly, they had the wealth, raw materials and an industrial base unhindered from attacks by the enemy. No blackouts or air raid sirens for them!

Ship	Naval Air Squadrons	Aircraft Type
HMS Indefatigable	1772	Firefly I
HMS Indomitable	1839	Hellcat I/II
	1844	Hellcat I/II
HMS Implacable	828	Avenger I/II/III
	880	Seafire F III/l III
HMS Illustrious	1830	Corsairs II
	1833	Corsairs II
HMS Formidable	1842	Corsair II
	848	Avenger I
HMS Victorious	1836	Corsair II/IV
	1834	Corsair II/IV
	849	Avenger II

Aircraft Carriers and Squadrons deployed in the Pacific[1]

During the RN Pacific Fleet's Okinawa campaign, 5,335 sorties were made against kamikaze attacks and 958 tons of bombs were dropped on Japanese airfields.

In summary, the British Pacific Fleet along with the FAA at this stage of the war in early 1945, were at the bottom end of a learning curve in respect of operating multiple carriers together and the subsequent launching of large air groups. However, by the time the Japanese surrendered in August 1945 it had come up to speed and was able to operate on a par with US operations over a relatively short period of time i.e. seven months.

The FAA was handicapped initially, due to the lack of modern naval aircraft at the beginning of WWII and this was result of the FAA being in the wilderness for over two decades equipment wise during the 1920s and '30s. This had led to a dearth of commanders at all levels with experience of naval air operations/tactics and equipment, which simply could not match the developments the US Navy had made in the same period. This was particularly galling for the embryo RNAS in 1918, as it could match and better anything the Americans had been developing during those early days.

Apart from the advantages of having armoured flight decks, another area at which the British carrier group excelled, was better fighter control techniques than the US. These techniques were finely honed because of the better quality of enemy pilots and the aircraft they encountered during the European air war. This led to fewer fighters being deployed for defensive purposes in order to protect the British fleet.

The one area of logistics, which needed to improve, was the antiquated method of refuelling at sea i.e. the trailing of a refuelling hosepipe astern behind the tanker. The Americans had fitted refuelling equipment, which allowed two of their ships to replenish alongside both sides of the tanker simultaneously whilst sailing along at 10 knots.

War Crime 1945

On the 15th August 1945, Sub-Lieutenant Fred Hockley a FAA pilot of the Royal Naval Volunteer Reserve, took off from HMS Indefatigable in a Supermarine Seafire of 894 NAS. He was part of a flight of five Seafires tasked to escort Fairey Firefly and Grumman Avenger fighter-bombers, whose combat mission was to attack airbases in the Tokyo Bay area. The aircraft were subsequently diverted to a different target, namely a chemicals factory in Odaki Bay.

Sub-Lt Hockley suffered a radio failure, was shot down and subsequently bailed out after being attacked by Mitsubushi Zeros. Emperor Hirohito announced the Japanese surrender at 12 noon on that day. After parachuting safely, he was duly captured where the actions and decisions of three senior Japanese officers some nine hours later, led to his execution by beheading.

A War Crimes Court was held in Hong Kong in May/June 1947 whereby all three were put on trial. Colonel Tamura and Major Hirano were hanged in September 1947 and Captain Fujino sentenced to 15 years imprisonment. It was an inexcusably barbaric act by these Japanese soldiers.

Sources

Further details can be found:
www.sohamgrammar.org.uk/fred_hockley_inmem.htm
[1] *Courtesy of the Squadrons of the Fleet Air Arm p398 to 402*

Chapter 6
Korean War 1950–1953

In just five years after WWII in 1945, another South East Asian conflict was to suddenly appear on the horizon. As with the FAA's involvement in the latter days of the Pacific war with Japan, the Korean War was also dubbed by the press at the time as the 'forgotten war', as it was one where many National Servicemen were to feature extensively and play a prominent part in the fighting. Again, British aircraft carriers and FAA squadrons were to play an important role in this conflict.

Going back to 1949, Kim Il-Sung pressed Stalin for an invasion of South Korea. Stalin was sceptical, however, a year later he relented after the Korean People's Army (North Korea) had been re-equipped with Soviet armaments along with the release of North Korean veterans from the Chinese Army. Therefore, once all the equipment and manpower was in place, the North Koreans boldly invaded South Korea across the 38th parallel towards Seoul, on the dawn of the 25th June 1950.

The North Koreans had expected a quick surrender along with a collapse of the Republic of Korea (ROK). This did not happen. President Truman did not press for an immediate declaration for action from Congress as it would take too long but instead, he went to the United Nations to call a halt to this invasion. Initially, divisions of US troops arrived from Japan and fought for two months until August 1950 when the first of the United Nations contingents started to arrive. The British Commonwealth Brigade also arrived shortly afterwards.

After the attack on South Korea, United Nations (UN) troops led by the US, landed in the country. China and the USSR backed North Korea and duly went on to equip them throughout the conflict. Whilst it took some time for the British contingent of the UN allied land force to arrive, the RN and FAA were soon in action when the carrier HMS Triumph was placed under the control of the US Naval Commander in charge of naval operations around Korea.

The first strikes, in conjunction with the American carrier USS Valley Forge, were carried out by twelve Seafire Mk FR 47s along with nine Fireflies Mk FR 1s on the 3rd July 1950 against targets in Korea. This was a remarkable achievement because only eight days earlier, HMS Triumph had left Japan following an exercise and was enjoying a peaceful cruise back to Hong Kong.

She was scheduled to return to the UK in order to retire its elderly Seafires and Fireflies. Therefore, in just over a week after the invasion, HMS Triumph was off to Korea and its FAA squadrons were launching fully armed combat aircraft against targets in North Korea.

During these early days, there had been several incidents of mistaken identity by the Americans, which led to 'D-Day' type black and white stripes being painted on to the wings and fuselages of all non-US type aircraft. Sadly, and in order to highlight the dangers of operating and working on a carrier, a freak accident occurred on board HMS Triumph on the 29th August 1950.

Lt Cdr MacLachlen RN, the Commanding Officer of 800 NAS was killed when he was inside the operations room located in the ship's island, when a Firefly crashed into the flight deck barrier. Fragments from its shattered wooden propeller came flying off at high velocity through an opened porthole and struck and killed him whilst he stood inside. Sadly, he was buried at sea with full military honours and he was to become HMS Triumph's only aircrew fatality during all of the Triumph's tours during the Korean conflict.

Hawker Sea Fury FB11 – Author's image

HMS Triumph was subsequently to do a total of three tours of duty, but by then, the immense operating strain placed on these old aircraft had begun to take its toll. So much so, that HMS Triumph on the 21st September 1950 was ordered to return to the UK. By then, she had only three Seafires and eight Fireflies ready for operations.

They were the last aircraft of these models left in the FAA squadrons as they had been denuded of all the spare airframes and engines for these elderly types, which were no longer available globally. Her sister ship, HMS Theseus was to relieve her within a week equipped with the much more capable Firefly AS Mk 5 and a new powerful fighter-bomber, the Sea Fury FB 11.

Throughout the period of 1950–53, four British aircraft carriers were deployed on station as follows:

HMS Triumph to September 1950
HMS Theseus to April 1951
HMS Glory to September 1951
HMAS Sydney to January 1952 (formerly HMS Majestic)
HMS Glory to May 1952
HMS Ocean to November 1952
HMS Glory to May 1953
HMS Ocean to the end of hostilities – 27th July 1953

Some fourteen Naval Air Squadrons of the FAA were embarked and participated as follows:

800 NAS – 1950
801 NAS – 1952 to 1953
802 NAS – 1952
804 NAS – 1951 to 1952
805 NAS – 1951 to 1952
807 NAS – 1950 to 1953
808 NAS – 1951 to 1952
810 NAS – 1950 to 1953
812 NAS – 1951 to 1952
817 NAS – 1951 to 1952
821 NAS – 1952 to 1953
825 NAS – 1952
827 NAS – 1950
898 NAS – 1952 to 1953

Seafires, Fairey Fireflies, Sea Furies and a later version of the Firefly were to operate from RN aircraft carriers, thus providing the only British tactical air combat and ground attack contribution to the Korean War. Also utilised for the very first time was the use of Search and Rescue helicopters, i.e. the Westland Dragonfly, which was particularly suited to this role. Its specific purpose was to rescue downed aircrew.

On the tactical air power front, Britain's contribution during this 3-year conflict was entirely provided by the Fleet Air Arm operating from x 5 light Fleet Carriers. Flying operations consisted of 14 days on, 14 days off throughout the conflict over a period of three years. No messing, no compromise. There was no direct RAF air combat contribution during this war although some pilots flew Super Sabres with the USAF.

RAF transports were utilised but their involvement was minimal. RAF Sunderlands of No. 205 Squadron gave air cover to United Nations naval forces bombarding Communist coastal towns. Aircraft of the Seletar Sunderland wing, made up of No's 88, 205 and 209 Squadrons were based at Iwakuni in southern Japan and operated on four-week cycle of deployments.

The Aircraft

It is worth briefly mentioning the aircraft that were involved and the problems they encountered in this conflict. It was to produce the first shooting down of a jet by a piston engine aircraft. The Seafire, which was based on the Spitfire design and although a splendid aircraft on land, it was to show during the Pacific War in 1945, that it was not sturdy enough for carrier operations. The Mk 47 version stood out because it had a contra-rotating three bladed propeller designed to counteract the enormous torque that the RR Griffon 87 engine produced.

In reality, even with modifications, the Mk 47 was never intended to operate from aircraft carriers. Apart from the many undercarriage failures and stresses, which caused wrinkling of the fuselage skin, it was also a very difficult aircraft to land on a carrier. Some creative squadron engineering was employed where a special measuring device was used to keep track of the wrinkling of the fuselage skin caused by these demanding combat conditions.

In any other circumstances, most Seafires would have been withdrawn from service for repair once any skin ripples appeared. At the end of one FAA operational period on the frontline, all Seafires of one squadron had to be completely removed back from embarked service for re-skinning and deep maintenance.

Seafire Mk III – author's photo

The specifically designed Hawker Sea Fury, eventually replaced the Seafire and it proved to be a more powerful and robust naval fighter/bomber aircraft.

This aircraft was to achieve fame in 1952 by being the first recorded piston-engine aircraft to have shot down a jet fighter in air-to-air combat. This occurred in November 1952 when Lieutenant 'Hoagy' Carmichael RN was credited with the shooting down of a MiG 15.

He was flying a Sea Fury FB11 from HMS Ocean belonging to 802 NAS and was leading a four aircraft formation. The targets were railway facilities between Pyongyang and Machon near Chinnampo, when his No 2, Sub-Lt Haines warned over the radio that a formation of eight MiGs were diving from behind and to their starboard side. They turned towards the MiGs and commenced a scissor turn, making themselves very difficult to target.

A MiG came at him, he held on and then fired a burst as the enemy rushed by, with others getting hits on to the MiG too. For this action, Carmichael was awarded the Distinguished Service Cross.

Recently, an update on this action has come to light and it appears other aircrew in this Sea Fury formation were probably more responsible for the shooting down of the MiG 15. It looks as if the Navy at the time was seeking some publicity and the senior officer involved, rightly or wrongly was attributed with this kill.

Hawker Sea Fury front fuselage (Mk T20) – author's photograph

The Fairey Firefly Mk AS-6 was primarily built for the FAA with the type eventually flying with a total of some 24 Naval Air Squadrons. It had a crew of two, separated in a tandem cockpit and was powered by different marks of Griffon engine throughout its service life. The Firefly operated in a variety of fighter, bomber, reconnaissance and anti-submarine roles. It became an early example of a truly multi-role combat aircraft. It remained in service until the mid-1950s with both the Canadians and Australians operating the aircraft following purchases of 108 and 65 aircraft respectively.

Fairey Firefly AS-6 – Courtesy of Richard Seaman

Research reveals some interesting facts taken randomly from the Korean War and FAA statistics, which are highlighted in the table below. One has to remember that each column represents but **one British aircraft carrier** with their embarked squadrons over a period of four months. There were over the three years of the conflict, three other carriers involved. These being HMS Glory, Triumph and Theseus (another if you include the Australian aircraft carrier HMAS Melbourne), which also produced similar sortie rates.

It is interesting to compare the difference in tempo of the operations being carried out by the RAF Akrotiri today in Cyprus, where many other support aircraft are required for the Typhoons, the F35Bs and Voyagers needed for flight refuelling, AWACS and other intelligence gathering aircraft. It has to be remembered that the base at RAF Akrotiri needs to be regularly supplied with rotating personnel, spares and equipment by Airbus A400s and C-17 Globemasters of RAF Support Command.

All the sorties figures represent a catapult launch (in some cases with rocket assisted take-offs) and arrester gear landings. At its peak, HMS Ocean during flying stations was launching an aircraft, on average, one every 35 seconds and upon their return from a mission, the ship could recover one aircraft every 18 seconds. By any standards, a phenomenal operational achievement.

Statistics – Aircraft Carrier v Fixed Base Sorties Comparison

The table below shows the sortie and strike rate of just two aircraft carriers involved in the Korean War over a period of several months compared with the strikes being flown out of Cyprus by the RAF between 2016 and 2019 against ISIS.

	Aircraft Carrier		RAF Akrotiri Cyprus
	HMS Triumph	**HMS Ocean**	
Embarked Aircraft	Seafires – 800 NAS Fireflies – 827 NAS	Sea Furies – 802 NAS Fireflies – 825 NAS	Typhoons Tornados
Period	July 1950 to Sept 1950	May 1952 to Oct 1952	Oct 2016 to Sept 2019
Sorties/Strikes	3,900	5,945	900
Weapons dropped/fired	x 3,400 rockets x 170,000 rounds	x 420 1,000 pounds x 3,464 500 rounds x 16,490 rockets	216 mixtures of missiles and bombs

In retrospect, these figures simply reinforced the potency of a fixed wing strike carrier even taking into account the different weapon loads of a modern-*day* strike aircraft – this is the reason why the Americans had three nuclear strike aircraft carriers on station when tensions arose recently with North Korea. This mobile strike capability is available immediately.

More tonnage of bombs was dropped during the Korean conflict by the UN forces than those used throughout WWII in the Pacific. The vast majority of it being delivered by naval air power of the RN and USN. Sadly, some 22 FAA pilots were killed during this conflict. Many of these were shot down and although captured, some were never seen again. Eventually, an armistice was signed in July 1953. However, no formal declaration of war or peace treaty has ever been signed. It remains so to this day.

In the initial phase of this war, it was the US, which was the main driving force. The British in conjunction with other nations, fought as allies under the umbrella of the United Nations going to the aid of South Korea. This was a brutal war with indescribable conditions being experienced on both land and sea. Unfortunately, some 3–5 million people were to be killed. Figures vary because neither the Chinese nor the North Koreans have ever released their true losses.

Also, one aspect of this war sometimes skimmed over, was the weather. Whilst those fighting on land faced atrociously freezing temperatures, with those on working on the flight decks suffered appalling conditions too. One FAA Korean veteran armourer said, that arming the aircraft in many tens of degrees below freezing was a personal challenge along with many of his squadron colleagues suffering from frostbite.

The wind chill blowing across the deck during launches made maintenance and refuelling even more difficult. To illustrate how cold it was, he remembers that even the stokers in the engine boiler rooms wore overcoats!

This conflict proved to be one of the triumphs of the FAA's strike capabilities over a prolonged period. It was able to match and even better the Americans in aircraft carrier operations. It was from the experience gained by Royal Navy pilots during this conflict that led to the developments of the angled deck, the steam catapult and mirror landing system, which were to emerge later – they all were British inventions.

Sources

https://www.britannica.com/event/Korean-War
http://www.royalnavyresearcharchive.org.uk/Article_Forgotten_Cruise.htm

Chapter 7
SUEZ – 1956

On the 26th July 1956, the newly elected Egyptian President Colonel Nasser nationalised the Suez Canal, which previously had been mainly owned by Britain and France. To gain back control of the canal, an Anglo-French force aided by Israel, military invasion took place on the 5th–6th November 1956.

This was to be a classic and successful FAA operation operating from recently modernised RN aircraft carriers carrying out the first amphibious assault utilising helicopters landing an embarked force of Royal Marines. The French contribution to this naval task force included the two aircraft carriers, the Arromanches and Lafayette.

What became known as the 'Suez Crisis', was originally instigated by the US and British Government's decision not to finance the construction of the Aswan High Dam in Egypt, which had been duly promised. A convoluted political game had been developing over a period of time and the Anglo-US decision was in response to the expanding ties Egypt was making with the communist Soviets and Czechoslovakia.

Colonel Nasser played a very cagey game between the East and West, especially with respect to arms sales. Commentators and experts at the time said he was a very difficult man to read but was astute in building up his pan-Arabic and nationalistic image and ideology. He wanted to see Egypt become the focal point of the Middle East and strongly opposed any security initiatives emanating from the West.

After this decision, Nasser declared martial law around the canal zone and seized the Suez Canal Company. He reckoned that the fees from ships using the canal would pay for the new dam's construction within five years. However, Britain and France feared Nasser would possible close the canal, thus choking off the oil from the Middle East Gulf States destined for Europe.

With diplomatic efforts failing, Britain and France made secret plans to invade Egypt militarily and re-establish control of the canal and if possible, remove Nasser. There was a willing ally in Israel as there was mounting hostility towards Egypt over their blockage at the mouth of the Gulf of Aqaba and the frequent raids by Egyptian-backed commandos into Israel during 1956–57.

The joint Anglo-French and Israeli forces prepared for their assault on Egypt during August/September 1956. On the 29th October, under the code name of 'Operation Musketeer', the Israelis attacked across the Sinai. On the 30th October, the Allies received their orders to initiate operations in the occupation of Port Said and capture the Suez Canal. On the 31st October in the late afternoon, allied air attacks commenced with the aim of destroying the Egyptian Air Force.

RAF Valiants and Canberras led these attacks operating out of airfields at Malta and Cyprus. At first light on the 1st November, in conjunction with French and British naval aircraft from three strike carriers joined shore-*based* RAF aircraft in initiating attacks on Egyptian airfields. Some 12 Naval Air Squadrons operated from the carriers, with six of them being equipped with Hawker Seahawks.

By the end of 2nd November, destruction of the Egyptian Air Force was all but complete. During 3rd November, the air effort switched from the airfields to other military targets such as camps and barracks sites. An attack was made on the railway marshalling yards at Ismailia with the view of stopping Egyptian reinforcements reaching Port Said. Attacks were also made by the FAA, when they came across three E-boats heading for Alexandria. Two were sunk and the third damaged but was allowed to pick up survivors and head back into Port Said.

On the 5th November, British paratroopers, who were on the west side of Port Said, carried out an initial airborne assault joined up with French paratroopers. This combined force landed on the south side. Airborne drops continued but, on the 6th November 1956, history was made by a seaborne landing utilising the Royal Marines of 40 and 42 Commando. The FAA squadron of 848 flying Westland Whirlwinds airlifted them from the two commando carriers HMS Ocean and Theseus.

Westland Wyvern – author's photograph
(9 Wyverns of 830 NAS operated from HMS Eagle during Suez)

Throughout the assault to capture the canal and Port Said, tactical air support was provided by Sea Hawks from embarked FAA squadrons, along with a squadron of Westland Wyverns and French F4U-7 Corsairs. The Westland Wyvern S4s of 830 NAS embarked on HMS Eagle, were flown during the Suez operation and were to become one of the last propeller driven aircraft to be used in combat operations by the FAA.

Between the 2nd and 6th November, Wyverns flew numerous missions, some 74 in all, attacking airfields, bridges, barracks and camps. Two Wyverns were lost to anti-aircraft fire with both pilots successfully ejecting over the sea. They were picked up and rescued by the SAR helicopter from HMS Eagle. It was remarked upon in the follow-up reports, how readily available and advantageous the carrier borne aircraft were.

Both French and British carrier aircraft were stacked and circling overhead likened to a taxi rank on a continuous basis and called down to support ground troops when required. It should be noted that the French Navy Corsairs attacked the airport at Cairo, when one was shot down by anti-aircraft fire. The pilot was captured and duly executed by the Egyptians allegedly by stoning.

Hawker Sea Hawk Mk FA 6 – author's photograph

Outcome and Summary

It was recognised at the time by both the French and the Israelis in the planning of this invasion, that only Britain had the necessary littoral naval air power to neutralise the Egyptian Air Force. Fortuitously, the RN went into this operation well equipped. Learning from the Korean War several years previously, an extensive carrier modernisation had been undertaken.

A total of twelve FAA squadrons (see table of RN participants below) took part and were embarked on the three RN strike aircraft carriers, plus the two French carriers. They provided the majority of tactical close air support to the Royal Marine Commandos plus the British and French paratroopers. The RAF's Hawker Hunters stationed at Cyprus were too far away and could only spend less than 15 minutes on station before having to turn back to base.

The other nearest RAF base was at Malta, which was 1,000 miles away to the west and therefore impractical for providing close air support during Operation Musketeer. Night time bombings by Valiants and Canberras were found to be ineffective.

Also, for the first time, Westland Whirlwind Mk 22 helicopters of 845 NAS airlifted Royal Marines, who were embarked and carried out the world's first sea borne assault by helicopter. Also in support, some Bristol Belvedere helicopters were used in the assault on Port Said. The Belvedere, a British built twin rotor type whose configuration was similar to that of the Chinook, was later to see service in the RAF. Ironically, this helicopter was initially designed for use by the Navy.

It was a textbook military operation and demonstrated the flexibility of getting troops into action quickly and efficiently from the sea. These troops were a self-contained battle-*ready* unit who could easily be resupplied from their 'home base' i.e. the aircraft carrier located off-shore. It was from here that the Navy developed the concept of 'Commando Carriers' and Commando carrying FAA helicopters.

In line with carrying this amphibious contingent of Royal Marines, the fixed wing aircraft carriers also operated jets for the first time using the new angle deck concept and mirror landing aids. Furthermore, some twenty-five Sea Venoms embarked on HMS Eagle and Albion were equipped with radar and were capable of night operations.

The Allied forces were well on their way in seizing all of its objectives, when on the 6th November a United Nations resolution called for a ceasefire at midnight. With a spearhead of troops reaching El Cap, some 23 miles south of Port Said, no further movements of Allied Forces would take place.

Unfortunately, the shenanigans of global politics led to a UN led ceasefire and effectively put an end to Operation Musketeer as it was known. It could also be considered that this operation was the beginning of the end of Britain as a major world power, mainly because there was no support from Britain's major allies. The US had also applied financial and diplomatic pressure to end the invasion.

The Bank of England had lost some £40 million at the end of October and the beginning of November 1956, and coupled with dwindling oil supplies because of closure of the Suez Canal, Britain sought a loan from the IMF. The US threatened to veto this loan and being unable to withstand a devaluation of the pound, Britain was forced to order a ceasefire.

It is worthy of note in the aftermath, that had the Prime Minister taken the decision to invade the Suez Canal earlier in the June when the world was still in shock over its nationalisation, the outcome might have been different. Also, it is interesting to note how America's foreign policy in the Middle East was changed dramatically some 35 years plus later in the Iraq conflict.

However, despite the political background, from a military perspective the assault and brief occupation of key objectives around the canal and beyond was an overwhelming success. All achieved quickly and efficiently with relatively few loses. The FAA operating from RN carriers played a vital part in that success. The operation also demonstrated once again the benefit of a carrier force being stationed a few miles off-shore, enabling it to provide close air support to ground assault troops both on the coast and inland.

These troops could be brought to bear quickly and rapidly moved as the tactical situation on the ground demanded. Now for the very first time with radar carrying aircraft at sea, the RN had the ability to provide 24/7-*day*, night and all-*weather* cover for both the fleet and combatants ashore. Surprise was the main feature, as this maritime force could cruise outside national territorial waters below the horizon without causing any diplomatic problems.

Disappointingly, no doubt due to the political climate of the time, no battle honours were awarded for this particular military action. On the individual honours front, the FAA was awarded x6 Members of the British Empire, x4 Distinguished Service Crosses, and x21 Mention in Despatches.

Role	Aircraft Carriers	FAA Squadrons
Strike carrier	HMS Albion	800 NAS – Seahawks 802 NAS – Seahawks 800 NAS – Sea Venoms
Strike carrier	HMS Bulwark	810 NAS – Seahawks 895 NAS – Seahawks
Strike carrier	HMS Eagle	830 NAS – Wyverns 849 NAS C Flt – Skyraiders 892 NAS – Sea Venoms 893 NAS – Sea Venoms 897 NAS – Seahawks 899 NAS – Seahawks
Commando Carrier	HMS Ocean	845 NAS – Whirlwinds 22
Commando Carrier	HMS Theseus	Ditto

RN Aircraft carriers and FAA Squadron participants – Suez 1956

Sources

https://www.naval-history.net/WXLG-Suez.htm
https://en.wikipedia.org/wiki/Suez_Crisis
https://www.britannica.com/event/Suez-Crisis

Chapter 8
The Middle East – 1958 to 1960

A prime example of the flexibility, rapid reaction capabilities and effectiveness of an aircraft carrier's ability to respond quickly to political decisions came to the fore in the late 1950s and early 1960s. In the early 1950s and even before the Suez crisis of 1956, the Navy had recognised the need to move away from a direct conflict with the Soviet Union and adopt a policy where mobility and more efficient use of resources was to become the order of the day.

Operation Musketeer for Suez, exposed the folly of relying on fixed bases, which were too far away from the Egyptian canal and invariably had restrictions placed upon their use. They also exposed to the potential banning and diplomatic issues of flights over former British colonies. The Navy quietly moved to a more littoral role with the use of two new assault ships, HMS Fearless and Intrepid.

Two light fleet carriers, HMS Bulwark and Albion were also commissioned as 'Commando Carriers' carrying some 16+ FAA designated helicopters called 'Commando Squadrons'. Initially, these were Whirlwinds but were soon replaced by the more superior performing Westland Wessex helicopter. Some 140 of all types of the Wessex were built for the FAA and saw service for over 37 years. The FAA Commando Squadrons were to become affectionately known as the 'Junglies'. (See Chapter 14 – The FAA's Unsung Helicopter Boys).

Jordan 1958

Following some years of turmoil in the Middle East during the late 1950s, Jordan in 1958 sought US/UK assistance against Iraqi aggression. There had been ongoing problems in the area, which included Iraq laying claim to Kuwait and a threat of invading them. (This was as history was to show, repeated some 30 years later in what later became known as Gulf War I).

The carrier HMS Eagle provided support for British airborne forces in Jordan. HMS Eagle's carrier borne fighters provided air defence cover because RAF fighter bases were out of range and unable to provide adequate air protection for RAF transport aircraft flying from Cyprus.

Problems in the area were again to be repeated, whereby under Operation Vantage in 1961, a British military operation was mounted to support the newly independent state of Kuwait against Iraq's aggressive claim and stance on its former's territory. Britain had previously accepted responsibility for the defence and protection of Kuwait.

Following a call for support from the leader; the Emir of Kuwait, British Naval forces and two Royal Marine Commandos Units (42 and 45) were deployed to Kuwait. The carriers HMS Bulwark and HMS Victorious led this operation, with the latter being eventually relieved by the strike carrier HMS Centaur.

HMS Bulwark had Royal Marine 42 Commando embarked, with their vehicles and equipment travelled over 1,000 miles to Kuwait within two days. Using her helicopters, the ship was able to deploy and support the Marines ashore by helicopters within 24 hours. Helpful intelligence had positioned HMS Bulwark in the right place, allowing two frigates and five tank-landing craft to quickly join her.

This whole task force was self-supporting due to the redeployment of Royal Fleet Auxiliary replenishment ships for logistics and fuel. HMS Bulwark's presence immediately brought calm and a steadying influence to the region. The newly commissioned commando carrier carried Whirlwind helicopters of 848 NAS and was at the time in Karachi, Pakistan.

The original intention for her was to transit to the Persian Gulf for hot weather trials. Although Bulwark was not originally part of Operation Vantage, she had been fortuitously positioned in readiness for the rising tensions taking place in the region.

To complete the support buttress, the strike carrier HMS Victorious with her escorts arrived several days later bringing the full 'power package' i.e. strike capability after having sailed from the South China Sea. A squadron of RAF Hunters, based in Bahrain, was deployed to Kuwait but lacked fuel, spares and ammunition. Most critically, there was no Ground Control Interception (GCI) radar coverage except that provided by HMS Bulwark.

The Hunters left once HMS Victorious was on station. One outcome of this operation in Kuwait, was that HMS Albion (the second commando carrier) was later to be equipped with better surveillance radar. This type was installed to enable the RN to provide better cover in the future in order to support RAF aircraft overseas, when operating away from their fixed overseas bases.

Operation Vantage was considered a success. Acting in a deterrent role, the rapid deployment of HMS Bulwark carrying 42 Royal Marine Commando along with 848 Naval Air Squadron operating Whirlwind HAS 7 helicopters were a key and deciding factor. With the experience learnt from the Suez operation some five years earlier, Bulwark was able to loiter off the coast out of sight waiting for orders and the arrival of further military assets.

42 Commando was fully equipped i.e. ammunition, fuel, spares and all the requirements to go into action at a moments' notice. Unfortunately, the second Royal Marine contingent 45 Commando arrived by RAF transport after being airlifted from Aden but during transit and stopovers, much of their logistical support had become stranded en route.

However, fortuitously, the fact that HMS Bulwark had undergone some 18 months intensive training in her commando role and was the only British military asset available to arrive immediately. She therefore, was primed and on a war footing able to fight immediately.

Another valuable point frequently overlooked by military planners was the temperature in Kuwait being encountered during the first two weeks of July. This ranged from 40 to 45 Centigrade (100- *and 112-degrees* Fahrenheit in 'old' money). Those already embarked on Bulwark were somewhat acclimatised to these temperatures and therefore those arriving 'out of theatre' were at a huge disadvantage as they could not go into action straight away.

Secondly, once the Marines had disembarked, the aircraft carrier was able to sit just off-shore and with its air conditioning, able to offer respite to those operating at the coal face on a rotational basis.

Although HMS Bulwark was only capable of giving limited radar coverage, this limitation was overcome by the arrival of HMS Victorious some nine days later. She came on station with her Sea Vixen FAW 1s, (893 NAS) thus giving a genuine day and night and all-*weather* capability. Also on board were Scimitars (803 NAS), which in its ground attack role soon added clout to the RAF's Hunters.

Regrettably, operations were to expose some of the Scimitars' limitations in hot weather i.e. lack of power. This meant they could not take-off with drop tanks fitted, thus limiting the time on station. This deficiency was soon recognised and accelerated their replacement with the introduction of the Blackburn Buccaneer.

Sea Vixen Mk1s – 766 NAS – Author's commission painting

Like Bulwark, Victorious arrived with a fully worked up air group ready for action. She was a fully operational strike carrier and self-contained floating airfield with her own sophisticated radar coverage. Having transitioned from the South China Sea during the nine days voyage, she also had the advantage of being acclimatised to the local conditions and was ready for action once on station. The 'Vic' was eventually relieved by HMS Centaur, which had been ordered to the Eastern Mediterranean at the same time HMS Victorious was sailing from the Indian Ocean to Kuwait.

In essence, some four British aircraft carriers (three strike and one commando) were involved. It once again demonstrated the versatility of the carrier and for the first time, Britain had a sophisticated and mobile, day and night air defence ability operating at sea. Little known at the time, the Royal Rhodesian Air Force transports were freely placed at Britain's disposal at the outset of the operation.

Sources

https://api.parliament.uk/historic-hansard/commons/1961/jul/11/kuwait

Chapter 9
The 1960s – The Defining Decade for the FAA's Future

The decade of the 1960s was one, which proved to be very turbulent and unsettling from a FAA perspective. It was equally turbulent for the RAF because the UK's nuclear deterrent was moving from the V-bomber force to the Royal Navy with the introduction of the Polaris type submarines carrying nuclear missiles. The RAF were also to experience the cancellation of several aircraft projects i.e. the TSR 2, P1154 and then the US built swing-wing Lockheed F-111(K) aircraft a potential replacement for the TSR 2.

A furious and bitter inter-service rivalry was to develop, where battle-lines were to be drawn over the requirements of the Navy against those of the RAF. The Navy requirement of at least two new aircraft carriers, was countered by the RAF, who tried to persuade the government that the UK's post-colonial responsibilities in the Middle and Far East could be achieved by an 'island hopping strategy'.

This inter-service rivalry was allowed to develop and this rivalry was partially manipulated by the politicians, culminating in the major involvement and influence of the then Labour Defence Minister in 1966, namely Denis Healey. The decisions made at this time were to have a profound effect on the FAA's future for the next 20 years and contributed to a further decline in Britain's naval airpower prowess.

My involvement with the FAA commenced when I joined the RN as an aircraft artificer in 1961. Five years later in 1966, I was eventually to join the 'coalface' of the FAA on a Sea Vixen squadron as a fully-fledged Aircraft Artificer 2nd class. My entry of around 35 aircraft artificers throughout the five years apprenticeship lived through uncertain times with regard to our FAA career, as there were to be several contradictory defence reviews during our apprenticeship.

One minute the RN was going to get two new aircraft carriers (CVA01 and 02) and at one stage, some 120 Phantoms were going to be procured to embark on them. The Navy manpower planners were astute because my entry in September 1961 as a sprog artificer was the largest entry ever to join and one assumed this number was recruited in order to meet the manning requirements of these new carriers and their escorts.

Manning the Navy post 'National Service' era with an 'all volunteer' service was a headache. As previously mentioned, also coming into service during the mid-1960s was the introduction into the RN of the nuclear deterrent in the shape of Polaris submarines. However, history was to show that the Navy did not get any of these new carriers and eventually only 48 Phantoms F4Ks (the Navy's version) were ordered.

Sounds very familiar to the scenario being faced today regarding F35B numbers? Actually, the FAA only got 29 of this version of the Phantom with the remainder being allocated to the RAF. This, in turn, meant only one FAA squadron of these aircraft would eventually embark on an aging HMS Ark Royal.

This decade throughout the 1960s resulted in being a tumultuous one for the FAA as a whole. In a matter of 8 years, the FAA's 'glass of wine' went from overflowing, to one where there only just a few drops left at the bottom of the glass. This was because of the decisions made during this period, which was to result in fixed wing flying from genuine strike carriers to cease by 1978. The cause of this change away from any carriers was due to a more competent and persistent RAF Staff Command.

They kept constantly pestering, lobbying and cajoling the Government on a wide front with their case. This was to prove in the longer term, not to be in the UK's best interests. However, it was in the best interest of the RAF, whose 'Island Hopping Strategy' was to be accepted by the Government of the day.

How did all this come about? It was fairly obvious in the mid-1950s that all of the existing RN aircraft carriers, which had been laid down and built with designs made before or during World War II, were due for replacement. Earl Mountbatten, who as a former 1st Sea Lord and then Chief of the Defence Staff was influential in steering through the new carriers in the late 1950s and early 1960s.

Preliminary plans were put forward that two carrier replacements were going to be needed. The 'rumour factory' within the FAA at the time thought that a third new carrier was also going to be included. The two new proposed carriers, which were going to be built in the UK, were preliminary designated as follows:

- CVA01 to replace HMS Victorious and/or HMS Ark Royal.
- CVA02 would be the replacement for HMS Hermes.

The rumoured third carrier CVA03 was a replacement for HMS Eagle. All this seemed logical because as Britain's operation of aircraft carriers had historically shown, that at any given time, one aircraft carrier was always in a dockyard for upgrades and refits. Another important factor in this post war era of the UK that needs to be highlighted, were the recurring financial crises centred on the economic and balance of payments problems which the country found itself in during the 1960s.

There was an eventual devaluation of the £ in 1968, which was the prime cause for the reduction in the exchange rate. Harold Wilson, the then Prime Minister was famous for the comment of the 'The Pound in your pocket'. Wilson was referring to a devaluation of the pound by 14.3% and interest rates being hiked to 8% and trying to explain that that the pound abroad was not worth less than the pound here in Britain, i.e. the one in your pocket/purse/bank had not been devalued.

He was widely derided but basically the country was under constant severe financial pressures, if not broke during the 1960s. Couple this with the dire economic situation and the political decisions to close all of Britain's overseas bases East of Suez and then withdraw from the Middle East, pointed to the fact that we were reverting back again to becoming a European based power.

In the early 1960s, Britain was still in the premier league with regard to aircraft carriers. Only the US Navy was larger and they were embarking on re-equipping their Navy with the 80,000 ton 'Kitty Hawk' class of aircraft carriers. While all four of the UK's largest carriers at the time could operate the Blackburn Buccaneer, only HMS Eagle and HMS Ark Royal were physically big enough as fleet carriers to take a viable mixture of the proposed US built Phantom and Buccaneers.

Aircraft were becoming larger and heavier, requiring longer flight decks for taking off and landings. Because HMS Hermes and Victorious could not take the necessary mixture of aircraft, it became imperative that Britain needed to replace two fleet carriers by the mid-1960s. Despite withdrawal from the Far East, there was still a Government geo-political policy of maintaining influence in the region. Many studies, enquiries, strategic papers and political arguments were put forward. Eventually because of the financial constraints pertaining at the time, only one new aircraft carrier was going to be built i.e. the CVA01.

Author's photographic artwork of RN Phantom F4K of 892 NAS and sketch of CVA01 planned for the 1970s

In order to cover any contingencies post the Far East withdrawal, an alternative strategy of 'Island Hopping' was being pushed; developed by the RAF staff, it began to win support from the Treasury. The latter could see savings, which the RAF alleged could be made over expensive aircraft carriers. This was in direct opposition to the Royal Navy's 'Carrier Strategy' in a post-East of Suez era.

The question of replacing the carriers was in truth going to have a major impact on the defence budget, which in turn would also have an equally significant impact on the RAF's share of this budget. They had at the time planned for the TSR2, P1127 (eventually to become the Harrier) and possibly development of the P1154 (an updated follow-on supersonic version of the Harrier) were all part of their future plans. Therefore, the RAF saw their 'Island Hopping' proposals as a way of safeguarding their new equipment procurements.

When the 'Island Hopping Strategy' ideas began to surface in 1962, the inter-service rivalry began to heat up considerably. The RAF and Air Ministry began to influence defence experts and of course politicians, on the use of four islands in the Indian Ocean and bases in Australia. These islands incidentally were Aldabra, Masirah, Gan and Cocos.

The basis of their argument was based on the idea that they could act as staging posts and could rapidly be reinforced from the UK by air. Any one of these bases closest to any trouble could be utilised, with troops, and radar and air defence systems being airlifted in to establish a forward operating base. The TRS2 would provide strike capability while the proposed P1154 (supersonic Harrier) would fulfil any air defence requirements.

Unfortunately, the RAF produced an infamous map in 1962 showing the air coverage these bases could provide globally. The RAF and Air Ministry used this map extensively during many discussions throughout the winter of 1963. Naval Air Staff received these maps with great scepticism alleging the RAF had 'moved' Australia some 400 miles nearer Singapore!

Many FAA veterans of all ranks to this day remain convinced that politicians and defence civil servants were deliberately misled by RAF Staff, who were economical with the truth beyond reasonable limits over the distances involved in support of their island-*hopping* strategy. The Admiralty then again had to defend its concept of a Carrier Task Force, so MOD decided to set up a scientific expert group headed and led by the then Chief Scientific Advisor Solly Zuckerman.

This final report was delivered in April 1963. The outcome was firmly in favour of a carrier task force in light of the Government wanting to keep influence and the capacity to intervene if required in the East of Suez. The scientific group based their conclusions on the proven use of fixed wing (strike) carriers and amphibious forces as used in Korea and Suez.

Although the alternative strategy appeared on the surface cheaper, the scientific advisors did not believe the RAF's 'dream scheme' of utilising island bases was realistic. Their scepticism centred on three key elements:

1. The political uncertainty of over-flights above unfriendly countries. Problems were envisaged, particularly in the Middle East and Gulf states.

2. Having sufficient capacity and the ability to achieve the reinforcements of these islands and sustainability.
3. The inflexibility of having permanently fixed bases, which would require a British skeleton crew to keep such bases operational.

The 1960–63 debates ended in July 1963, when the RN won its case for carrier-based task forces against the RAF's island strategy that had been aggressively pushed by them. The Cabinet agreed with the Navy and the political decision was made to proceed with the carrier replacement programme. An order for the first new carrier was placed by Peter Thorneycroft, the then Conservative Minister of Defence, in early 1963. This new carrier CVA01 construction programme was not to last long.

Artist Impression of the CVA-01

Though the Admiralty had won this round, the battle was still to carry on and the Navy would come into conflict with the Treasury. The inter-service rivalry was to deepen further. The Air Ministry and RAF resolved at every opportunity to push, repeat and reiterate their Island Strategy to all and sundry. The RAF considered that carrier-based strategy was expensive, which had been picked up by the Treasury and although the decision to order had been agreed, no funding was forthcoming.

Major political changes were to take place when there was a General Election in October 1964. Without going into too many details, the Labour Government came into power under the Premiership of Harold Wilson as previously mentioned. A major player in this inter-service battle of carriers versus island bases came on the scene in the figure of Denis Healey, the new Secretary State for Defence.

He became the foremost influencer in this battle, which the RAF was quick to pick up on. The Wilson Government initially, did not want any major changes to the previous Conservative policies. However, the Labour Party's chief modus operandi at the time was one of disarmament and to deal with international bodies only, such as the United Nations or other similar organisations. In other words, they wanted to pursue a less interventionist stance.

By 1965–66, the same arguments and lengthy debates were pushed forward as in 1963, with the Admiralty not coming out with anything new. Though their arguments were strong and viable, the Admiralty failed on the PR front as they did not communicate their case adequately to the MOD, public, or more importantly the Defence Minister and politicians.

However, at the same time, the Air Ministry subtly changed the 'Island Hopping Strategy' into one entitled 'Land-based air power' as the alternative. The RAF became even more aggressive and cleverly linked and aligned their ideas to British foreign policy on defence spending. In particularly, they won the support of the Treasury by stating that their strategy was the most cost-effective.

Denis Healey was against any new carriers confirming Labour's stance whilst in opposition. The Defence Review White Paper was published in February 1966 and the following is an extract of the White Paper covering the future of the Royal Navy under this review:

The Navy of the 1970s

33. "The Royal Navy will exploit to the full the most modern technologies in the maritime sphere, particularly in nuclear propulsion and guided missiles." When the Polaris-carrying, nuclear submarine fleet becomes fully operational in 1969–70, the Royal Navy will take over from the Royal Air Force full responsibility for the strategic nuclear deterrent, at a planned cost of under 2% of the total defence budget.

By the early 1970s, we reckon to have in service four nuclear-propelled hunter-killer submarines, which, with their long endurance and immunity to detection, will be a formidable part of our anti-submarine defences. We shall complete the conversion of the Tiger class cruisers to carry anti-submarine helicopters and we are planning a 'new type of ship' to succeed them.

We shall shortly order the first of a new, more powerful class of guided missile ships-the Type 82-to be equipped with the surface-to-air guided weapon Seadart, the Ikara anti-submarine weapon and the new Anglo-Dutch radar. We shall develop a small surface-to-surface guided weapon for use against missile-firing craft. Our amphibious fleet-the commando ships and assault craft carrying Royal Marine commandos-will greatly strengthen our forces outside Europe.

34. *The present carrier force will continue well into the 1970s; but we shall not build the carrier (CVA 01). This ship could not have come into service before 1973 when our remaining commitments will not require her and the necessary elements of carrier capability will have been replaced as explained below.*

35. *The conditions under which we intend to operate our forces outside Europe are set out in paragraph 36. There are limitations on the use of our present forces; we must face the fact that these limitations are likely to grow more severe. This is the background to any assessment of the case for keeping a carrier force in the Far East in the 1970s.*

Experience and study have shown that only one type of operation exists for which carriers and carrier-borne aircraft would he indispensable that is the landing or withdrawal of troops against sophisticated opposition outside the range of land-based air cover. It is only realistic to recognise that we, unaided by our allies, could not expect to undertake operations of this character in the 1970s, even if we could afford a larger carrier force than planned.

36. *But the best carrier force we could manage to in future would be very small. The force of five carriers, which we inherited from the previous Government, will reduce to three in a few years' time. Even if CVA 01 were built, the force would be limited to three ships throughout the 1970s.*

The total cost of such a force would be some £1,200 million over a ten-year period. For this price, we should "be able to have one carrier permanently stationed in the Far Fast with another available at up to 1.5 days' notice. We do not believe that this could give a sufficient operational return for our expenditure."

37. We also believe that the tasks for which carrier borne aircraft might be required in the late 1970s can be more cheaply performed in other ways. Our plan is that, in the future, aircraft operating from land bases should take over the strike/reconnaissance and air defence functions of the carrier on the reduced scale which we envisage that our commitments will require after the middle of the 1970s.

Close anti-submarine protection of the naval force will be given by helicopters operating from ships other than carriers. Airborne early warning radar aircraft will be operated from existing carriers, which we intend to keep as long as we can for this purpose. Strike capability against enemy warships will be provided by the surface-to-surface guided missile already mentioned.

38. In order to give time to reshape the Navy and to provide the necessary parts of the carriers' capability, we attach great importance to continuing the existing carrier force as long as possible into the 1970s. The purchase of Phantom aircraft for the Navy will, therefore, go ahead, though on a reduced scale.

The Buccaneer 2 will continue to enter service, and the ARK ROYAL will be given a major refit in Devonport to enable her to operate both these aircraft until 1974/5. The gradual rundown of the Fleet Air Arm will be carefully arranged in order to give adequate alternative career prospects to officers and ratings who have served the Navy so well.

Details are being promulgated to the Fleet.

(In the same review the RAF, the Government planned to buy some 50 F-111As to be supplemented by the V-bomber force in their strike role).

Summary and Outcome

The above was 'promulgated' to the Fleet and was received with great dismay, and disappointment. It was quite demoralising to have the building of a new carrier overturned. The 'no carrier' decision immediately caused an extensive political and military fall out. Christopher Mayhew, the then Labour Navy Minister resigned in February 1966 as he strongly felt the new carriers were crucial for the RN. All the Sea Lords resigned, but were persuaded to stay by the First Sea Lord Admiral Sir David Luce (1963–66) to ensure continuity and pursuance of the new policies.

He too resigned as he headed up the Navy's team advocating aircraft carriers and their replacements. All this was to cause in 1966, the resignation of many experienced aviators, who felt there was no future in naval aviation. Ironically, the RAF was to suffer equally, because following the middle 1960s, they were also to suffer cuts under the same Labour Government. No TSR2, no P1154 and then no UK version of the General Dynamics F-111 swing bomber.

The Navy and those in the training pipeline did take the decision hard. Having been personally involved at the time, my future FAA career was forever changed and I watched events develop during the next few years. For many who had been tracking these developments, it was professionally disappointing that the RAF had got its way again. During the research for this particular chapter a sneaking suspicion began to creep in wondering whether it was coincidental or otherwise, that by the end of the decade all Britain's world beating aircraft designs would never come to fruition.

The exception being the Harrier, which was to become the last 'All British', manufactured aircraft. Despite its development costs, the TSR2 had the possibility of becoming a world beating aircraft with export potential and the supersonic P1154 with a plenum chamber engine would have enabled both the Navy and the RAF to leapfrog into the 21st century.

It was criminal that on the day the TSR2 was cancelled, all the production machine tools, jigs and even completed airframes at the factory were towed outside by tractors and broken up before the very skilled manufacturing technicians, who had been involved in the production of the aircraft. Not one-person, group or defence expert has ever justified this decision to immediately destroy the airframes and production jigs. It had never occurred previously nor been repeated since.

If the UK had built the two new carriers, they could have covered the phasing out of the aging WWII carriers and covered all the UK's political commitments post the 'East of Suez' policy. Eventually, we were to build three Dinky toy aircraft carriers in the mid-1970s under the politically correct guise and treasury smoke screen of 'through deck cruisers'.

These were in truth, light fleet carriers to be known as the 'Invincible Class'. It was also by sheer luck that HMS Hermes was kept in service until 1982, as she was earmarked to be sold to the Indian Navy prior to the onset of the Falklands War.

As a final comment on this dreadful period for the FAA, was the 'smoke and mirrors' tactics as employed by the RAF; it was not in the UK's interest either in the short or long term. In addition, the existing carriers would be phased out by the mid-1970s. Veterans wonder if the politicians and Defence Chiefs had any clue on the demoralising effect this defence review had on the FAA. My particular aircraft artificer entry was coming to the end of our apprenticeship in 1966 and gloomily thought they could not see themselves staying longer.

It was concerning to observe the feelings of those who had made the FAA their profession either as aircrew or engineers. Not long after this announcement, the first of several redundancies took place and many of my contemporaries volunteered for them. Additional redundancies where to take place during the next 2-3 years.

By default, the early manning plans of the 1960s described went out the window and the FAA found itself oversubscribed in all ranks, rates and trades. It was muted at the time that Denis Healey had enjoyed pitting the Defence Chiefs of the Navy against those of the RAF. Whatever political games were being played at the time, the RAF had once again won the argument.

Author's sketch – Buccaneers of 809 NAS – HMS Ark Royal 1970

History was to prove that this decision was wrong, as the advent of the Falklands War in 1982 was to expose. At that time, politicians repeatedly asked the Defence Chiefs, "Where is our strike carrier? Sorry sirs, but you got rid of them all by 1978". Had HMS Ark Royal (or its replacement the CVA01) still been operational, Argentina would not have invaded the islands. Labour's Defence Minister Denis Healey's review just continued the slow decline of the Royal Navy, Britain's maritime influence and of course, that of the FAA.

Sources

https://commonslibrary.parliament.uk/economy-business/economy-economy/pound-in-your-pocket-devaluation-50-years-on/
https://www.globalsecurity.org/military/world/europe/history/cva-01-hms-queen-elizabeth-cancelled.htm
https://web.archive.org/web/20150421014446/http://www.jepeterson.net/sitebuildercontent/sitebuilderfiles/dfdgar03.pdf
http://filestore.nationalarchives.gov.uk/pdfs/small/cab-129-124-c-33.pdf
https://www.wikizero.com/en/1966_Defence_White_Paper
https://en.wikipedia.org/wiki/CVA-01

Chapter 10
Fleet Air Arm – Success May 1969
(With Help from the RAF)

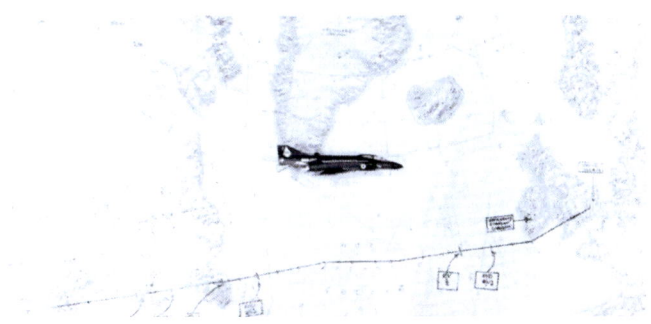

Air Race Programme – Author's collection

Recently, during a clear-out of old photos and memorabilia, I came across a first day cover given to me as a 'thank you' by the CO of 892 Squadron some 55 years ago. It had been one of twenty as carried on the fastest flight during the

Daily Mail Trans-Atlantic Air Race in May 1969. The Fleet Air Arm eventually took the honours of winning the prize of the quickest west-to-east flight with a naval Phantom i.e. the F4K version with Rolls Royce Spey 203 engines.

Signed 1st Day Cover carried on Fastest Flight 11th May 1969 – Author's collection

The basic premise of this Trans-Atlantic air race, as sponsored by the paper, was to see who could produce the fastest time possible across the 'pond', i.e. the Atlantic from the top of the Empire State building in New York to the top of the Post Office Tower in London and vice versa. In other words, there were prizes for the West to East crossing and also for an East to West crossing.

Entry was open to all under a number of natural categories i.e. civilian, military, sub-sonic, light aircraft et al. Celebrities of the day such as Stirling Moss, Clement Freud and Mary Rand were also to take part. The RAF, the Navy's main rivals were to enter a Harrier.

The FAA had decided to enter the Daily Mail's air race for a number of reasons by utilising the Phantoms of the newly formed 892 Naval Air Squadron, which was based at RNAS Yeovilton. The squadron had formed from the recently disbanded 700P the Intensive Flying Trials Unit with the 'P' standing for Phantom. The 700 number had always been traditionally allocated to the naval squadron when a new service aircraft were being introduced and trialled prior to them entering into FAA.

At this time, the FAA's morale was low as the demise of the UK's big strike carriers with fixed wing aircraft embarked was on the horizon. They were due under Labour, to be withdrawn in the mid-1970s, (eventually the last carrier i.e. HMS Ark Royal was finally decommissioned in 1978). The concept of 'Through Deck Cruisers', the 'Invincible class' flying the Sea Harrier, had not yet been developed or funded. Secondly, the FAA wanted to demonstrate that it could rapidly deploy its strike capability across the globe. It was to be a West to East supersonic attempt for the Navy's Phantoms.

Having just been promoted as a 1st Class 'Tiffy' (aircraft artificer), all bright eyed and bushy tailed, the hierarchy in their folly decided to put me in charge of a small technical working party at the then British Aerospace Corporation's airfield at Wisley in Surrey. It was here that we were to receive the three of the 892 NAS Phantom aircraft entrants during the period of 4th to the 11th May 1969.

Also, at Wisley with us was a detachment of 'Junglies' with two neatly camouflaged Wessex 5s from Culdrose. Their job, piloted by a former Borneo veteran Lt John Dines, was to whisk the FAA race contestant, (in the FAA's case the Phantom's observer), directly from Wisley's runway to a temporary helicopter landing pad built at the bottom of the Post Office tower in central London.

There were many other service and civilian support teams at the Wisley airfield and the lads took great delight in stuffing FLY NAVY stickers everywhere possible! During that week's stay at Wisley, a Super VC-10 based there was undergoing automatic landing trials i.e. hands off approaches.

Putting on the usual Naval charm and chat to the VC-10's aircrew and engineers, we managed to scrounge a flight. Most of the seats had been removed and this particular VC-10 was fitted with numerous test instrumentation and data recording equipment. I clearly remember doing circuits with the pilot doing complete 'hands off' landings at both RAE Bedford and Heathrow.

This race generated a lot of publicity in the media and the late Simon Dee adopted the FAA's race attempt. During that period and apart from being a popular DJ, he hosted an early evening family orientated programme, which was very similar to today's 'One Show'. He even made a visit to Wisley to film background shots for his evening programme. Numerous 'takes' had to be shot of him climbing into and out of the 'junglies' Wessex with a pilot's helmet under his arm.

The helmet being discretely carried so as to hide the nude artwork under his arm, as it was unsuitable for his family programme! Incidentally, Simon Dee arrived and departed in the boot of a large Rover limousine much to the bemusement of the Naval contingent because of the large crowds that had gathered around the main entrance to the Wisley airfield. The car was driven into the hangar and the said boot was opened revealing him climbing out into the world.

A fairly large RAF contingent were also stationed at Wisley in order to support their Harrier race entry and others. They naturally had numerous security personnel in the shape of the RAF Police and people from their Regiment, who are affectionately or otherwise referred to as 'Rock Apes' by the RAF themselves. When it came to overnight security of the Navy's Phantom following the three trans-Atlantic flights, we simply towed the aircraft to the hard standing adjacent by the main gate at Wisley.

Author's Collection: The author is on the right inspecting the damaged tires as fitted to Phantom 002.

Due to the fact we only had a few guys, I had previously arranged with the BAC's security manager to see if they would look after our aircraft overnight. There were always two security guards on duty giving excellent 24-*hour* coverage at the main gate, which was extremely brightly floodlit and just adjacent to the hangars. It was probably the most secure aircraft at Wisley!

After much practising and reiterations on calculations around fuel consumption of the Phantom and its Spey engines, plans were finalised and the Navy's West to East attempts was on. It was going to be accomplished by three air-to-air refuelling points across the Atlantic, rendezvousing with Victor tankers of 55 Squadron based at RAF Marham. The last refuelling rendezvous would be under the radar control of HMS Nubian, which would pre-positioned mid-Atlantic, as air traffic was very congested in this part of the North Atlantic.

Because of favourable weather conditions, it was decided that the Navy's first attempt would take place on the opening day of the competition, namely the 4th May 1969. The observer, Lt Paul Waterhouse RN left the top of the Empire State Building on Sunday morning at 0800. Phantom 002, flown by the pilot Lt Cdr Doug Borrowman RN, enabled them to record an actual time of 5hrs 30mins upon reaching the top of the Post Office Tower. No mean feat on the first attempt. It should be remembered at the time in the late 1960s, the non-stop train journey from London to Edinburgh took six hours.

Whilst the transit from Wisley went smoothly, when 002 landed it subsequently proceeded to burst both the main tyres, thus leaving the aircraft stuck on the main runway. Unfortunately, the starboard wheel had fully locked whilst braking and the hub had been ground flat by contact with the runway. See photograph below. This caused a headache for us maintainers, as we could not get access to the single wheel jacking point on the main undercarriage leg.

Eventually with welcomed support from Wisley's airfield services, we chiselled out a recess in the runway, thus enabling the positioning of the small bottle wheel jack into place. The said wheel now reputedly resides in the FAA's museum at RNAS Yeovilton. After all the necessary functional checks and inspections, the aircraft safely returned to Somerset the following day.

Phantom 002 – landing and bursting its tyre – Author's photo

Many lessons were learnt on this first flight and were fed back to the 892 NAS team based in New York – US Naval Air Station Floyd Bennett located just outside New York. With more favourable tail winds expected, the second attempt was made on the Wednesday. Phantom 003 was crewed by the pilot Alan Hickling with observer Lt Hugh Drake, the latter clocking on at 0800 at the top of the Empire State Building.

Having encountered warmer temperatures in mid-Atlantic, they were able to attain a slightly faster air speed and also experienced improved tail winds. The time to the top of the Post Office Tower from the Empire State Building was brought down to 5hrs 19mins – a saving of 11 minutes plus over the first flight flown on the 4th.

A weather front approaching the USA East Coast and 892's CO overcoming a head cold, the third and final attempt was made on Sunday 11th May 1969. Phantom 001 (XT859) was crewed by 892's CO Lt Cdr Brian Davies RN and Senior Observer, Lt Cdr Peter Godard RN.

By delaying the third refuelling until it was further eastwards (nearer the UK), aided by 50 knot tail winds and juggling heights to obtain the optimum fuel consumption/speeds, the time was further brought down another 8 minutes. The time from building top to building top was 5hrs 11mins, which became the fastest flight for the west to east element of the Daily Mail competition.

Author's commissioned painting of Phantom 001 being refuelled mid-Atlantic

Without doubt, winning the 'Alcock and Brown' Trophy and the Daily Mail's £5,000 prize money gave a much-*needed* fillip to the Fleet Air Arm when it was facing an uncertain future. The media followed the race closely as did the public and they became more enlightened about the Navy's air arm operational capabilities. It goes without saying that such an event was only achievable by the input and contribution of a wider team.

For example, the planners of 892 Squadron, those of Naval and RAF Staff, the contribution by the Victor tankers of 55 Squadron, HMS Nubian's controllers and the assistance of the US Navy, all played their part. One must not forget the positioning of a Shackleton MR3 in mid-Atlantic as precaution against any mishap.

For once, a rare piece of inter-service co-operation played its part in helping the FAA win this trophy. Of course, the RAF also learned lessons on carrying out long-range deployments of the Phantom aircraft as the all the calculations and requirements equally applied to their own version of the Phantom FGR 2 (F4M), which basically had the same RR Spey engine.

The FAA was to get an upgraded Spey engine later, which had a rapid reheat modification to enable a faster thrust response in afterburning when carrying out 'bolters' (missed arrestor wires) when landing on HMS Ark Royal.

Author's collection – 892 Squadron's Air Race Engineering Team 1969 (Author 3rd from left back row)

Postscript:

During a visit to a UK air show a few years ago, I happened to meet by chance a former RAF 55 Squadron Victor ground crew member, who was involved in the 1969 air race. They had also supported and refuelled the RAF's Harrier entry. When I asked him how many times, they had to refuel the Harrier across the Atlantic during the 1969 Daily Mail Air Race, he said, "It wasn't refuelled, the refuelling hose was permanently connected and to the Harrier and virtually towed it across!"

Chapter 11
Falklands Naval Air War 1982

This conflict, where neither side formally declared war, stemmed from a lengthy dispute with Argentina over the sovereignty of the Falkland Islands and its dependencies of South Georgia and the South Sandwich Islands. The Islands had been a Crown Colony since 1841 and the conflict started by the occupation of South Georgia by Argentine scrap merchants followed by an invasion of the Falkland Islands on the 2nd April 1982.

At the time, Argentina was in the middle of an economic crisis compounded by ever growing civil unrest against a military Junta. The UK immediately severed diplomatic ties with the country and commenced a diplomatic push to gain support and military actions at the United Nations (UN). The UN Security Council approved a resolution calling on Argentina to withdraw its forces from the islands and that a diplomatic solution be sought by both countries. A further resolution was passed for a ceasefire, which both the UK and US vetoed.

The political background and circumstances prior to the Argentinean invasion are described in depth in other publications. However, the UK government found itself once again having to consider how to deal with invasion on a British Overseas territory and the possibly of having the means to retake it militarily. Echoes of Suez and Korea came flooding back.

When the Argentineans invaded the Falkland Islands on the 2nd April 1982 and South Georgia on the following day, there was at the time a collective groan by FAA veterans. They knew the Argentineans would not have attempted an invasion if the UK had a genuine strike carrier still in service. A plaintive cry was heard throughout Government and Westminster, "Oh, where are our Phantoms, Buccaneers and the intrepid Gannet with its Airborne Warning Radar (AEW)?"

A comment no doubt reflected by older MPs in Westminster along with Naval Air Staff in MOD, who remember the decisions of no more strike carriers made during the mid-1960s. The UK no longer had a genuine 'strike aircraft carrier' as HMS Ark Royal had been scrapped some four years earlier in 1978 along with the promised CVA01 replacement, which was scrapped back in the 1966 Defence Review. Whilst 'Ark' may not have been in her prime, she would have definitely acted as a deterrent.

The Argentineans were also emboldened by the potential sale of the 'through deck cruiser' HMS Invincible to Australia and HMS Hermes being sold to India. Also, the other RN presence in the South Atlantic, HMS Endurance the ice patrol ship, was going to be scrapped with no planned replacement. This mixture of ships being sold and disposed of, led the Argentinean Junta to conclude that the UK was no longer interested in the importance of the Falkland Islands along with its territorial dependency of South Georgia and the South Sandwich Islands.

The RAF's 'Island Hopping' strategy plans put forward some sixteen years earlier in place of having aircraft carriers were briefly dusted down, but because of the vast distances involved with the Falklands Islands, this strategy was not a viable option in this unforeseen and forthcoming skirmish. The nearest 'island hopping' base was the Wideawake Airfield on Ascension Island, which was approximately 4,000 miles from the Falklands and itself some 4,200 miles from the UK.

The vast distances were going to be a major factor from a logistical point of view and the airfield and its use at Ascension Island was going to be critical. Without doubt, this was going to be predominately a Naval, Army and Merchant Marine operation, which was to become known as Operation Corporate. A Naval Task force was assembled, which was to eventually consist of some 127 ships, spearheaded by the aircraft carriers HMS Hermes and Invincible.

The FAA was to come to the fore once again and prove its worth with its twenty-eight Sea Harriers and a handful of Harrier GR3s. Not only was the FAA's fixed wing element going to provide combat air patrols but also carry out ground and ship strikes for the Task Force. Equally in support of all this, the FAA's rotary wing element was also to give sterling service in anti-submarine, anti-ship, special operations and troop deployments throughout.

Even the diminutive Wasp helicopter with its AS12 guided missiles and a Sea Skua as fitted to the Lynx helicopter were able to disable the Argentinean submarine, the Santa Fe, which was located and operating adjacent to South Georgia. These Navy helicopters were the first to successfully use missiles in anger at sea. The Navy's helicopter boys were in the 'thick' of it right at the beginning of combat hostilities, long before the Task Force was on station.

The RAF realised after the first month that it could only play a secondary role in the protection and the retaking of the Falklands. Because of the ranges involved, it could not provide air cover for the RN Task force in the South Atlantic, neither could it carry out anti-submarine patrols with its Nimrods. The Navy had to rely on its hunter killer subs and its own organic anti-submarine helicopters operating from the two carriers and escorting destroyers and frigates. The RAF also attempted to establish unsuccessfully, a covert photographic reconnaissance base in Chile utilising Canberras.

Ascension Island in the mid-Atlantic essentially became a staging post for the conflict by Britain and during the next few months, it became the nearest airbase to the Falklands. Nearly every type of aircraft flown by the RAF at the time was to be based there. Hercules, VC10 transporters, Nimrods, Victor tankers and eventually the Vulcans were to be stationed at the Wideawake airfield.

When the Task Force was within range and passing by, a lot of shuffling took place logistically in both materials and manpower terms. It all had to be transferred from ship to ship and ship to shore and vice versa. Also additional stores in support of retaking the island had to be flown to Ascension before the Task Force could finally continue on its way.

Some 20 Sea Harriers were embarked on HMS Hermes and Invincible as 800, 801 and 809 Naval Air Squadrons, with the latter being absorbed into 800 and 801. 809 NAS had been formed from the residue of aircraft belonging to the Sea Harrier training squadron i.e. 899 NAS and those held by the manufacturer and aircraft research establishments.

HMS Hermes had undergone three 'face lifts' during her career after being initially launched as a fixed wing carrier. At one stage, she did excellent work carrying Sea Vixens and Buccaneers. Following a refit, she was converted for a short period into a Commando carrier transporting Royal Marines. She then underwent a further refit in order to have the ski-jump fitted for Sea Harrier operations.

It is ironical that the disposal of these two carriers was one of the catalysts, which precipitated the Argentinean Junta's thinking reinforced by the planned withdrawal of HMS Endurance. The Task Force, commanded by Admiral 'Sandy' Woodward was to set sail from Ascension Island on the 18th April 1982. This UK armada was in position by the 30th April 1982 and was able to set up an exclusion zone of 400 miles centred on the Falkland Islands.

Hostilities and the first shots fired in anger of the air war were by rotary wing elements of the FAA on the 25th April 1982. The radar of a Wessex HAS 3 spotted the Argentinean submarine Santa Fe off South Georgia. This helicopter was the ship's flight from HMS Antrim. It proceeded to drop two depth charges with one bouncing off the submarine's deck. The second one exploded adjacent to the port ballast tank causing it to split and perforate an external fuel tank.

Because of this, the Santa Fe could no longer dive and therefore it was forced to reverse course back to Grytviken. A Lynx from HMS Brilliant launched a Mk 46 torpedo, which passed underneath because unfortunately it had been pre-set to 'home' in on submerged submarines. Two Westland Wasps from HMS Endurance and one from HMS Plymouth all armed with AS12 missiles came on the scene.

Plymouth made a single attack but because Endurance was nearer, her Wasps were able to rearm and make repeated attacks. The submarine was reputedly hit below the waterline and the last missile damaged the periscope and pumps. The crew eventually abandoned it after being moored at Grytviken.

'Humphrey' the nickname for HMS Antrim's helicopter, was to achieve fame during the retaking of the Islands of South Georgia (Operation Paraquet). Initially on the 21st April, in conjunction with two Wessex HU5s helicopters, they dropped Special Forces to the Fortuna Glacier for the purpose of observing Argentinean positions. Because of appalling weather conditions the Special Forces were forced to withdraw. Details of the exploits and phenomenal airmanship of this withdrawal are given in Chapter 16.

For the fixed wing boys, the shooting began on the 1st May, when the day started with Sea Harriers from HMS Invincible carrying out both ground attacks and Combat Air Patrols (CAP). During one of these patrols, some six Mirages appeared at 35,000 feet. There followed a 'cat and mouse' session where the Mirages did not come down to engage but neither did the Sea Harriers go up to the Mirage's height where it was considered to be a dangerous adversary.

This first air-to-air engagement therefore reached a stalemate and was called off due to the lack of fuel. This sparring continued throughout the day until two Mirages were shot down. The AIM-9L Sidewinders as launched by the Sea Harrier caused the damage, with one them being shot down directly and the other Mirage so badly damaged, it tried to limp towards Port Stanley airfield. It was subsequently hit by 'friendly fire' by the Argentineans, and was eventually brought down.

As with any war, there were to be many cases of friendly fire incidents throughout the conflict. In the meantime, three Daggers and two more armed with Israeli Shafrir heat seeking missiles descended on the Task Force. The Argentinean pilots were unsuccessful after firing their missiles at extreme range with one of the attacking Daggers being hit and downed. Also, an approaching flight of six Canberras were scattered with one of them being shot down too. It has to be pointed out that a mixture of FAA and RAF pilots manning the Sea Harriers, achieved success for the British.

Thus ended the first day of defending the Fleet from the Argentinean Air Force (AAF). Both sides counted up the costs, which resulted in the loss of four aircraft by the Argentineans without any Sea Harrier losses. The UK realised some of its new missile technology worked well, while the AAF decided to avoid contact with the Sea Harrier wherever possible. It was to be dubbed by Argentine pilots 'La Muerta Negra' or in English, the Black Death.

The Harrier's profile was very small and coupled with its new sea-grey finish, was difficult to spot over both land and the ocean. When the reserve Sea Harriers were earmarked for the formation of a third FAA squadron i.e. 809 NAS, they were re-sprayed to an all-over mid-grey with the barest of identification markings.

Following advice from RAE Farnborough and no doubt feedback from the Task Force, the traditional post WWII colour for Navy aircraft i.e. dark sea-grey topside and an all-white underside was changed to the low visibility mid-grey all over. This new adopted colour known as 'Barley' grey was in recognition of the camouflage expert at Farnborough. It was to match the conditions the FAA experienced on a day-to-day basis i.e. low grey misty clouds and murky dark seas.

The Sea Harrier's air war continued in the same vein throughout the conflict. Argentinean fighters were operating at the limit of their endurance. The Mirage IIIEAs were only able to reach the Falklands with some twelve minutes of fuel for combat at altitude, with only 5–6 minutes loiter time when fighting at low level. The Israel Aircraft Industries (IAI) version of the Mirage 5, sold to Argentina from 1978–80 was known as Daggers.

They too could only manage ten minutes over the islands. These were to make some 145 sorties throughout the 45 days of operations and were to damage five RN warships. A total of eleven Daggers were shot down with the Sea Harriers accounting for nine losses using the Sidewinder AIM-9L air-to-air missile. The remainder were shot down by surface to air missiles. A4 Skyhawks, although they had slightly better endurance with the assistance of in-flight refuelling, suffered the same disadvantage of the lack of loiter time over the Falklands.

This amounted to only ten minutes at a time. However, they were to inflict considerable damage and losses with their 500-pound 'Snakeye' bombs. They were to lose seven A4s throughout the air war.

On the 9th May 1982, the Sea Harrier also found success in a maritime strike role when two aircraft led by Flt Lt D Morgan RAF and Lt Cdr G Batt RN of 800 NAS took off on a combined CAP/ground attack mission. They had taken off from HMS Hermes each carrying 1,000-pound bombs on the centreline fuselage rack, with the intention of dropping them initially on Stanley airfield.

They encountered low cloud and visibility on their way to the designated holding station, when Ft Lt Morgan spotted a target blip on his radar screen some 50 miles away. They dropped down low and were breaking cover at around 350 feet to investigate when they discovered a sizeable trawler, the Narwal, flying a large Argentinean flag. This trawler had been spotted on the 29th April within the British Total Exclusion Zone (TEZ) and was suspected of carrying out intelligence gathering missions.

The pair radioed HMS Coventry, who responded some minutes later with a terse message from the Command, 'Engage'. Flt Lt Morgan decided to attack the Narwal with their bombs. He made his approach at around 500 feet and at a mile and a half from the ship; he pulled the nose up and hit the bomb release button. The ejector release unit on the centre fired, thus releasing the bomb.

As he pulled and rolled left, he saw a flash and then a splash some sixty feet beyond the trawler. He had missed. Because of the low trajectory and height, the bomb had failed to fuse and therefore explode. Meanwhile, Lt Cdr Batt had made an attack with his bomb and it made a direct hit on the forecastle of the Narwal passing through two decks. Again, because of the shallow dive the bomb did not arm and therefore did not explode.

Unfortunately, this bomb's trajectory through the decks had caused one fatality. The decision was then made for them to both strafe the vessel with the Sea Harrier's two Aden 30-millimetre calibre guns. The aircraft came in from either side of the vessel with one aiming alongside the vessel in an attempt to hit the waterline and/or cause damage to the engine room, whilst the other aircraft aimed for the bridge.

Their strafing runs caused considerable damage to the hull and bridge superstructure of the trawler, which came to a halt. A boarding party of British SBS men reached the target via a Sea King Mk 4 of 846 Naval Air Squadron and captured the ship dead in the water, taking off all of the men and the body of the boatswain of the Argentine trawler plus an injured seaman.

It later emerged that the Narwal was a 13,000-ton stern trawler requisitioned by the Argentine Navy a few weeks previously as an intelligence-gathering asset. She had been previously warned to leave the area but had not done so. Flt Lt 'Mog' Morgan went on to become an 'air ace' shooting down two Skyhawks plus two helicopters (one shared) and was later awarded the DSC.

The Sea Harrier also suffered from being unable to stay on station i.e. Combat Air Patrols (CAP) for any length of time. This was exacerbated by the defensive positioning of the Task Force in having to protect itself by remaining well clear to the east of the islands in order to stay out of the range of the Super Ètendards armed with Exocets.

The Sea Harrier was to gain a combat proven reputation during the Falklands War, downing 25 enemy aircraft by embarked Sea Harriers deployed in the conflict. The FAA did not sustain a single air-to-air loss and this tiny British built aircraft was to inflict 28% of Argentina's air losses.

Meanwhile, the rotary wing element of the FAA were extensively utilised, consisting of some ten Naval Air Squadrons, which included three that had to be formed in order to support the subsequent push towards Stanley. Flying predominately from the warships and Royal Fleet Auxiliary's (RFA), they carried out transport and vertical replenishment (Vertrep) duties, Special Forces landings and naval gunfire support, and anti-submarine and anti-ship missions, the latter by Lynxes carrying Sea Skua missiles.

Unfortunately, there was no airborne early warning radar carrying helicopters for the Task Force at the beginning of the conflict. In total, some 17 helicopters were lost.

One audacious raid involving a Wessex 5 of 845 NAS (the Junglies) occurred on 12th June 1982 when it attacked Port Stanley's Police Station. Special Forces namely the SBS, had observed that every morning, a sort of conference seem to take place at this building. The road outside appeared to have a large number of vehicles parked and there was speculation that Generals Menendez and Joffre, plus their senior staff officers were in attendance for these daily meetings.

Whilst not knowing precise details of what the Special Forces were doing in Port Stanley, it appears a possible idea developed of attacking this requisitioned school where there was a high chance of wiping out the entire Falkland's Argentine command structure. Such a raid had historical precedence because in WWII, both the Allies and the Germans made plans to utilise commandos and make several attempts to destroy each other's high commanders.

It is thought that such an idea was put to a pilot in 845 NAS, which was wholeheartedly supported. A plan was formulated and put forward to Command and it was approved, so on the morning of 12th April, an armed Wessex 5 carrying two AS12 missiles swooped low over Port Stanley having flown at low-level through the mountains.

The first missile hit the school roof and blew part of it off, whilst the second missile missed and after hitting some telegraph poles, it hit the sea. Because of the intensity of the heavy defensive flak, there was no time to make a second pass, so the helicopter retreated rapidly along the mountain route. Once again during this attack, the Argentineans shot down one of their own helicopters.

It was indeed a daring raid by a single FAA helicopter and although not 100% successful, it resulted in several white-faced and shaken Argentine Commanders emerging from the school. Had it been successful, perhaps it might have precipitated an earlier surrender.

The author was running the Air Engineering Workshops, which included the dope (spray paint) shop at RNAS Yeovilton, throughout the Falklands war. During the early phase as the Task Force was making its way south using 6–8 Sea Harriers the workshops were called upon to re-spray these aircraft in a new 'all over' barley grey scheme.

These aircraft were being made ready for the formation of 809 NAS and its deployment to the South Atlantic. The workshop personnel at HMS Heron

RNAS Yeovilton, toiled tirelessly on 24/7 basis, in not only producing these re-sprayed aircraft in record time, but throughout the conflict supporting many FAA squadrons and flights. A total of the 141 Naval aircraft with the Task Force were sustained by these workshops.

In parallel to the initial attacks against Port Stanley airfield on 1st May by Sea Harriers, a lone Vulcan also bombed the airfield. This Vulcan had flown from Ascension Island, supported and refuelled by virtually the total tanking capability of the RAF with some thirteen Victor aircraft. Of the twenty-two 1,000-pound bombs dropped by the Vulcan on this first attack, only one hit the main runway. This operation was given the name of 'Black Buck' and was the first of three missions flying the vast distance to and from Ascension in order to attack the runway.

Of the 63 bombs dropped, only one hit the runway. A further four missions were carried out utilising the SHRIKE missiles in order to destroy the radar and gun installations around Port Stanley. Of these attacks, only one was successful. Furthermore, some twelve other Black Buck missions were aborted whereby 1.1 million gallons of fuel were used.

From the 21st until 25th May, a concentrated air war took place following the landings at San Carlos in East Falklands. The Argentine Air Force and its Naval Air Corp began low-level raids so as to avoid detection by ship borne radars of the Royal Navy. This resulted in loss of nineteen aircraft belonging to the Argentine forces.

Although the Argentineans inflicted major damage and fatal losses to four RN ships, the bridgehead was established. By the end of these five days, it was deemed at this point of the conflict that the Argentine air forces had lost the momentum in forcing the UK from the Falklands.

HMS Invincible was relieved by her sister ship, the newly completed HMS Illustrious in July 1982. 'Lusty' remained on station with 809 NAS giving cover until the runway facilities at Port Stanley airfield was ready operate its RAF Phantoms. The retaking of the Falkland Islands was a classic aircraft carrier and amphibious ship operation, because, without the two carriers central to the Task Force, Britain would not have been able to retake the islands from the Argentines.

The air defence of the Task Force was dependent upon the organic embarked aircraft based on the two carriers, HMS Hermes and Invincible and the escorting ship's air defence missiles like the Sea Cat, Sea Dart and Sea Wolf. There has been an inference contained within several recent documents/papers written by senior RAF staff officers, on the support it gave the Naval Force in 1982.

Because of the distances involved, the RAF was unable to provide air cover or provide flight-refuelling facilities to carrier borne Sea Harriers, which were operating around the Falkland Islands. Neither did the Nimrods carry out critical anti-submarine patrols around the islands.

Despite recent publicity backed up by some biased propaganda books by former Air Vice-Marshals, the RAF played only a supportive role in the conflict, although the embarked Harrier GR3s did sterling work in its ground attack role. It is generally considered that the 'Black Buck' Vulcan raids were totally ineffective. It took an inordinate amount of aircraft and support just to land one bomb on Port Stanley's airfield.

This crater was filled within minutes. This bombing raid required some 14 Victor tankers refuelling in relays and transferring some 1,000,000 pounds of aviation fuel (this was the amount fuel consumed on each of the total number of 18 raids, which includes both actual and aborted missions) to get a Vulcan there and back from Ascension Island.

In other words, this involvement from a military perspective was bordering on the ludicrous and at best an embarrassing failure. One Sea Harrier could drop five bombs at a fraction of the cost and utilise only 4,000 pounds of fuel. Perhaps these raids had a secondary purpose of making the Argentineans wary of raids on their homeland, which was a political, no-go area for the UK.

Whether Britain would have carried out such raids and stirred up negative world opinion remains speculative. The RAF's role in Operation Corporate was basically a logistical, albeit an essential one where men, materials and stores were channelled via an air bridge between RAF Lyneham and Brize Norton to Ascension Island.

At no time was the mid-Atlantic base under any serious military threat and it was noted how much the Victor and Vulcan's tankers took up valuable dispersal space on the island.

With respect to the Vulcan raids, once again history was repeating itself, as the above seems to reflect what happened in 1944 during the raids to cripple the Japanese-held Palembang refineries of Sumatra in the Dutch East Indies. Here some 50 USAF B-29 Superfortresses were unable to put out of action the actual refineries and the resultant bomb craters made at the attacks on the defensive airfields surrounding these refineries were filled in within hours.

It took naval aircraft of the British Pacific Fleet i.e. the FAA from carriers to eventually negate the effectiveness of these Japanese airfields in Sumatra.

Basically, Argentina's military junta grossly underestimated the determination of the UK Government to retake the Islands. It also took a relatively small naval air force i.e. the Fleet Air Arm, which had an excellent esprit de corps within its pilots, aircrew and maintainers, to bring about success for the Naval Task force.

It is well remembered and understood that the crews of the two aircraft carriers, plus all the other ships involved, did excellent work in supporting FAA air operations. Fate was once again to play its part; because Britain had at the time a war winning British built aircraft in the Sea Harrier, which simply re-enacted the legacy left by the Spitfire and Lancaster.

It was flown by highly motivated, experienced and skilful pilots, who knew their aircraft inside out and were on top of their tactical game. All this did not come about by accident as the Sea Harrier was intensively tried and tested during the trials unit.

This trials unit 700A NAS was led by the indomitable Lt Cdr 'Sharkey' Ward RN DFC AFC and he was also the CO of 801 NAS flying off Hermes. He was to be promoted to Commander RN and became known universally as 'Mr Sea Harrier'.

A really brief and astute summary of the Falkland Island's war was succinctly made by Admiral of the Fleet Sir Henry Leach, First Sea Lord and Chief of the Naval Staff, when he said:

"Without the Sea Harrier, there could have been no Task Force"

I also contend, that:

"If HMS Ark Royal or its planned replacement, the new aircraft carrier CVA01 had been operational, the invasion of the Falkland Islands would not have taken place."

Sources

https://en.wikipedia.org/wiki/Falklands_War
https://military.wikia.org/wiki/IAI_Nesher
https://en.wikipedia.org/wiki/ARA_Narwal
https://medium.com/@CarlUpshon/sbs-operators-prove-argentinian-trawler-was-a-spy-ship-c15ea8f3177f
Hostile Skies by David Morgan – paperback version published by Phoenix in 2007
The Falklands War – 'Day by Day record from Invasion to Victory' published by Marshall Cavendish Ltd – 1983

Chapter 12
The Joint Force Harrier Fiasco

The immediate reaction on learning of the formation of the Joint Force Harrier (JFH), speculated at the time, was the Fleet Air Arm going to get control of all the Harriers? Logical thinking was centred around the two aircraft carriers HMS Illustrious and HMS Ark Royal, which were still in-service, one assumed there was going to be a nicely balanced capability of an embarked air wing of Sea Harriers FA-2s, with a mixture of Harriers GR7s and eventually the GR9s.

This basic concept appeared to be an updated version of the same mixture of aircraft as used by the Task Force carriers during Operation Corporate in the Falklands War.

Alas, how wrong was this logical thinking. The outcome following the 1996 Strategic Defence Review (SDR) turned out to be the other way round i.e. all the Harriers were going to be under the command and control of RAF Strike Command. The RAF was still envious of the FAA's success some sixteen years earlier during the Falklands War in 1982.

There was a popular school of thought amongst some defence minded observers, that this was an initial move by the RAF Staff as part of their long-*term* tactical plans, to absorb the fixed wing element of the FAA. A decade later was to show; this earlier sceptical viewpoint was confirmed by the subsequent procurement of the 5th generation fighter, the F35B. It was simply a continuation of their absorption policy.

The amalgamation of all the Harrier aircraft assets seemed at face value, to be a sensible proposition. The UK was in financial difficulties once again, the era of austerity was just beginning and savings had to be made by the MOD as part of the Government's overall cost reduction strategy. However, like all good intentions it became somewhat bit of a fiasco because instead of the FAA getting overall command off this Harrier Force, lo and behold, the RAF did.

Thoughts lingered back to 1918, whereby history was made by the absorption of the Royal Naval Air Service into the newly formed RAF under Lord Trenchard in 1918. Like then, a confusing disjointed approach developed and this was to be reflected in the frequent changing of names of this embryo Harrier force.

This led to a 'who would do what' situation, especially during embarked operations. Adding to this confusion were the changes and retirement of Harrier types that were to take place, along with the reduction in squadron established numbers, sadly, all adding to the detriment of the FAA as a viable fighting force.

Under the 1996 SDR, it was going to be called the Joint Force 2000 (JF2000), which was then changed to Joint Force Harrier (JHF). On 1st April 2000, two Sea Harrier FA 2s squadrons namely 800 NAS and 801 NAS were amalgamated along with four RAF Harrier squadrons. These being No 1, No 3, No 4 and No 20 RAF Squadrons respectively.

In 2006, No 3 RAF Squadron converted to the Eurofighter Typhoon. Also in the same year, the Sea Harrier was unfortunately retired and 800 NAS was re-equipped with the Harrier GR7s and GR9s formerly of No 3 squadron. Occurring at the same time, the sizes of the operational squadrons were reduced from 12 aircraft to 9.

More importantly and significantly, the Navy operated these new ground attack types, but did not own them! The second FAA squadron 801 intended to reform with GR7s/9s in 2007, but this was halted by the formation of the Naval Strike Wing (NSW). This new structure consisted both 800 and 801 NAS merging into a single operational squadron for deployments on the two remaining Invincible class carriers i.e. HMS Ark Royal and Illustrious.

This merged squadron could also double up for ground use in Afghanistan. At the same time, NSW reverted to just 800 NAS. On the 31st March, the JHF was reduced by one squadron – the disbandment of No 20 RAF Squadron along with No 4 Squadron becoming a reserve unit based at Wittering. The name was changed again given the Joint Strike Wing (JSW) name. All the Harrier Mk GR7s were retired.

The intention up until 2010 was that the Harrier GR9 aircraft would continue until the Lockheed Lightning II F35B came into service around 2018. As events have shown even this was to be changed, because the Harrier's end of service life as defined in the SDR 1996 was brought forward to April 2011. The final flypast of Harriers took place on the 15th December 2010 with all Harriers squadrons being disbanded at the end of January 2011. From that date, the FAA no longer had any sea going fixed wing capability and therefore, no fleet air defence.

Without any real military knowledge, which even a layman can detect, the previous paragraphs, exposed a complete lack of joined up or logical thinking of the consequences and the repercussions, which were to follow. That is, the retirement of the Sea Harrier FA2 with its excellent and up to date integrated radar/weapons fit, was some 10 years too soon. Not only was the Navy unable to provide Carrier Air Patrols (CAP) for its ships, it was to create a 10-*year* gap until the F35 came into service.

With no Sea Harriers, the interest in naval fixed wing waned considerably and the Invincible class carriers became vulnerable to the 'bean counters'. It came as no surprise when HMS Illustrious and HMS Ark Royal were scrapped with very little opposition.

This decision was to come back and bite the political/military planners in March 2011 regarding the Libyan upheaval, as Britain had no immediate military means to assist in supporting allies there. This led to a costly operation by the RAF, with its aircraft and support personnel spread at bases and hotels all around the Mediterranean.

One basic question stands out, how on earth did planners think an aircraft specifically designed for ground attack operations i.e. the Harrier GR7/GR9 would be able to replace the raison d'être of the Sea Harrier? Neither was the GR7/9s designed for a maritime role both operationally nor robust enough to withstand the harsh salt laden environment it would find itself in.

Overnight in 2006, the carriers HMS Ark Royal and Illustrious were neutralised with regard to their embarked air defence capabilities. These floating platforms simply became ferries for the RAF's Harriers, with woeful maritime or fleet defence usefulness.

Some planners thought that the GR9 would be able to operate providing fighter cover for any sea going task force using ship-borne anti-aircraft weaponry. This was simply unrealistic, impractical and militarily naïve.

To operate aircraft carriers efficiently, squadrons need to work up, which the FAA has long experience of and it was known that it could take some 12–18 months of continuous embarkation to become effective. This effectiveness depending upon being able to fly day and night in all weathers and integrating with the ship's weapon system and flight deck crews. In reality the RAF Harrier squadrons and aircrew were dependent upon a fully worked up naval controlled 'ship to air' environment, many RAF pilots had not had any previous experience of operating at sea.

There was a gradual decline in pilots being night qualified at sea and along with less and less embarked time, the JFH and its Navy element morphed basically to a land-based ground attack force. Hence, the use of the Navy Strike Wing during Afghanistan in support of the 'Herrick' operations. In short, the RAF procured the Harrier fundamentally as a land-based attack aircraft, so there was little enthusiasm in seeking embarkation time. This being no doubt due to pressures from the commitments in Iraq and Afghanistan.

Harrier GR9 of Naval Strike Wing – Author's photograph

From the SDR of 1996 until the implementation of the Joint Force Harrier in 2000 and then beyond, there must have been utter confusion within this force on what was going on. In the background, the financial crisis of that era was biting and cuts with the Armed Forces having to bear its share. Whether these cuts to the Harrier fleet were cost effective is speculative. The uncertainty that was occurring must have had a major impact on morale and efficiency to both aircrew and maintainers, especially to FAA aircrew personnel.

To move from RNAS Yeovilton (HMS Heron) to RAF Cottesmore and amalgamating with the RAF must have been bit of a cultural shock. With the demise of the Sea Harrier and having to re-equip with the GR7/GR9 version must also have been bemusing along with the knowledge that the FAA did not own these aircraft.

One minute, they were Naval Strike Wing in March 2007 merging both 800 and 801 NAS into one operational squadron. Then during April 2010, the NSW reverted back to being 800 NAS. On the engineering front, it would be interesting to learn of how the two different servicing doctrines were solved. The FAA had for many years adopted a flexible serving approach and the Navy's concept of only withdrawing aircraft for deep servicing when their material condition warranted it.

The FAA had all its aircraft surveyed by an independent unit on an annual basis. This flexible maintenance system had been developed since the 1960s by the FAA in order produce the maximum number of aircraft for flying operations. The RAF maintenance at the time was still based on flying hour's i.e. 100, 200, and 500 hours, which meant aircraft were withdrawn from at these breakpoints irrespective of operational needs.

We now come to vexed question of command and control and which command staff controlled which squadron? It looks as if Flag Officer Naval Air Command (FONAC) and by default Navy Board, relinquished control of its Sea Harriers to RAF Strike Command when the JFH was formed in 2000. However, when they embarked did all the Harriers revert back to Naval control or did Strike Command keep command and control of the Harrier fleet including the Sea Harriers?

Were RAF Staff familiar with understanding the implications of the integration of an air group into both a ship-borne naval environment along with associated operations at sea? Here we have history repeating itself because the same confusion, dithering and command ownership also occurred between 1918 and 1937.

Throughout the maritime embarked exercises and operations between 2000 and 2010, there were on many occasions many RAF pilots who were not conversant with ship borne operations and in particular, night flying whilst embarked. Those pilots, who were cleared for night flying, were mainly Sea Harrier trained aircrew.

To give a flavour on the high-level use of Naval assets throughout the 'Harrier Strike Force' period, the following are the hectic movements of 801 NAS throughout 2004:

- *5th May 2002 – Embarked HMS Invincible-10-day Atlantic crossing and deployment to the US for exercise 'Aurora 04'. 3 weeks at test ranges Port Mugu and China Lake.*
- *Mid-June 2004 – Exercise 'Blinding Storm' with the USS carrier John F Kennedy.*
- *4th July 2004 – HMS Invincible makes port visit to New York and then transits home to UK in mid-July.*
- *18th September 2004 – Sea Harriers of 801 NAS attend RNAS Yeovilton Air Day.*
- *Autumn 2004 – Embark twice on HMS Invincible for two weeks apiece for fixed wing refresher operations. Exercise 'Hold Fast'.*
- *Early October 2004 – Embark HMS Invincible to sail to the Mediterranean for exercise 'Destine Glory04'.*
- *10th December 2004 – Final detachment of the year working in the air defence role with F16s from Belgium and Mirages of the French Air Force.*

It should be pointed out that while these deployments listed above, range from two weeks to several months long, they were continuous and the same sort of pattern was to be duplicated for the next 18 months, until 28th March 2006 when 801 NAS was disbanded.

History shows that the Sea Harriers were deployed constantly all over Europe, all the way to the US, the Middle East and flew in two conflicts in Iraq and Sierra Leone. Embedded within all these movements and deployments were the logistical headaches, which occur when a squadron embarks and disembarks. On top of all this, was the disruption to family life.

It also appears that during this period of the JHF and NSW, RAF Staff Command saw an opportunity to clip the Navy's wings. How much of a fight did the RAF put up and what arguments did they put forward in order to save the Sea Harrier, whilst in the background they wanted to keep their own version? Conversely, how strong a case did Naval Air Staff and the general Service Admirals put to the Prime Minister and Defence Minister on keeping the Sea Harrier and the ships they flew off?

The financial pressures of the time fell right into the RAF's lap once again and the resultant evidence shows the RAF was proportionally the least affected service by the SDR of 1996. Subsequently, the JFH would become one equipped with their version. From an established number of 83, the reduction to 51 completely diminished the capability of carrier-borne aircraft for fleet air defence.

This decision also ensured that the Navy would not have any genuine fixed wing air defence for a decade. UK MOD also used a false premise of the Sea Harrier's capability and its withdrawal by saying it would be covered by other means such as the new Type-45 destroyers. It also said the UK would in future operate in a littoral role with major allies and the UK could rely on the US to provide additional air cover if required.

All the information in decrying the Sea Harrier must have been fed to the Ministers and MOD civil servants from somewhere. Whatever the source and content, that information was absolute garbage. It is worthy to note the comments from former Air Engineering Officer (AEO) Commander Steve George RN after having brought the Sea Harrier FA.2 into service:

"For ten years, the FA.2 was the best fighter in the Western world – it could beat anything, including the F-15s and F-16s. It was probably the first aircraft in the history of the British aircraft industry that entered service that worked on day one! Not only did it work magnificently, and the integration with the Advance Medium Range Air-to-Air Missile (AMRAAM) was fabulous. The guys from the US who made the missile said that FA.2 was the best platform the missile had at

the time and we were ahead by some distance. The only thing that came close was the F-16 Block 60 model.

"By 1992, we were the first coalition aircraft to be declared swing-role (off the coast of Bosnia). We had Sea Harriers launching with 1,000-lb bomb, two AMRAAMs and a very good F95 camera. We were declared in three roles at once – I don't know of any other coalition aircraft that was. Quite an astonishing achievement and one that reflected huge credit on the UK companies and FAA personnel involved."

As soon as the FAA relinquished control of the Sea Harrier, its fate was sealed. In summary, it was folly to retire the Navy's version of the Harrier as it left the UK with a capability gap, which remained for a decade. The Sea Harriers with very modern and up to date avionic and weapons fits, were sold to the US at a knock down price. Incidentally, talking to several USM pilots at USMC Yuma and technicians in the AMMARG 'bone-yard' in Arizona, they were unanimously amazed that the UK had scrapped the Harrier.

One comment made, was over the large amounts of modern avionic equipment removed from these aircraft, which had been purchased at bargain prices when they were scrapped. The Americans said, thank you very much. As of 2022, the US Marine Corps is still flying the AV-8B Harrier.

At the time in early 2011 and in parallel circumstances, the Tornado came under threat with the 'bean-counters' and in order to save it, the RAF offered up the Harrier as a sacrificial lamb. Had the Tornado or a portion of it been retired instead, the RAF Command suddenly would have found itself with an air force no larger than that of the Belgium Air Force. The RAF was not going to let that happen!

A more sensible solution at the time perhaps would have been the retention of the Sea Harrier. It was undoubtedly retired 10 years too soon. It did after all have a dual role and had an excellent weapon fit i.e. fighter and attack. A permanent Naval Air Wing under FONAC could have been formed and alternatively operate between HMS Ark Royal and Illustrious allowing one to be in dockyard, whilst the other was at sea.

There would also be the advantage of having sufficient pilots permanently familiar with flight deck operations and having the necessary hours for night flying. In this scenario, the RAF's Harriers numbers could have been reduced without significant loss in aircraft establishment numbers in either Iraq or

Afghanistan. There were still sufficient numbers in the Tornado fleet to cover these overseas operations.

HMS Illustrious operating Sea Harriers FA 2 – authors image

To an impartial outsider, all the changes to titles to the combined force the Harriers came under during this decade was very confusing. One minute, it was Joint Force 2000 then, Joint Force Harrier, and then Navy Strike Wing with squadrons merging, being disbanded and then being commissioned again. Embedded within all these name changes, was the eventual demise of the Sea Harrier in March 2006, which had been cleverly camouflaged and disguised within all those changes.

The RN was suddenly lumbered without proper air defence cover. Many defence commentators collectively said that this decision was 'bonkers' with the same being said about the withdrawal of the HMS Ark Royal and Illustrious. It was a complete folly to pretend that the Harrier Mk GR 7/GR 9 could carry out the same functions as the Sea Harrier with its Blue Vixen radar. The impact on FAA aircrew and maintainers was utterly demoralising, not only from a personnel point of view but also from a historical perspective.

Naval fighter pilot's careers ended and many did not want to become mere ground attack jockeys or mud-movers, whilst FAA naval technicians wondered what the future held for them?

Sea Harrier FA2 – 800 Naval Air Squadron – Author's image

Sources

http://www.aeroflight.co.uk/aircraft/types/type-details/british-aerospace-sea-harrier.htm
https://en.wikipedia.org/wiki/Joint_Force_Harrier
Commander S George RN page 256 – 'The Fleet Air Arm Boys Volume 1' by Steve Bond
Gabriele Mollineli dated 25th April 2011 – 'Fleet Air Arm, RAF, the past and the future'

Chapter 13
The Lockheed Lightning II F35B Saga

Introduction

As from November 2021, the UK is now one F35B down. Now, only 23 remain of these from the initial tranche of 24. Unfortunately, one of the F35Bs serving on the carrier Queen Elizabeth crashed in to the Mediterranean shortly after take-off. It transpires that the aircraft lost power whilst negotiating the ship's ski-jump ramp. Fortunately; the pilot ejected safely and was rescued by a RN Merlin helicopter and was soon returned back to the carrier.

Each of these F35Bs cost £100M. At the present moment, the cause for abandoning the aircraft is unknown and whether the pilot was an RAF or FAA one. The UK was scheduled to purchase a total of 138 of the B variant and so far, only 48 of this type have been confirmed. Currently, a total of £9Bn has been allocated for equipping the UK's aircraft carriers with these new aircraft. What stands out most prominently in the British press in coverage of this incident is that it was an RAF aircraft belonging to an RAF squadron namely 617.

The press has released very little information about the Royal Navy's involvement except for the fact that this accident occurred on one of its major sea-going assets i.e. a 60,000-ton aircraft carrier. The RAF's publicity machine has made the most of this misfortunate ditching by ensuring the British public know it was a Royal Air Force aircraft. What this loss indicates most clearly, is the inherent difference of operating at sea when compared to flying from a fixed land-based airfield, which was only lightly touched upon by the press.

Hopefully, this chapter will enlighten readers of the significant differences and highlight the historical and long-standing issues surrounding command and control between the FAA and the RAF. As described in a previous chapter, the Royal Navy experienced the same problem, which occurred in the 1930s.

Historical Background

After fighting the Navy over many decades for the need for aircraft carriers, the RAF has fought its corner both tooth and nail in maintaining the distinct demarcation between embarked aircraft and their own 'land based' aircraft philosophies. It was many a wry smile that some FAA 'old-salts', welcomed the sudden interest and keenness that the light blue uniform force were to show in the Navy's new aircraft carriers.

This interest included the potential equipping of the FAA with a new stealth fighter-bomber aircraft, i.e. the Lightning II F35B. However, this newly welcomed interest is somewhat off-set by the way the UK has gone about procuring this new aircraft and how it is being integrated into the UK's armed forces. Apart from questions over its capability, there are some serious questions to be asked over the operational control and ownership of this aircraft between the FAA and the RAF.

This will become particularly critical when the F35B is flown whilst at sea, as the UK does not have a very good historical record of inter-service co-operation and understanding at the Chief of Staff levels. It should be highlighted at this point, that no other nation has allowed a land-based air force with no in-depth experience of operating at sea, to take the lead in the introduction of a brand-new aircraft for its Navy.

The use of aircraft from a dynamic moving platform on the ocean in all weathers, day or night is totally different to flying from a fixed air station. Would the US Navy or US Marines have allowed the American Air Force to carry out all the trials and introduction into service of their particular version of this aircraft i.e. F35B or C models on their behalf?

Unfortunately, there is a sense of déjà vu, as the British have history in this area whereby the FAA/RAF have clashed repeatedly over procurements of their aircraft The development of the F35 is reminiscent of the Vixen/Javelin and RN/RAF Phantom 'buys' that took place in the late '50s and '60s respectively.

The Vixen and Javelin were based on post WW II and 1950s requirements with both having similar specifications. However, the two services could not agree on a common aircraft. With some forethought, the UK could have had an opportunity to streamline its procurement for both the RAF and FAA, which would have led to substantial savings.

Across the Atlantic during the same period, the US proceeded to amalgamate their future requirements across three services (USAF, Navy and Marines), which was to result in the very successful McDonnell Phantom. Despite this US example of inter-service co-operation, the UK still continued to pursue and build two completely different aircraft.

The RAF went for the Gloucester Javelin and despite the early set-backs, the Navy chose the De-Havilland Sea Vixen with the latter becoming the better aircraft and having greater longevity once in service.

In the mid-1960s, the UK eventually purchased the Phantom, which proved to be expensive; especially the Royal Navy's version (designated the F4K). This was because eventually only 48 naval versions were to be built. Originally in the 1960s, some 250 plus Phantoms were going to be procured, with half going to the RAF and the other half going to the FAA in order to equip two new aircraft carriers designated CV01, 02.

There were plans to equip both HMS Ark Royal and Eagle with Phantoms following a major modernisation programme. The decision to re-engine the British version with the Rolls Royce Spey, caused long delays and major airframe alterations to accommodate it. The advantages of the more powerful Spey turbofan with reheat were cancelled out by the extra drag that the redesigned airframe generated, especially the need for much larger intakes.

Another factor, in these delays were the modifications specifications required of the original radar. This increased the unit cost, which was required to develop the Westinghouse AN/AWG-10 radar as carried by the F-4J, which led to the procurement and building under licence by Ferranti leading to the AN/AWG-11 for Fleet Air Arm aircraft and AN/AWG-12 for those of the RAF.

As previously mentioned, there was an intention to procure up to 250 plus aircraft for the Royal Navy and the RAF but the development cost associated with the changes specified by the UK to accommodate the Spey turbofans meant that the per unit price eventually ended up being nearly three-times the price of an 'off the peg' McDonnell F-4J.

At the time and because the Government of the day then had a policy of negotiating fixed-price contracts, it meant that these costs could not be evened out by a large production run. The contractual conditions reduced the total UK order to 170. There has never been a rational explanation why the more cost-effective original order of 250 plus 'off-the-shelf' Phantoms aircraft was not followed through.

Similarly, the Blackburn Buccaneer was another example of this inter-service rivalry, because following its development from the early 1950s until its introduction to FAA squadron service in 1963, the RAF did not want to know this new aircraft – it was too navalised. Coming forward some thirty years or more later, the Buccaneer suddenly found an important and unexpected role in the twilight years of its service in Iraq as part of Desert Storm.

After ignoring this aircraft whilst the FAA was using it, RAF crews were unstinting in their praise for this transonic tactical bomber when they eventually operated it. They were handed all the Navy's Buccaneers following the decommissioning of HMS Ark Royal in 1978.

From 2000 onwards, it had become politically expedient for the RAF to go along with the building of the two new strike aircraft carriers i.e. HMS Queen Elizabeth and the Prince of Wales. If one recalls, following the rundown of the Afghanistan conflict and since the conclusion of the Iraq war, the UK's air force i.e. the RAF was coming under serious existential threat.

This emanated from many directions such as defence experts, commentators, military gurus and defence minded Members of Parliament with the question "What is the purpose of the RAF?" Such questions at the time were being critically discussed and considered. With the building of the new carriers containing their organic strike capability, it was being queried why did the RAF really need a new aircraft like the F35 when the build-up of Typhoons numbers into squadron service was starting?

Why not build a further tranche of Typhoons and save money in the longer term? There was a general consensus that the UK Government had a major opportunity to realign its defence policy and consider leaving any overseas strike commitment to the FAA, but unfortunately this never came about. The change in the RAF wanting to be part of the new carrier programme resulted in a complete 180° turn in policy.

As previously discussed, it should be remembered that during the 1960s the RAF fought tooth and nail against having the Buccaneer and the building of any new aircraft carriers. They stated at the time they could have provided maritime cover anywhere in the world. Similarly, they were also half-hearted and sketchy on their attempts to support the Harrier on sea operations throughout existence of the Joint Force Harrier (JHF).

There was no real resistance from the RAF (or the Navy) when the Sea Harrier was prematurely retired ten years too soon from this so-called Joint Force. A decision, which incidentally was to result in the UK having no fixed wing carrier capability for over a decade, that is, until the arrival of the new Queen Elizabeth class aircraft carriers.

However, because of the change in the political wind at the time, the junior service's hierarchy saw this commitment to the building of two new aircraft carriers as a potential lifesaver with an opportunity to get its hands on another aircraft type and add further flying assets to its inventory. Crucially, the F35 was a 5th generation aircraft, which also had genuine stealth capabilities.

Also on the horizon at the time and reflecting Britain's monetary problems then, the question of whether to retire the Tornado or the Harrier fleet was under discussion (the FAA still having fixed-wing squadrons as part of this fleet but equipped with the Harrier GR7/9s).

The RAF's Chief of the Air Staff and its Board, suddenly realised that if 174 Tornados were prematurely retired along with some 350 plus aircrew, they would be in charge of an air force smaller than that of Belgium! No wonder the Joint Harrier Force became the victim of cuts as only some 70 aircrews would be affected and made redundant.

Procurement, Acquisition and Comments

The Joint Strike Fighter (JSF) requirement for the US evolved during the mid-1990s with the UK becoming a founding member of the programme and it became the only Tier 1 partner. The intention of JSF was to replace USMC's AV-8 Harriers, F16, F/A-18, and A10. The UK likewise was also investigating a replacement for the Sea Harrier, Harrier and Tornado.

The original plan by the US was to build some 5,000 aircraft, but the final number has been whittled steadily downwards during the last decade with the latest figure to be released at the beginning of 2022, is around 2,500, although some aviation sources say it will eventually be nearer 3,500. Some 900+ F35s have been manufactured and delivered by April 2023. The majority are for the US and will form the basis of manned tactical airpower for the USA and its allies until 2044.

There are three types:

- The F-35A built to meet an USAF requirement with conventional take-offs and landings (CTOL).
- The F35B built for Short Take-offs and Vertical Landings (STOVL). Trials have been carried out with the UK's F35Bs on the Queen

Elizabeth class carrier for Shipborne Rolling and Vertical Landings (SRVL). This model's range is curtailed by a third because of the lift fan's deadweight during conventional flight. Unsurprisingly, this version is limited to a maximum of 7.0 G, whilst the A and C models are limited to 9.0 and 7.5 G respectively.
- The F35C the aircraft carrier-based version Carrier Version/Catapult Assisted Take-Off but Arrested Recovery (CV/CATOBAR).

F35B transitioning to the hover – RIAT 2016 – Author's image

The UK's original Royal Navy's Operational Requirement centred on replacement for the Sea Harrier with the Future Carrier Borne Aircraft (FCBA). The RN joined forces with the USMC and wrote the F35B Joint Strike Fighter Operational Requirements Document (JORD). During its drafting, the US DoD decided to use the F35 as a pathfinder project joint acquisition and the JORD was expanded to cover three variants. All the UK RN requirements were incorporated into an approved US/UK JORD.

All this began in 2001, when a Memorandum of Understanding with the US Defence Department was signed by the UK to become a full member in the Joint Strike Fighter programme. This joint programme was to eventually materialise as the F35. In September 2002, the MOD announced that both the FAA and RAF would operate the STOVL version i.e. the F35B variant.

This meant that the new carriers would be conventional and would have a life of 50 years plus but not have catapults and arrestor wires (CATOBAR).

However, the carriers were deemed to be future proofed and that CATOBAR capable aircraft could be utilised beyond the life of the F35B. In 2001, there was a Strategic Defence and Security Review stating that only one carrier would be commissioned, the future of the second carrier being left undecided.

Also announced at the time, was the decision to accommodate the carrier version of the F35 i.e. the C model, which meant the fitting of catapults and arrestor wires to the Queen Elizabeth. Financial considerations and attention then focussed on the possibility of fitting the new electromagnetic aircraft launch system (EMALS) alongside the new advance arresting gear (AAG), which was being developed by the US.

Fitting, or conversion, to this new system would have been very expensive if carried out by UK contractors, as it would have virtually doubled the price of the two new carriers. For that price, two further new aircraft carriers could have been built. As an aside, some commentators speculated at the time that if the UK had built a third Queen Elizabeth class carrier along with the first two, selling the third would have paid for the whole aircraft carrier project for the UK.

The EMALS system takes up a lot of compartmental space and requires large and virtually unlimited amounts of electrical power. The UK's design and intention was to have only two catapult launchers compared to the four as fitted to the American's 'FORD' class carriers, which coincidently are all nuclear powered. The modifications to meet the UK requirements and with two carriers to fit out, costs would spiral upwards.

The decision to also fit CATOBAR to the Prince of Wales carrier was also reviewed and because the costs of such a fit had escalated to an unacceptable level (nearly £2Bn); so in May 2012, the Government decided to revert back to the F35B instead of the F35C. In the SDRS of 2015, it was confirmed that both carriers would be brought into service with one being available at all times.

The Government also confirmed some 138 F-35 Lightning IIs would be ordered although the specific model was not mentioned but the first 24 would be made available for the carriers by 2023. The only definitive comment made in the review was "**The RAF F-35B Lightning Force** size will be increased beyond the 48 aircraft that have already been ordered." Note that once again, it only says with no reference to the RN – The RAF F-35B Lightning Force.

Although the UK's initial procurement was for 138 F35s, with the first 48 being the F-35B model, there has been much discussion and speculation recently in 2020–2021 on what model the UK's next batch of deliveries might eventually be. Curiously, it has never been disclosed over what time period the original number of 148 F35s were going to be delivered.

Speculation was rife with rumours that the remainder, some 100 aircraft, were going to be the F35A model. If such a purchase were to go ahead, how would the FAA and RAF reconcile these numbers with only 48 F35Bs allocated across, four squadrons, (x2 FAA, x2 RAF), plus one training squadron? Sharing these aircraft for embarkation on two aircraft carriers on a war footing is problematical.

A minimum of x24 aircraft would be required for both the Queen Elizabeth Class carriers in this scenario. Maintaining this number would be difficult to achieve, especially when attrition rates caused by accidents and those undergoing upgrades etc. are taken into consideration. The confirmation of further numbers was not readily confirmed in the Strategic Defence Review of March 2021. It seems fairly obvious that further numbers of the F35B model are going to be needed to take into account the inevitable attrition rates.

Even now, the US is retiring earlier models of the F35 to the bone-yards in Arizona because it is cheaper not to fix the major deficiencies or do retrofit upgrades. If the Navy, at the behest of the RAF were to stick to just one carrier being fully operational at any given time, then upping the current number to be delivered by another 24 would possibly just suffice. Ideally, the barest number required to sustain one carrier on a war footing would be between 60–70 aircraft.

As for the possibility that the remaining purchases being the F35A model would be an absolute folly. Apart from the major logistics problem of maintaining two different types, which have only 35% compatibility, the reasons for having carrier force would be completely negated.

If we retrace a few steps to the formative decision-making process under Gordon Brown and his government, it makes additional interesting reading on what type of new aircraft carrier the UK was going to build. Initially, plans to build two conventional strike carriers with 'cats and traps' were being considered and at that time the RAF appeared to be uncommitted and showed little interest when the full carrier version i.e. the F35C was in the frame.

However, as their commitment became more prominent the decision was made to revert to the F35B model. Here was an opportunity also to get the VSTOL land-*based* version into their inventory.

The first F35B squadron to be commissioned and embarked operationally on the Queen Elizabeth, the Royal Navy's major sea going asset, will be 617

Squadron (The Dambusters), a RAF squadron. This is indeed a historical misnomer and goes against all normal FAA service traditions. This prestigious occurrence should have been a pivotal moment for the RN and particularly the FAA in the 21st century, following the absence of 'flat-tops' for nearly a decade.

Unfortunately, it appears that the Navy's PR has permitted itself to be subsumed into the RAF's slicker PR machine. The latter now no longer mention aircraft carriers but refer to both the Queen Elizabeth and the Prince of Wales with the terrible non-entity description as 'alternative basing' options. This alternative basing term being used regularly in many of its briefing and future policy documents.

One suspects that the RAF by being the first to embark on the new carriers, will keep them in the public eye. Secondly, there has been another break from naval tradition, the MOD have decided not to allow the Lightning II to be called the 'Sea Lightning'. This thus breaking lineage of the Seafire, Sea Hurricane Sea Gladiator, Seafox, Sea Hawk, Sea Vampire, Sea Venom, Sea Vixen and Sea Harrier et al.

It is noted that several other naval aircraft did not have the 'Sea' prefix but the Buccaneer, Barracuda and Gannet names have a strong and obvious maritime association. On top of all this, the new aircraft were going to be based at RAF Marham. It is a shame that the Navy Board allowed this to happen.

USMC – F35B at RAF Fairford 2016 – Author's photo

F35 Impressions

Personal observations from a general aviation perspective have unfortunately somewhat clouded my overall opinion of this aircraft. I saw the F35 for the first time in March 2013 at USMC Yuma and because it had just been delivered, it was only on static display and did not give a flying demonstration. Now, having seen it perform both here in the UK and at subsequent US air shows I am left with some critical layman comments.

The initial impressions have been, that notwithstanding its stealthy looking appearance, it is visually quite an ugly squat aircraft. If one refers back to the old adage 'if it looks good, then it must be good', which is the category the Spitfire and Hawker Hunter fall into. Furthermore, looking at video footage of the F35B launching from both British and US carriers, it looks very ungainly and has many openings.

These access openings appear to vibrate wildly, especially the lift fan cowling when it trundles down the flight deck and the same vibration is apparent when being recovered vertically. On the positive side, at its debut at Fairford it was noted how smooth the transition from conventional flight to the hover and successive manoeuvres, when compared to the Sea Harrier.

The large access panel of the vertical lift fan behind the pilot looks incongruous and again, it was noted how much it was whipping during a ski-jump take-off. One wonders what fatigue stresses are being induced on the airframe during this phase of flight.

Talking to many people not familiar with the F35B, it seems they are under the impression that this new aircraft can replicate the capabilities of the former Harrier in respect of vertical take-offs and landings. Especially on minimally prepared landing sites. The F35B is a Short Take-off and Vertical Landing (STOVL) aircraft not a Vertical Take-off and Landing (VTOL) one, because it requires extensive preparations on the ground before landings can take place.

Similarly, it does not have the flexible 'in the field' operability in a battleground environment that the land-*based* Harrier could exhibit. Neither does it have the same flexibility nor wherewithal of the carrier-*based* Sea Harrier of being able to operate from a variety of platform bases with the minimum of preparations.

When the F35B made its first public appearance at the Royal International Air Tattoo at Fairford, special airfield type tracking had to be laid on the grass adjacent to the airfield taxiway. It was also noticed that before doing its vertical landing, the metal tracking was extensively cooled by two-airfield fire fighting vehicles spraying water on to this landing site. It should be borne in mind that the engine of the F35B in a hover is producing some 50,000 pounds plus, twice the output of the Sea Harrier.

The reason for the restriction for both vertical landings and take-offs is because the whole of the rear engine exhaust rotates 90 degrees (and beyond) downwards and operates in reheat (afterburning) mode. In other words, the F35B has to have specially prepared landing sites e.g. either on selected spots on the flight decks of the HMS Queen Elizabeth class aircraft carriers or on special prepared hard standings, which have only been built at RAF Marham.

In other words, in order to cope with the very high exhaust temperatures, special materials have had to be applied to the carrier deck. To date, since its debut in the UK, the F35B or other versions, none have done any high-speed manoeuvres to show off its agility.

Similarly, having seen all versions of the F35 flying in the US, once again aerobatic manoeuvres displays at these public air shows were somewhat restrictive. Whilst this may be for operational reasons, normally display pilots like to show off their newly acquired aircraft.

Capabilities, Observations and Perceptions

Recently, a BBC documentary showed F35B trials on the QE off the coast off America, where rolling landings were being conducted. It should be noted that these rolling landings will only apply for a UK requirement. Former Sea Harrier FAA Commanding Officer and Falklands veteran, Cdr 'Sharkey' Ward (known as 'Mr Sea Harrier' and considered to be the most combat proven and carrier experienced VTSOL pilot on Sea Harriers), has repeatedly warned of the danger and hazards of rolling landings.

Rolling landings at approximately 70kts in good visibility and weather, stable flight deck conditions, relatively slow approaches and in the hands of test pilots, look benign. The purpose and rationale behind these types of landing exposes one of the weaknesses of VSTOL operations, i.e. on landing vertically, the weight of the aircraft can only match the thrust of the engine.

Therefore, if you lower this landing weight or alleviate to some extent this weight, the greater the operational flexibility of the aircraft. By performing an element of forward movement whilst landing, some wing lift is created and this reduces the aircraft's landing weight. This type of landing allows operators to use more fuel on actual missions, rather than on expending it on vertical landings.

Secondly, it has the added advantage of increasing the flexibility of being able to bring unused ordnance back to the carrier. Landing back on a carrier with a weapon 'hang up' is very critical within the VSTOL world.

All the above sounds great in theory, but what about bad weather and sea conditions, slippery deck, poor visibility and the F35B being flown by ordinary squadron flying 'jocks'? One would suggest rolling landings in these conditions on a heaving deck would be extremely 'hairy' let alone downright dangerous. What about doing it at night and in low visibility along with a wet and oily deck?

The need for rolling landings appears to be rather retrospective, so why not land at faster approach speeds and permit even heavier fuel/weapon landing loads? Oh furthermore, why don't we put in arrestor wires and have deck hooks to compensate for these higher speeds to stop the aircraft?

Although this attempt to be sardonic is poor, this may not be so far-fetched, as it seems because the Indian Navy has fairly recently been doing ski-jump trials with a McDonnell-Douglas F/18 Hornet in the US. It seems we are within maybe but one step of going back to the use of arrestor wires on a ski-jump fitted ship. These are known colloquially as 'traps'.

Hiccups and Setbacks

One area, which will come to light or otherwise during the F35B's deployment to the Far East in the later part of 2021, is the problem of operating in a salt-water laden corrosive atmosphere. The FAA has long experience of dealing with this environmental difficulty whilst embarked and should be able to greatly assist their embarked RAF counterparts when dealing with corrosion on both aircraft and helicopter structures.

Any magnesium alloy component or of similar composition when subjected to any dents or scratches in its protective paint coat, would immediately begin to froth and bubble when exposed to salt water on the flight deck. Naval personnel could, when working on the flight deck whilst embarked, hear the aircraft of the 1960s and 70s (particularly the Sea Vixen and Scimitar) sizzling on the undercarriage oleos or wing fold mechanisms when they were exposed to salt water.

This occurred even when there was only a small chip of paint missing. The effect was reminiscent of the reaction of bicarbonate salts when spooned into a glass of water. For the FAA, corrosion became a very serious and expensive problem during the 1960s. Consequently, the scientists in the FAA's materiel laboratories carried out extensive research and investigations on how to implement and carry out preventative methods in its maintenance routines.

The result of this research also included the aircraft/helicopter manufacturers and led to corrosion teams being formed on every Naval squadron and flight. Corrosion prevention and training became mandatory and formed a major part of the general engineering training for all trades. The routine of washing aircraft and spraying the aircraft, including helicopters with the oil-based product WD 40, informally known as 'Rocket' by naval air mechanics, was mandatory at the end of each day's flying whilst at sea.

Incidentally, WD 40 was known to affect the radar signatures of aircraft. The F35B is one of the first aircraft to go to sea with a stealth finish. Hopefully, this aircraft's finish is beneficial to the improved robustness of the application of the latest generation of stealth coatings. The F117 and B2 being of the earlier generation of stealth finishes.

It is predicted that it is going to take a lot of man-hours of specialist work to maintain the stealth finish's integrity on top of the normal corrosion preventative measures for this aircraft. Perhaps research into the aircraft finishes when embarked are sufficiently robust and all the lessons learnt during the 1960s–70s have been taken into account.

One deficiency that has recently arisen in the US, which on the face of it looks serious, is the question of sustained supersonic flight. Cases have occurred where there is a risk factor whereby damage is caused to the tail section. Also, the reliability of the stealth finish diminishes when supersonic speeds need to be maintained. The USMC F35Bs, including the UK's F35Bs and the USN's F35C version, can only fly at sustained supersonic speeds for short periods.

Some commentators may consider this a major setback for an aircraft, which was procured and advertised to fly at supersonic speeds. However, feedback from F35B and C pilots is that whilst it is advantageous to get out of a sticky situation fast using afterburners, it is not the main tactical feature as it is only a small part of the combat envelope.

However, not going supersonic as originally envisaged might not be as critical as first thought. The F35 was designed as a weapons system for dealing with targets Beyond Visual Range (BVR) with the aircraft never going within 50 miles of a target. Hopefully, the pilot would have destroyed the target and disengaged the interception. Secondly, going supersonic reduces some of the main advantages on which the F35 was originally marketed e.g.

- The aircraft's radar footprint is greatly increased and therefore, the likelihood of being detected.
- Engine fuel consumption goes through the roof and consequently, reduces the aircraft's range and time on station.
- Engine wear and tear is increased thus, reducing the life of the engine.
- Increased wear and tear on the stealth finish.
- The aircraft's fatigue life will be reduced due to the additional stresses and vibrations that are induced at high speeds.
- Places restrictions when there is need to carry external weaponry on the wings hard points.

One factor concerning some USN planners is that many of the above defects resulting from prolonged supersonic flying are going to require a 'return to depot or manufacturer' fix. In other words, these problems may not be rectified at squadron or station level i.e. RAF Marham. Not really helpful to have a valuable asset out of commission on a long sea-going deployment.

With good squadron management on its aircraft, especially as these aircraft get older, these supersonic flight restrictions can be managed. How the UK will deal with this developing problem has yet to be revealed. It may be dealt with at RAF Marham or elsewhere by civilian contractors.

Defence Policy Analysis

The consequences of the F35B decision of not having 'cats and traps' were far reaching because as defence experts have pointed out, the flexibility of the new carriers has be greatly reduced. The UK will not be able to cross operate with fellow NATO allies i.e. US F-35Cs and French Rafale aircraft. Although with the UK having the ski-jump fit, it would provide a suitable additional platform for the US Marines, as they are the only other service flying the F35B version.

This came to fruition during the Far East deployment in 2021, when a contingent of USMC F35Bs joined the Queen Elizabeth for the trip. Furthermore, another opportunity has been lost whereby had the UK gone for the CATOBAR system, it would have opened up an alternative potential option to purchase Super Hornet F/A 18Es.

Additionally, this would have enabled a tried and tested AWAC aircraft to be embarked i.e. the E-2D Hawkeye. The Super Hornet purchase could have been the new proposed Tranche 3 version, which is being considered by the US Navy as a way of increasing the service life of the Super Hornet for a further 25 years. This route would have given the UK an aircraft with a proven capability and track record thus, saving many millions of pounds.

There is a history in the UK for offsetting costs for such large contracts from the US as the Phantom and Hercules purchases in the late 1960s were but examples. Perhaps, further savings could be made if the UK could outsource all its flying and maintenance training if it went down this route?

French Navy 'Hawkeye' AWAC – Author's photo

On the Defence Policy front, it has been very difficult to track down who was making these decisions behind the scenes. Was it the MOD, military advisors, the various staff officers of the Royal Navy, FAA and the RAF? This, of course, includes politicians who were involved. A Freedom of Information request was made recently but unfortunately the fee to get the necessary documents to carry out research were too prohibitive at a cost of some £3,000 plus.

The research for this book had to rely on the rather sanitised parliamentary and MOD papers to obtain some background information. During the cyclic 5

Yearly Strategic Defence and Security Review of the time, the UK's military tasks were reviewed and the MOD then restructured these tasks to meet the new requirements of the Foreign Office.

Perhaps, one compelling reason for this 180-degree change of tack and reversion back to a ski-jump option, was the sheer cost of installing CATOBAR equipment. The two new aircraft carriers were going to be conventionally powered i.e. gas turbines and not nuclear. This meant the installation of steam catapults was out of the question. Attention then turned to the possibility of fitting of the new electromagnetic aircraft launch system (EMALS) alongside the new advance arresting gear AAG, which was being developed by the US.

Fitting or conversion by UK contractors of this new system was forecast to become very expensive as the price would have virtually doubled. Another setback was the fact that the UK carriers were designed to be conventionally powered and any additional electrical power requirements would be limited. US carriers are nuclear powered with virtual unlimited electrical power.

Summary

To summarise, it should be remembered that the F35 is now in its 16th year of gestation. Not for the first time, the UK defence procurement system has been sorely tested and outcomes made worse because no one realised the long-term repercussions of those legacy decisions made a decade or so ago. Decision makers, who are no longer around due to retirement, political or other reasons (and probably indifferent to the outcome), are the ones, who made these somewhat incoherent plans.

Inter-service rivalry also played its part, as the UK was probably wrong to go for an unproven and untested aircraft with the number of aircraft ordered, manufactured and to be delivered over such a long-protracted period. The F35B will undoubtedly become a fine combat aircraft in due course when its avionic and weapons packages mature in the mid to late 2020s, but it is still less capable than its sister aircraft, the F35C version. All this has left the FAA with some serious potential shortcomings with the current carrier and aircraft combination:

- The Navy's share of the defence budget will be put under severe strain in order to maintain and operate a carrier task force on a permanent basis. Even more so if such a task force is based in the Pacific as there is a

- secondary problem of crewing escort ships, which includes getting the crews for the Queen Elizabeth and Prince of Wales.
- Operationally, the FAA/RAF embarked squadrons will not be supported by an on board organic inflight refuelling capability unless a RAF Voyager circles the QE when she is operational at sea! Perhaps the UK should integrate and join with the US Marines as they have been investigating and developing the possibility of refuelling their F35Bs from a shared V-22 Osprey platform? However, this would be an expensive and long-winded route to take.
- The Airborne Early Warning (AEW) under the guise of CROWSNEST as fitted to the Merlin helicopter (at the time of writing) is way behind schedule. Even on its maiden deployment, there will only be a partial AEW capability as the system is still undergoing development. The Merlin is restricted to flying below 10,000 feet due to having no oxygen or cockpit pressurisation systems, making it far less capable than the conventional twin propeller Hawkeye AEWs as flown by the French and US Navies. The CROWSNEST system is two years late and means the sensor integration is only partially completed between the Merlin and the F35Bs. Therefore, the QE's first operational deployment is going to be devoid of a fully integrated sensor system until the development work is completed.
- The UK is out on a limb with regard to the lack of interoperability with both the US and French CVA strike aircraft carriers, both current and those planned for the future.
- The RN needs to be at the forefront with respect to the use of drones (UAVs) on the Queen Elizabeth class carriers for the future.

As previously stated, with the building of the new carriers containing their organic strike capability, it could be argued, did the RAF really need a new aircraft like the F35 when the build-up of Typhoons into squadron service was taking place? Why not build a further tranche of Typhoons and save money in the longer term by operating only one type.

If this had taken place, the air force could have a clear run financially in developing the 6th generation fighter i.e. the TEMPEST. There was a general consensus that the UK Government had the opportunity to realign its defence policy and consider leaving any overseas strike commitment to the FAA but unfortunately this never came about.

The Joint Programme costs for the F35 for the design and development expenditure paid the Department of Defence (DoD) was in the region of $50Bn. The UK's contribution of circa $2Bn makes it the only nation having access into Tiers 1, 2 and 3 of the project. The building of this aircraft by Lockheed, has been a colossal industrial undertaking, which only the US with its vast aviation industry could have implemented.

It probably is one of the largest aircraft projects ever to be undertaken by the aviation industry worldwide. From an economic and political point of view, it has got to be seen as being a success. Although, some 13% cheaper than the very early models, the fly away cost of each F35B model in 2021 is hedging around $100M per unit figure. This figure is changing constantly and in the British press as of May 2021; the cost was still given as £190M per aircraft.

The reason why production costs per aircraft are still high is because the programme has still not started the Full Rate Production (FRP), which is likely to begin in 2022. The JSF programme's target for FRP is to keep the cost per aircraft to below $100M. Therefore, with an aircraft of such complexity, requirements and not without controversy, its development was going to be monitored closely by all and sundry outside of the military.

In conclusion, the author's opinion is, that the UK plumped for the wrong aircraft and aircraft carrier type, which should have had cats and traps (catapults and arrestor wires). Additionally, the UK carriers cannot cross operate with our NATO allies in the fixed wing arena. Secondly, is the RAF going to provide a Voyager tanker aircraft 24/7 in the vicinity of the Queen Elizabeth anywhere to make up for not having an organic flight refuelling facility?

The MOD should have allowed the Naval Air Staff to carry out a full cost/benefits analysis of procuring the 'Tranche 3' of the Boeing F/18 Hornet, including the Growler (Electronic Counter Measures) and tanker versions. In addition, the Merlin helicopter is only a partial solution for AEW coverage and that a genuine Aircraft Early Warning aircraft like the Tracker could be included in any such procurement from the US.

This would have given the UK a truly cost-*effective* strike carrier capability for the next 25 years. Furthermore, this capability would have been up and running many years ago. In a quarter of a century's time, drones will be masters of the battlefield at sea and looking at some of the potential all up weights of these 3rd generation drones, they too are going to need catapults to get them off the flight deck anyway.

Author's impression of F35B in the Fleet Air Arm colour scheme of 809 NAS (Stealth finish permitting!)

An interesting postscript was made by Bill Covington, a former Joint Force Harrier commander, who in a recently published book gave a very incisive view on the FAA's involvement with regard to the Harrier and the introduction of the F35B and QE class carrier:

"The dismay with which the RAF viewed the loss of cockpits to FAA pilots, meant the RAF's enthusiasm for the Joint Harrier Force and the Invincible Class carrier programme waned. They preferred their natural comfort zone of the Tornado and Typhoon aircraft, wholly under their control, operating from airfields they understood and were set up to support.

"In my view, these and other factors together led to the demise of the UK Harrier Force and the CVS carriers. One needs dedication and enthusiasm to argue the strategic case. If the perceived needs of the services do not align, then the result is bad news for one side. What was interesting was that forward thinking RAF officers could see the need for the Queen Elizabeth class carriers to underpin the procurement of the F-35 Lightning.

"I think it is fair to say that there must have been stunned silence, when even without the Sea Harrier, the FAA devised a plan to maintain the Royal Navy's

fixed wing expertise. In conjunction with US Navy and Marines and other navies, it has positioned itself, with its normal 'can do' attitude and innovation, to be very well placed to participate in today's F-35B Lightning Force and carrier operations – a formidable achievement."

"It should also be said that the F35 is a totally new aircraft, very different from past UK aircraft. Gradually and sensibly building up the Force up over time will avoid the visceral issues that JFH endured. I hope so."

By permission of Bill Covington and John Bond (author of Fleet Air Arm Boys Vol 1 Page275)

Chapter 14
The FAA's Unsung Helicopter Boys

Originally, the author wanted to give a slightly quirky title to this but decided it might detract from the valuable service and unpublished efforts of this element of the Fleet Air Arm i.e. the rotary wing squadrons and flights. On a wider front, these helicopter boys generally receive very little publicity or recognition.

It is the same in most of the world's air forces, fixed wing aircrew (the strike/fighter jockeys) get all the glory and have macho images published regularly. Quietly, but just as importantly, Royal Navy helicopter pilots go about their daily business both in peace and war without any fuss.

They often fly in conditions that no right-minded fixed wing pilot would ever do. Yet, they equally have as many exploits to tell as their blowlamp/stovie (jets) colleagues. These rotary wing flyers fall into the following but not necessarily official categories:

- Junglies
- Search and Rescue
- Pingers
- Baggies
- Small Ships' Flights.

The FAA can be credited with the development and initial use of helicopters in deploying troops from a sea-going platform. The RN was the first to utilise the concept of the 'Commando Carrier' with the insertion and support of a Royal Marine Commando from the sea via a converted aircraft carrier. These landings from the sea by commandos were successfully achieved during the Suez Canal crisis in 1956.

These operations were further developed, whereby two commando carriers were specifically dedicated to this role namely: HMS Albion and HMS Bulwark. The FAA squadrons of 848, 845 and 847, who carried these Royal Marines and others from ship to shore and vice versa. These were affectionately known as 'Junglies'. Their exploits along with their 'can do' philosophies reach legendary levels in the jungles of SE Asia during the Malaya/Indonesia/Borneo confrontations in the 1950s–60s.

The Royal Marines, the Ghurkhas and special forces could rely on these Junglies whatever the circumstances, to transport, insert, search, rescue, supply and extract casualties on a 24/7 basis throughout this confrontation period in SE Asia. A lot of these operations were carried out in appalling weather conditions.

Sea *King HU5/SAR of 771 Naval Air Squadron – Portsmouth Harbour 2008 – Author's photo*

Although 'Search and Rescue' was contracted out to a civilian organisation in 2015–16, it was up till then that the FAA was responsible for carrying out some of most daring sea rescues ever encountered around the UK. One of the most spectacular involved many civilians with a total approaching some 800 people being rescued, was from the East Coast of England and the Netherlands during the North Sea tidal surge flood of 1953.

It was the result of this exploit that gave birth to the FAA's Search and Rescue organisation. During the disastrous Fastnet Race of 1979, the Naval Air station at Culdrose was heavily involved in rescuing many crews and individuals of that race. Culdrose had regularly become the epicentre of many rescues in the dangerous waters off the South Western approaches to the UK.

Lastly during the Falklands war, there was the dramatic and unprecedented rescue by HMS Antrim's anti-submarine helicopter of special-forces personnel from the Fortunna Glacier located on South Georgia. Also, quietly hidden in the FAA's search and rescue repertoire and what could potentially be regarded as a boring and tedious role, was that of the 'Plane Guard'. It was indeed a deadly serious role.

Every aircraft carrier, which operated fixed wing aircraft since the 1950s, carried a flight of some two or more helicopters dedicated to guarding and rescuing aircrew whenever a carrier was at flying stations i.e. the launching or recovery of aircraft during flying stations. It is a well-known statistic in aviation terms that during the take-off or landing phase, the vast majority of flying accidents occur. This is particularly true during maritime flying operations particular over the sea at low level.

These statistics increase greatly when flying from a carrier. Even the Queen Elizabeth on return from her first deployment to the Far East, the ship's Merlin plane guard rescued a F35B pilot as he ejected whilst taking off from the ski-ramp.

Much to the irritation of the FAA personnel, many of these rescues in the UK were regularly attributed incorrectly to the RAF by the press, even though they were clearly operating from the Navy based helicopters air stations at Culdrose, Prestwick, Portland or Lee-on-Solent.

The term 'Pingers' applies to a group of FAA aviators, who are the Anti-Submarine Warfare helicopter specialists, where the nickname is derived from the pinging sound made by active dipping sonar. They provide an anti-submarine screen around a task force or an individual ship. One of their major tasks in particular was and still is, guarding the aircraft carriers from submarine attack.

Lastly, since the 1960s, nearly every HM ship carries a helicopter, some even carry two and many are also embarked on the Royal Fleet Auxiliaries, the Navy's supply ships. They are generally known as Small Ships' Flight and over recent years have probably become the major weapons system a ship can possess.

Apart from being a valuable aggressive asset enabling an over the horizon range to the ship's command, they additionally provide a flexible workhorse capability to that command. For example, they can provide emergency disaster, aerial reconnaissance, medical evacuation, logistics and probably most important of all from a ship's morale point of view, collect and deliver the mail.

These small ships' flights are manned by a dedicated and tightly knit group of FAA personnel. The establishment crew levels consist of a Flight Commander plus the additional aircrew of pilot(s) and observers along with an engineering support crew of some 6–8 or more led by a FAA Senior Maintenance Rating (SMR) depending on the type of helicopter employed.

These flights used to operate out of the busy Royal Naval Air Stations of Yeovilton, Culdrose, and Portland. The latter station being dedicated to small ships' flights was one of the busiest but unfortunately is no longer operational.

The roles of these FAA's SMRs, who head up and are in-charge of the engineering team of any small ship's flight are worthy of further explanation, The FAA has always had technical personnel, who were dual trade i.e. airframes/engines, weapons/electrical and radio. A small ship, or even an aircraft carrier, simply does not have the on-board accommodation space that a land-based air force maintenance team requires. Space is at a premium.

This dual technical trade philosophy incidentally also applied to those who serve on the FAA's fixed winged squadrons. The SMR has full technical and engineering remit for the embarked helicopter(s). An embarked flight does not carry an engineering officer, so therefore the SMR has a very important role as a key member of the ship's company and is held in high esteem.

One has to remember that the embarked helicopter is the ship's major weapons system. Whilst the flight commander has executive and operational responsibilities to the ship's Captain, the embarked helicopter could not fly without the say so of the SMR.

The safety of the aircrew, availability of the helicopter as a major weapons platform depended upon the SMR's certification in the aircraft's logbook. These SMR's are highly competent and experienced engineering personnel and important part of any ship's company.

Another factor to note, is the atrocious weather that a ship and its helicopter experience whilst at sea. These whirly bird machines land and take off in conditions of nearly hurricane winds and mountainous seas day or night. They invariably fly in such terrible weather, which prevents their fixed wing contemporaries from even considering flying. Conditions on the flight deck at the back end of a frigate require the helicopter support crew to be tied or lashed down for landings, and assisting in the rearming and refuelling evolutions.

These conditions were experienced frequently during the Falklands Island's war in the South Atlantic. Blade sailing is a danger to ground crew whereby the rotor blades 'bend' due to the unpredictable wind and rotational forces can nearly strike the deck. This blade sailing phenomenon can easily decapitate a person as their rotational momentum energy is in the region of 40–50 tons.

FAA helicopters save 75 sailors – The Fastnet Race of 1979

The Fastnet Race of 1979 was the Royal Ocean Racing Club's 28th race, which has been held biennially ever since 1925. The course consists of some 605 miles starting at Cowes on the Isle of Wight and then sailing south of the Scilly Isles to the Fastnet Rock. Known as 'Ireland's Teardrop' because it was the last part of Ireland that emigrants saw in the 19th Century when they sailed to America. It lies 4 miles (6.5 Kilometres) southwest from Cape Clear and some 8 miles (13 Kilometres) from County Cork on the Irish mainland.

The race started on the 11th August 1979 with the shipping forecast predicting SW winds of Force 4 to 5 increasing to 6 to 7 for a time. On 13th August, winds Force 6 were being reported with gusts up to 7. Forecasters were predicting winds of Force 8. During the weekend of 11–13th August, a large deepening depression had formed in the Atlantic and moved over the race area on the 14th.

This caused storm Force 10 with wind speeds of 55–63 mph, although race competitors reckoned that it was actually a violent storm Force 11 with wind speeds of between 64 and 72 mph, with a low pressure reading of 979 Mbars.

With these devastating winds of 60 mph being unleashed on the yachtsmen on the night of 11 August 1979, there unfolded the UK's largest peacetime rescue, which centred on RNAS Culdrose.

303 yachts had set off and over the 11th/12th August, some 75 boats capsized with five of them sinking. Tragically, 19 sailors died, which included four spectators, who were in a yacht following the race from a distance. Some 140 people were rescued with FAA helicopters rescuing 75 of those survivors.

The remainder being picked up by RNLI lifeboats and shipping. Fifteen helicopters, made up of Wessexs, Sea Kings and Lynxes flew over 200 hours carrying out rescue sorties, which were operating and being controlled out of

Culdrose. On 14th August, HMS Broadsword, which was on sea-trials was tasked as the Scene of Search Coordinator in the area. Additional FAA aircrew with search and rescue experience were to be called in from both RNAS Yeovilton in Somerset and Prestwick in Scotland to assist and supplement this rescue.

Wessex HU 5 in Search and Rescue of 771/772 NAS – author's image

Falklands War – South Georgia 1982
29 Special Forces personnel rescued

A small task group consisting of HMS Antrim, HMS Plymouth, HMS Conqueror and RFA Tidespring, had detached itself from the main Task Force heading for the Falkland Islands. This little flotilla then rendezvoused with HMS Endurance. They headed to South Georgia and its adjacent chain of small islands known as the South Sandwich Islands.

These have been British Overseas Territories since 1775 and 1908 respectively. They lie some 800 miles southeast from the Falkland Islands and were seized by Argentinean Naval forces on the 3rd April 1982.

In order to show political resolve, the British War Cabinet directed that South Georgia be recaptured from the Argentinean military occupation. This operation was officially name as 'Operation Paraquet' but was soon changed by British Troops to 'Paraquat' – a commercially well-known weed killer of that period.

Following the redistribution of Special Forces amongst the Task Group, which included six SBS men on to the SSN submarine Conqueror, the scene was set for reconnaissance of the targets earmarked for recapture. Whilst the SBS patrols were inserted to set up observations posts around Grytviken, the SAS had plans to insert their Mountain Troop, D Squadron, on to the Fortuna Glacier some 20 miles southeast of Stromness Bay.

The thinking behind this approach from the glacier was that it reduced the possibility of being detected by the Argentines, as they would not be expecting an attack from such a direction. Officers and the Captain of Endurance including members of the British Antarctic Survey opposed this glacier insertion. They had knowledge of the local conditions and felt the difficulties of travelling on and over the glacier were being underestimated.

Following strong political backing for the SAS operation from the UK Government, the Officer Commanding D Squadron decided to put into action the reconnaissance plan.

On 21st April 1982, following three reconnoitering trips by Antrim's Wessex Mk 3 helicopter, 15 men of the SAS Mountain Troop were airlifted by two Wessex Mk 5 helicopters from RFA Tidespring and Antrim's helicopter on to the Fortuna Glacier. Antrim's helicopter was affectionately known as 'Humphrey' and with its fit of equipment, was able to guide the three helicopters up and down the glacier walls and was able to reach the top.

It should be pointed out the differences in these two Marks of Wessex helicopters. The Mk 5 is a twin Gnome engine helicopter designed for carrying troops. It was a utility workhorse, flown by just one pilot aided by an air crewman in the rear cabin. It had radio altimeters, flight stability system but no 'blind' navigation equipment.

The Wessex Mk 3 with a single engine was built as an anti-submarine helicopter designed to carry a crew of four. This consisted of two pilots, an observer plus an air crewman both located in the rear. Fortunately, the Wessex Mk 3 had an observer, who was responsible for navigation and radar operation with the scanner built on top of the fuselage.

Although the helicopter's gearbox restricted scans forward, it had a wide view and some collision avoidance capability. It also had an early-computerised Automatic Flight Control System enabling the helicopter to be held at a particular height and location – a critical system for when hunting submarines with the dipping sonar. An ungainly concoction of systems and equipment, which proved to be a mixture of pluses and minuses for such an insertion as it could be removed to make space.

From the moment, the SAS were landed by these three helicopters the weather on and around South Georgia worsened with conditions becoming atrocious and dangerous. The disembarked troops tried to move off before nightfall but with wind speeds ever increasing, the mission became one of survival.

Therefore some 15 hours later, the Troop Commander requested evacuation as they were unable to move and the weather conditions had deteriorated even further. Even veteran members of the Mountain Troop had never experienced such diabolical environmental conditions. The following morning, the Troop had survived but were soaked to the skin, had equipment blown away, with some members showing signs of frostbite and hypothermia.

The decision was taken to get them off the glacier as soon as possible. Upon hearing this, the three helicopters led by the nickname 'Humphrey' the Wessex 3 once again took off immediately but found extreme flying conditions due to fierce winds and snow squalls reducing visibility to just a few yards. A rescue attempt was on its way.

After instructing the two Wessex 5s to shelter on the ground as best they could, Humphrey's crew discovered that the Fortuna Glacier was closed in by cloud and katabatic winds and had no choice but to delay the rescue attempt. Returning down the glacier, they picked up the two waiting Wessex 5 helicopters and returned to their respective ships to await an improvement in the weather.

An hour later, another attempt was made and this time the three-helicopter flight successfully found the stranded Troop. However, they landed in marginal conditions where visibility was being hampered by snow blown along by high gusting winds. Having embarked the Troop members across all three helicopters, one of the Wessex 5s was hit by a snow squall from the front and side, which created 'whiteout' conditions.

A whiteout is where snow reduces visibly to virtually zero with the helicopter being surrounded by a thick white blanket of snow. This produces no discernible horizon. With the radio altimeter giving wild readings, pilot and aircrewman in the back lost all external visual references and became disorientated.

The pilot noted the radio altimeter showing a rapid loss of height and realising what was about to happen, he raised the collective lever to increase power and lift to reduce any impact. The helicopter crashed into the snow where it tipped over on its side and slid into a gulley. The 'gods' were on their side as there were no casualties.

The remaining two helicopters, which had observed the Wessex 5 crashing and tipping over, air taxied to it. The serving troops abandoned their equipment and were distributed between the two. Unfortunately, another mishap was to occur. As Humphrey lifted over the ice ridges to apparent safety, the pilot in the second Wessex 5 lost sight of the lead helicopter due to another snow squall.

The pilot immediately faced the same conditions i.e. disorientation brought on by confused sensory messages, no visual references front or back and fluctuating instrument readings. He then noted the rapid unwinding of the altimeter and tried pull on power via the collective to gain height to get over the glacier ridges but the helicopter blades impacted these ridges on to soft snow.

The helicopter tilted, whereby the rotors then hit rocks and were wrecked until rotational energy was absorbed and the blades came to a standstill. By this time, it had also ended up on its side.

Having ascertained that there were no serious injuries Humphrey's Flight Commander made the decision to return to Antrim with their load and come back later. Having once having landed onboard and off loaded the rescued personnel, Humphrey then made another and final attempt to return to the glacier as the weather had cleared briefly.

Up went Humphrey again struggling in still atrocious weather conditions to pick up the remaining 17 people. This was successful. Loaded with 17 people on board (made up of Humphery's crew, x2 Wessexes aircrew and x11 SAS) onboard and with the Wessex Mk 3 (Humphrey) very near its torque limits the machine could take, it took off. With the heavy load, take-off was assisted by the dense cold air and galeforce wind through the rotors.

Intent on getting back to Antrim as fast as possible, the pilot without ceremony flew alongside the ship, moved sideways and dumped Humphrey on to the flight deck. They were all back safely. These rescue operations enabled some 29 personnel in total to be saved by HMS Antrim's Wessex 3. i.e. Humphrey. This helicopter features regularly as part of the Falkland's War display at the FAA Museum at Yeovilton.

As a postscript to this rescue, weather conditions even worsened once the SAS insertion was completed; the ships faced even further bad weather whereby Storm Force 11 conditions prevailed. These sea-state conditions had become so treacherous that Humphrey could not be moved from the flight deck into the hangar. Such a move would have been a threat to life and limb.

The flight deck crew had to be tethered by ropes for their safety just to lash the helicopter down. The same occurred on RFA Tidespring where a Wessex 5 had to be left exposed to the elements. Humphrey on her trips back and forth, the crew had registered wind speeds in the region of 90 knots (103 mph).

For their bravery and the operating in extreme conditions, the crew of Antrim's Wessex 3 helicopter received bravery awards with the pilot Lt Ian Standley being awarded the DSO for his airmanship.

One should not forget the fortitude and unstinting efforts of Humphrey's engineering crew ably led by an experienced Senior Maintenance Rating (SMR) i.e. 'Fritz' Heritier. This crew beavered away, regularly working intensely long hours in very unhospitable conditions into the night and beyond without breaks to ensure the ship's helicopter was readily available.

They also risked life and limb every time when moving Humphrey back and forth from the flight deck to the hangar. There were occasions where work required personnel to be lashed with ropes to prevent them from being swept overboard. This engineering team are credited with the following:

- Throughout the conflict, this engineering team were able to maintain a 97% availability rate to the 'Command'. For this achievement, the Chief Aircraft Artificer of the Flight was awarded a BEM.
- This serviceability rate was achieved despite an engine change, many removals and replacements of the sonar equipment.
- The helicopter suffered extreme 'battle' damage requiring the repair of 125 fuselage holes, a shredded main rotor blade and damaged tail rotor blade.

North Sea Floods – 1953
Over 800 lives saved by FAA helicopters

This particular rescue by a FAA Squadron, namely 705 NAS in February 1953 following this rescue, was to precipitate the formation of the Royal Navy's Search and Rescue units.

Over the weekend, starting on Saturday 31st January and during Sunday 1st February 1953, a deep low weather system combined with spring tides and gale force winds (recorded at 126 mph in the Orkneys), caused a storm surge in the North Sea. This surge peaking at 18 feet (5.6 metres) funnelled the high tides southwards to the relative shallows English Channel.

This peak occurred during the night and catching communities unaware, resulted in devastating floods to the low lying areas of East Anglia, mouth of the Thames and to the Netherlands. This disastrous event in terms of loss of life and damage was to become the one of the worst floods of the 20th century. At sea, the MV Princess Victoria sailing out of Stranraer was sunk with the loss of 133 lives.

On land, the Netherlands lost over 1,836 people, whilst the UK lost 307 and Belgium lost 32. All 12 Dragonfly helicopters of FAA's 705 NAS were put on standby to help in either SE England or Holland. Some went to Kent for use over the flooded areas of England. Nine helicopters with aircrew and mechanics from their base at the RNAS Gosport were sent to Gilze-Rijen in Holland.

These aircraft worked at full pitch for four days from the 4th to 7th February inclusive, during which period the nine pilots flew a total of 237 hours and rescued 752 people. Two Navy pilots between them saved 257 people in one day.

From 8th February onwards, the Squadron was held at immediate readiness to deal with the effects of any further flooding that might occur during the next series of spring tides. In fact, they were used mainly for supply dropping. In a week, the pilots had flown 185 hours and rescued a further 58 people.

In total, some 422 hours were flown and 810 people saved (80 of whom were hoisted into the aircraft by winch).

For these life-saving efforts, the Commanding Officer of the 705 NAS Lieutenant Commander Bob Spedding, received the MBE and Air Crewman Craig received the BEM.

It was realised by the FAA hierarchy by the results of this particular rescue that flood relief work by these Dragonfly's, which were just the 1st generation of helicopters, led to an expanding use of them in maritime rescues. 1953 heralded the birth of the FAA's Search and Rescue.

An Untold Story – Falklands
Royal Fleet Auxiliary (RFA) Regent and its Wessex 5 Helicopter Flight

The following is an extract from a transcript from Electrical Air Artificer 1st Class 'Ed' Cole, the Senior Maintenance Rating of RFA Regent's Flight during the Falklands' war. This involved a tale of 'can do', 'make do' and pushing Health and Safety to the very limits. For example: like successfully carrying out a sea rescue on the end of dangling cable, without any proper training. It should be understood that for this Falklands conflict, RFA Regent had no passive weapon systems fit.

Early one Saturday morning in April 1982, I was recalled from leave and told to assemble a team of engineers to maintain a flight of two Wessex Mk 5s, which was to embark on the RFA Regent and sail south to the Falklands two days later. 'A' Flight was to be part of 848 Squadron newly formed from 707 Squadron, a training unit for aircrew and maintainers.

As well as being appointed as the Senior Maintenance Rating (SMR) for the first time, I was also designated the flying maintainer, a role for which I had been trained for but not employed in previously. The flying maintainer's jobs included inflight main rotor blade tracking, vibration recording and analysis and various test flights as required.

The ship sailed from Plymouth in company with HMS Argonaut and RFA Orangeleaf. After a few days, the Argonaut was instructed to steam on ahead to join the main fleet. In order to make our passage as covert as possible, the ships sailed well outside of the main shipping lanes. One lunchtime, when we were somewhere south of the Cape Verde islands, well out into the Atlantic, the flight personnel were ordered to the flight deck at the rush as there was a man overboard situation, possibly voluntary, on the other ship.

Both ships turned around and backtracked. We scrambled on our deck aircraft and it returned after 2 hours searching for refuel and crew change. While this was happening, I volunteered to go up as a fresh set of eyes. The aircraft was now being piloted by a pilot, who had been a trainee on 707 Squadron, with myself and a Petty Officer Air crewman in the cabin.

After about 30 minutes of flying, the air crewman spotted the missing man. The next thing I knew was that he was strapping me into the rescue harness and hooking a rescue strop and me onto the winch. This was not something that I had been trained for, however a few years earlier I had been rescued from the sea in a Search and Rescue (SAR) demonstration for Weymouth Carnival, so I had some idea of what to do.

As he lowered me towards the swimmer, the thought went through my mind 'does this man really want to be rescued?' There was a small breakdown in communication between pilot and the crewman, as the pilot didn't know I was on the winch, he thought there was just the rescue strop. So, when I was in the water and the crewman called for the aircraft to move left/right 10 etc. the pilot made rapid corrections and I virtually water-skied over the water, exhilarating if nothing else.

I'm glad to say that he did want rescuing and I managed to get the rescue strop around him and enable his safe recovery to the aircraft. Besides being somewhat wrinkled by being in the sea, he was none the worse for his swim. The only casualty of the incident was my Casio watch, which didn't take kindly to its dip in the Atlantic.

On the transit to the Total Exclusion Zone (TEZ), we had our first air raid warning and went to our assigned action station, which was down at the waterline. Having spent 30 minutes there, I vowed that we would never go there again. From then on, at air raid warning we manned the flight deck and hangar roof with our rifles, 2 GPMGs and a Bren gun. Dad's army to the fore! The ship was fitted for chaff dispensers, but not actually with them. Great I thought!

Our armourer (bomb-head) stripped down Schermuly flares, removed the parachute and flare and packed them with hand held chaff. As soon as I hit the flight deck at air raid warning red, I would wet a finger, assess the wind and fire them off, don't know if they did anything but it made me feel good and I'm here to tell the tale. I think that we had 12 air raid warnings red, always during the evening meal. We were two miles from the Atlantic Conveyor, when she got hit.

When we eventually joined the Task Force and the Round Table class landing ships logistics (LSL) also known as the Sir Lancelot class arrived, I eventually received the chain lashings we desperately needed. We spent most of our time doing VERTREPS (Vertical Replenishment by Helicopter). The Task Force remained on Zulu time, the thinking being that there would be no air strikes by night, so we would all be up and have breakfast by first light.

The downside to this was that we would keep flying until about nightfall, which was around 22:00. So, by the time we had done After Flight Inspections, etc. and had a nightcap, it was usually gone midnight before we got to bed. On several occasions, we would be roused during the night to carry out an emergency VERTREP with ships that had suffered damage.

VERTREP being preferred to Replenishment at Sea (RAS) as they were quicker and enabled the fighting ships to get back on station quicker. From time to time, we would detach to South Georgia to restore ships coming from the UK. During this period, I was able to visit and see Shackleton's grave. The only other Flight Deck Officer (FDO) was the 1st Officer, who always ran the RFA's deck when replenishing at sea.

Therefore, if there was also a Vertical Replenishments (VERTREP), I was also the FDO. Once, I ran four different ships at once. During one of these episodes as FDO, I had a weird experience whilst doing this. I had started both engines and called the ship's bridge for permission to engage rotors (this is done to make sure that the ship isn't about to manoeuvre), the normal response from the bridge is, "engage rotors," but on this occasion the response was "standby, the ship is manoeuvring to avoid a torpedo." To this day, I have not heard of there being any torpedo attacks, so had no idea what was going on.

On one trip to South Georgia, the boss (Flight Commander) and I were summoned to HMS Endurance for a war brief! It had been decided to send a small force to retake the island of Southern Thule (the southern most of the South Sandwich Islands) from the Argentines and we were to embark one of our Wessex 5s on to Endurance for troop insertion.

This force consisted of Endurance, a frigate (HMS Yarmouth I think) and a tanker. It was strange going to war on a ship painted bright red. The flight deck on the Endurance was minuscule but the hangar big enough for two Wasps and a Wessex. In order to fold the rotor blades, we would have to shuffle it to one side in order to get the blade fold pole onto the blades on the other side. Fold them and then shuffle the cab (helicopter) to the other side and repeat the procedure, then shuffle back to the middle in order to get it in the hanger.

The whole procedure had to be reversed to range the cab ready for flying. All the more difficult as the flight deck had quite a steep rake on it and we didn't have a mechanical movement handler. Just to add a bit of spice, the flight deck was prone to icing up. Accommodation was tight on board, myself as SMR and Brian Hunter (the senior airframes and engine CPO) had foam mattresses, which were placed on the deck between benches in the instrument laboratory.

On the plus side, the ship had enough captured wine (from S Georgia) for six bottles to be placed on the table in the wardroom and senior rates mess every night. They gave a couple of crates to us when we left. When we got there, we launched our Wessex to pick up some RM Commandos from the tanker for a covert insertion the night before the invasion of the island. The purpose of this was so they could take up positions for the following morning. As it happened, the Argentines had left by the time they got there.

We spent a day anchored off the base liberating some Argentinian stores and more wine, then returned to South Georgia and re-embarked on Regent. We returned back to the TEZ after having to carry out an engine change on one cab. I and the boss did take the opportunity to fly over to the Atlantic Conveyor to touch base with the CO of 848, Sqn, Lt Cdr Baston.

We were given a guided tour of the holds, where there were stacks of 1,000lb bombs amongst other munitions, and a critical roll out runway for the Sea Harriers and the GR 3s. Ongoing to the bridge to call up our cab for the return flight, I met up with my old CO from 899 NAS, now Captain Layard, who was later to become 2nd Sea Lord.

On one rare day when we weren't flying because of dense fog and we had just celebrated the 18th birthday of one of my lads, we decided to have a bucket of moose's milk in the rarely used flight recreation room. Just settling down to half a pint and a King Edward, when I was piped to go to the flight deck. Called the bridge on the flight deck intercom and told that one of the Fort RFA boats had just joined the fleet and was lost in the fog and in danger of colliding with the Regent.

I was to launch a string of smoke and flame flares (normally used for poor visibility approaches of helicopters) to try and give them some visual clues as to where we were. You may well ask why they couldn't see us on radar, there was a total EMCON silence in operation for most of the time. Eventually, the RFA did appear on the starboard quarter and steered clear.

Strangely, on the day of the landing we weren't scheduled to fly and this was the day the Atlantic Conveyor was hit. We weren't tasked as SAR but sailed away, possibly because there was still lots of high explosives in the holds.

A few days later, we were tasked to go into San Carlos waters, by this time we knew what was going on in there, via the BBC World News for one and our PO Air crewman 'Scouse' Hogan had a brother, who was a chock-head (aircraft handler) on the HMS Hermes. When the cab stopped off on Hermes for a refuel during VERTREPS, he would talk to his brother and get all the latest gossip on what was happening.

We were due to go into San Carlos overnight, so I slept fully clothed that night. I can't tell you of the relief I felt when I lifted the dead light (porthole) in my cabin in the morning and saw that we were still in open sea. Apparently, command had decided that with the loss of the Atlantic Conveyor, they couldn't put us at such high risk. Also, possibly because most of the fleet had been disembarrassed (as it's called) by passing their special weapons to us.

Once the surrender had happened, we sailed into Port William waters and anchored up. We were then told to get rid of one of our Wessex helicopters for transit back to the UK with some of our crew, including the boss. This left just one pilot, Tom Mason – top guy. I was glad to get rid of the cab as I chose the one, which had a multitude of LIFEX (critical life expired) components, which required to be changed shortly.

We sailed once a week or so in open water in order to make freshwater. During this time, Brian and I took the opportunity to go ashore into Port Stanley to visit the squadrons ashore there. While walking around Stanley, we got a bollocking from an MP for not wearing our berets. I had taken a grip full of Argentinian wine to give the guys ashore.

Talk about coals to Newcastle, when we found them in tents inside a warehouse, each camp bed had a bottle rack alongside it full of wines and spirits. In order to get back to Regent, we had to go to the racetrack in Stanley where we managed to scrounge a lift in another Wessex. When we climbed in to the cabin, we found there were no seats, so we just had to sit on the floor. During this time, the ship was issued with two chaff and flare dispensers, which had been removed from RFA Tidepool and had been sold to Chile.

On our very last operational flight, we had our first flying incident of the trip. It was an under-slung load that included a ships ladder. Part way through the flight, the load decided to take charge of itself and flew up and struck; puncturing the underside of the helicopter just below the cabin door. Still it gave Brian something to do on the trip home, a bit of proper 'tin bashing'.

On the way home, Brian and I decided to take our helmsman ticket for something to do to pass the time. This involved a total of 10 hours, with each of us doing one hour stints at the wheel. This meant taking the ship off autopilot and the bridge watch-keepers reckoned that we cost them about a nautical mile each one hour stint with our meandering.

We now have helmsman tickets for vessels over 100 tons. We kept up our airframe husbandry on the way back but had run out of drab olive paint, so I took the decision to use black, which included the repair. We stopped briefly at Ascension Island on the way back and eventually disembarked at Hartland Point in the Bristol Channel with the help of a Sea King Mk4.

We did the usual fly by with smoke flares attached to the cabin doorstep but only to be told that that this had now been banned when we landed. The cab was given a survey on return and was put straight back into service, complete with all the black spots.

As a footnote, several years later I was called into the Station AEO and was asked what I had done with the aircraft's tool box for the cab when we got back to RNAS Yeovilton. I said it was in the back of the cab the last I saw of it. All I was interested at the time, was to hand over the A700 (helicopter's maintenance log) and go on leave.

Apparently, this toolbox had turned up in a private garage along with a great deal of other 'pusser's' (belonging to the Navy) equipment. A squadron stores Petty Officer was convicted of appropriating these missing items.

Reflections of effectiveness and efficiency

It is worthy to highlight the background and work of just one FAA helicopter squadron, which it carried out year by year. That squadron is 815 NAS, whose motto is 'Strike Deep'. It was formed originally in October 1939 at Worthy Down with Swordfishes and was part of the successful attack at Taranto. For the next twenty years, it was basically equipped with fixed wing aircraft like the Fulmar, Avenger and the Gannet.

In January 1959, it became equipped with helicopters, with the Whirlwind HAR 3 being the first type. Another twenty years were to pass when the squadron was re-commissioned in 1981 with Westland Lynx HAS 2s. They were to be stationed at RNAS Yeovilton and became the Headquarters Squadron for embarked Lynx Flights.

In 1982, the squadron moved back to RNAS Portland and shared flights with 829 NAS, which operated the Wasp helicopter. In the same year, both types operated from destroyers, frigates and HMS Endurance and were heavily involved in the Falklands War of 1982. Eventually, they were amalgamated in 1993 and became the world's largest helicopter squadron and with the closure of the air station at Portland, the squadron moved back to RNAS Yeovilton.

In September 2000, a Lynx took part in the successful Special Forces and Paras raid under Operation Barras, which led to the freeing of British Army hostages held by rebels in Sierra Leone. Flown by Lt Cdr Al Jones RN and with his observer Lt Nigel Cunningham RN, flew deep reconnaissance missions into the jungle.

815 NAS principal task is to prepare Lynx (the current helicopter is the Augusta Westland Wildcat HMA 2) aircrews and engineering personnel in readiness embarking on to small ships. These being Type 45 destroyers, Type 23 frigates, RFA Ships with some flights being deployed on the Queen Elizabeth carriers. A Maritime Interdiction (MI) flight is kept at a high state or alert for maritime counter-terrorism.

Wildcat and Lynxes breaking – RNAS Yeovilton Air day 2015 – Author's photo

To give an idea of the diverse operations undertaken, the following reflects and highlights what took place in just one year in 2010–11 by 815 NAS:

1. It deployed 13 embarked Flights to RN ships.
2. 815 Squadron Lynx helicopters participated in 22 UK based exercises, one NATO exercise and took part in 20 operational sea training periods.
3. The Lynxes accumulated nearly 7,000 flying hours.
4. 3,600 sorties were flown, of which 700 were operational. This equated to 10 sorties a day continuously.
5. Four 'drug busts' worth £10M confiscated.

6. Carried out searches for pirates in a length of sea larger than the coastline of the whole of the UK. This relates to a period when piracy was rife along the coast of Somalia.
7. A total of 18 pirate action groups were intercepted and seven pirate boats destroyed.
8. Some 43,000 machine gun rounds were used in support of the above operations.

On paper, all the above activity on 815 NAS looks a little benign but beneath the surface, it represents a high level of activity done at fast tempo and under trying conditions. These flights are part of the ship's weapons system but can be rapidly used in other roles like humanitarian i.e. earthquakes, floods and other disasters.

These activities had a disruptive impact on family life as a deployment can last up to nine months or more. Also, a small ships flight can quickly be transferred lock stock and barrel from one ship to another, should the need arise. Life on 815 was never boring and probably still isn't.

Augusta Westland Wildcat HMA 2 and Westland Wasp HAS 1 – Compton Abbas – 2015 – Author's photo

Sources

https://en.wikipedia.org/wiki/File:Royal_Navy_Wildcat_Helicopter_MOD_45158434.jpg

https://en.wikipedia.org/wiki/815_Naval_Air_Squadron

https://www.seaforces.org/marint/Royal-Navy/AIRCRAFT/Sea-King-RN.htm

Source – HMS Antrim – notes and conversation with Chief Aircraft Artificer David 'Fritz' Heritier BEM

Source – RFA Regent – Electrical Artificer (Air) 1st Class Ed Cole – notes.

Hansard 18th March 1953 vol 513 cc14-6W

Chapter 15
Very Different Animals – FAA vs RAF culture

Cartoon courtesy of Steev (2021)

The purpose of this chapter is to briefly describe the differences in the terms and conditions, and to a lesser degree, what influences the attitudes of those serving in the FAA and the RAF. This has developed due to the historic background and length of time each service has been in existence.

The FAA, formed a few years before the junior service but has its roots set in the senior service i.e. the Royal Navy, which in turn has centuries of traditions and a long established reputation of getting things done. This stems from the need for self-sufficiency and operating for long periods away and on occasions, many thousands of miles from home.

Whilst the RAF and FAA fly through the same atmosphere, some of it saltier than others, the philosophies of both fighting forces are different as chalk and cheese. This applies irrespective of whether you are a pilot/observer or maintenance technician/mechanic. If you want a 9 to 5 job, virtually every weekend off and minimum disruption to family life, then join the Royal Air Force. One has to remember that it has a very high ratio of officers with the majority being pilots. At times, it is very top heavy.

It also has the advantage of operating from airfields that do not move and where you take off and land in familiar surroundings i.e. local roads, buildings and landmarks etc. Having a large expanse of open space with long runways to operate from, these give RAF pilot's far wider safety margins and tolerances for when errors occur.

These tolerances are far more forgiving than those of a heaving deck. Furthermore, should inclement weather descend on a land-based air station or an incident blocks a runway, there are several diversionary airfields on hand. These diversions always form part of the pre-flight briefings, day or night and are normally at familiar airfields. As an airfield is fixed, far more accurate weather forecasts can be made and therefore landing in marginal conditions are considered to be safer.

For the Navy pilot, operating to and fro from a carrier at sea creates a totally different environment and mind-set. It requires 100% concentration 100% of the time. This applies to both fixed-wing and rotary pilots and aircrew. The sea is an unforgiving master. Whilst the UK decided not to have the F35C, which would have required catapults and arrestor wires, it is still demanding when taking off from a ramp and then coming back and having to land vertically with the F35B version.

Pilot stress factors and concentration levels increase especially in inclement weather, with the carrier rolling unpredictably in all three dimensions. Couple these environmental conditions, which occur regularly at sea with the possibility of weapon hang-ups, these stress factors increase exponentially. It was known that if any Sea Harrier returned with a variety of weapon hang-ups on one side only, this ordnance has to be blown off i.e. explosively released from the pylons.

If these cannot be released and the aircraft has such an asymmetric load, there is a distinct possibility that the aircraft might have to be ditched. No doubt, the F35B will present the same problems but some of these legacy problems might be alleviated with the development of 'rolling' landings.

Fixed wing pilots tend to get all the glory but naval helicopter pilots face exactly the same dangers when at sea. There are many 'hairy stories' of ship's flights, especially during the Falkland War, having to return to their 'mother' ship at night and land without any visual references i.e. a fully darkened ship.

A factor, when considering operations at sea, which is generally overlooked, is the subject of combat stress. For the land-based pilot, you go into combat and once your dogfight or bombing run is over, there is an immediate natural psychological release of tension and euphoria of having survived.

Not for the Navy pilot. Once any combat action is over, you then have the additional stress of finding the carrier or the back end of a frigate in all weathers; day or night and invariably it will not be in the same place from where you were launched. During the Falklands war, the RAF's involvement whilst embarked with the Harrier GR 3s, took some adjustment to recognise that these ground attack weapons systems were only a small integral part of the defensive and offensive systems available to 'Command' of the Naval Task Force.

It took time for aircrews to absorb Naval operations and in fairness to these crews; this was the first time many of them had ever operated from an aircraft carrier.

When personnel join the FAA, they invariably know full well and expect that they will go to sea. Therefore, as well as learning their aviation craft and airmanship, their training will include wider naval-related aspects such as operating and fighting in confined spaces (in grey coloured compartments or be accommodated in similarly coloured living spaces – something akin to prison).

They may be involved in supporting the ship's damage control and fire-fighting teams. There are the expectations of long periods away from home and family. Many FAA personnel during the Cold War period, who have done full careers of 22 years plus service, found the chances of a married accompanied overseas opportunity were extremely rare.

Due to the various carrier deployments, it was also rare to enjoy a short break or perhaps get your spouse or partner to join you on a rare indulgence flight. It was just an accepted part of service life in the RN.

Apart from the physical side of living on board a RN ship, there is a complete new language to learn. Fortunately, many naval phrases are embedded into everyday English. There is a well-known saying embedded in the English language i.e. "There's not enough room to swing a cat". One has a mental image of swinging a furry cat around by its tail.

However, whilst it does imply a small space, it actually refers to the time when sailors were flogged (lashed) by a cat-o-nine-tails whip in confined spaces. RN ship's operate 'watches' or for non-naval personnel, shifts. These watches for the ship's company are normally of four hours duration, with two 'dog' watches of only two hours duration with the 1st dog watch between 1600–1800 and then a 2nd dog watch between 1800–2000.

This ensures that no one has the same watch each day. This has been researched over a number of years with regard to aircraft operations and maintenance that different watch (shift) patterns than the general service Navy were developed. This is but one of a myriad of RN sayings and procedures, which have built up over a number of centuries. All have to be absorbed and learnt.

Commissioned by author and created by Steev (2021)

One area, which might give useful background for RAF personnel before going to sea, the author suggests as a little light reading before embarking, is the late Rick Jolly's book entitled 'Jackspeak' – a Guide to British Naval Slang and Usage. It is an encyclopaedia of both historic and modern terms used by both matelots (sailors) and bootnecks (marines).

Within the book, there are some hilarious cartoons illustrating some of the terms used. Alternatively, if you wish to have a good understanding of how sailors think, act and use their nautical language, it can be found in the nautical songs of the folk singer Shep Wolley, a former Navy seaman. His music and lyrics, which can be rather salty at times, reflects the thinking and traditions of British sailors.

Forget the demanding element of core skills required, whether you are a pilot or technician, being on an aircraft carrier you become interdependent with your fellow crewmembers, which becomes critical when the ship goes to action stations. Whether you may be on a FAA fixed wing squadron providing the Carrier Air Patrols (CAPs) covering the outer air defence of the fleet, or on embarked helicopter squadron providing an anti-submarine screen, you are in essence embedded into a fairly sophisticated fleet wide weapon system.

The same applies to a small ship's flight. You rely on the ship's company personnel to provide logistics i.e. food, stores and weapons, etc. Nobody is exempt when a ship is replenishing at sea (known as a RAS) when it is 'all hands' (all ranks and rates) to the pumps. Even this latter old nautical term harks itself back to the days when ships were either badly damaged or holed in battle and taking on water, meant your life depended upon keeping the vessel afloat with these pumps.

The safety of the ship as a fighting war machine is paramount. This in turn means, whatever your position on a ship you automatically become part of the ship's damage control set-up. Ships, even in peacetime are dangerous places to live and work, requiring 24/7 vigilance. Everybody has to learn fire-fighting techniques along with the ability to use breathing apparatus, wear fire protection suits and use such equipment in a confined space.

When you were drafted, whether to a ship or squadron and going on board for the first time, you had to attend the fire-fighting school at Whale Island, Portsmouth. In conjunction with the fire-fighting side, you also have to attend the damage control course at HMS Excellent Phoenix Damage Repair Instructional Unit in Portsmouth.

The structural safety and integrity of any RN ship is critical both in peacetime and war. It is assumed that RAF personnel will also have to be called upon to form part of damage control parties. Added to all this, the Nuclear Biological and Chemical Defence (NBCD) requirements on board have to be understood and learnt. At any given time, a RN ship has many different NBCD states whilst at sea or when tied up alongside in harbour. All this being rather daunting for those not familiar with such routines and from a different branch of the armed services.

Even for a maintainer working below in the hangar, it can be arduous with the aircraft being constantly moved and shuffled around in order to get serviceable cabs (kites in RAF parlance) up on the flight deck and vice versa. It can also be quite nerve racking trying to jack up a 20 ton plus aircraft like the Phantom or Buccaneer even in a gentle swell. Judicious use of chain lashings has to be employed whilst carrying out a jacking evolution whilst on the high seas.

As the supervisor of any such evolution requires liaison with the ship's Officer of the Watch (OOW) on planning whether to raise the aircraft during a relatively quiet period of minimum manoeuvres. The hangar can become extremely hot and smelly with the distinct mixture of aviation fuel, oils and the circulation of jet exhausts from the flight deck. Alternatively, the hangar can become equally as cold even in temperate climates with chilly draughts, especially if you are working by one of the aircraft lifts.

Making fine adjustments in engine or flying controls and electronic systems becomes problematic, when the tool box you are sitting on moves one way and the aircraft moves in the opposite direction straining against the deck tie down chain lashings. If you are 1st line trouble-shooter, you have to become used to working on the flight deck between launches and recovery (or even during both).

It is recognised by those who have served on aircraft carriers, that working on an aircraft carrier, especially on the flight deck, is one of the most dangerous places in the world. You have to be alert, both whilst working or when you are 'off watch' as life on board at sea never ends. Many veterans did not mourn the demise of the midday 'tot' i.e. rum ration at the start of the 1970s as to go anywhere near the flight deck with alcohol in your blood was suicidal.

To ensure your own personal safety and awareness, when joining a new carrier, it was always sensible to carry out a reconnoitre around the hangar/flight deck and living spaces. Escape routes and hatches, fire-fighting equipment and breathing apparatus locations to be duly noted and mentally stored wherever you went i.e. to remember what deck, section and compartment you were located.

Also equally important was to orientate yourself i.e. port or starboard and whether you were forward or aft. It has been reported that crew on the Queen Elizabeth have an app, which gives your location at any time, whenever you are on board. Whilst this is in keeping with modern trends, it would be wise to memorise and learn your physical location whilst embarked without electronic aids. Mobile phones become useless during electronic warfare scenarios as all SIMS have to be removed for security reasons.

Other abiding memories, which are readily recalled by carrier veterans, were the occasions when you did not see daylight for many weeks at a time. You can be on a prolonged anti-submarine patrol in the seas of the Iceland/Faroes gap for six weeks or more and if you were on a war footing, this could be so much longer.

Of course, seasickness could be a debilitating condition for many crewmembers. Aircraft carriers have unique handling characteristics when they experience heavy weather such as corkscrewing or wallowing on top of the waves, even in moderate sea conditions.

This is probably more relevant today with the introduction of the F35B, which of course is due for embarkation on the QE class of aircraft carrier. As of June 2021, the Queen Elizabeth is undergoing a long voyage to the Far East in 2021 with a distinct possibility of her being permanently deployed out there. It is envisaged that a mixture of FAA/RAF aircrews and engineers will man these squadrons.

Ignoring the difference in training, one of the fundamental problems, which hopefully will be harmonised, is the difference in separation criteria between the FAA and RAF personnel. There has been a historical problem over separation and leave compensation rules for being away between the two aviation branches.

In 1939, when the Admiralty gained back control of the FAA from the RAF, personnel from the latter were used to assist in the manning of embarked squadrons. This was inevitable as the FAA needed to rebuild its sea going support capability before the onset of WWII.

It was well known that RAF personnel, who served on aircraft carriers before and during early WWII as part of their conditions of service, received $1\tfrac{1}{2}$ times more leave than their Naval counterparts for doing exactly the same job and spending the same time at sea. They were paid more than their FAA counterparts.

Harmony Guidelines

One area that needs to be touched upon briefly is the question of separation away from home and family. Over many years, the RAF has enjoyed far fewer separation periods than the other two services. It is envisaged that these differences in separation rules, will have operational impacts when a mixed manned F35B squadron goes to sea.

Normal carrier deployments, which were the norm with respect to the US, French and British navies lasted between 6 and 9 months. With their harmony rules, the RAF personnel on a carrier would need to rotate at the fourth month period. The FAA squadrons historically sailed and returned with the ship without breaking RN harmony rules. The separated Service guidelines by each force is:

- Naval Service-in any 36-month period, no one to exceed 660 days of Separated Service.
- Army-in any 30-month period, no one to exceed 415 days of Separated Service.
- RAF – in a 12-month period, no more than 2.5% of personnel to exceed 140 days Separated Service.

The potential impact of these harmony rules unless they are aligned, could see RAF crews being rotated on a 4 monthly basis, whilst FAA crews could stay with the carrier to the end of the deployment. This would have a detrimental effect on the continuity of embarked squadron/ship 'workups', as well as the transportation and cost of transferring and replacing of such personnel.

There is, of course, the consideration for the sensitivities of FAA personnel watching their RAF counterparts returning home early. Since 2009, RAF tours of duty are being formally uplifted from 4 to 6 months, a process underway since 2009 as part of Armed Forces wide harmonisation policies following the Iraq and Afghanistan conflicts. Hopefully, this problem area is being addressed on a continuous basis.

On the aircrew front and prior to the beginning of flying, officers of the FAA and RAF receive specialised induction as pertaining to their particular service either at BRNC Dartmouth or RAF Cranwell. This initial training sets the scene, expectations and idiosyncrasies of their individual service. This period is crucial as the new officer entrants develop their views of life in that service.

Each Service has traditions with a different ethos and culture. Historically, the Navy by default has centuries of such traditions to fall back on, whilst the RAF has only just recently celebrated its centenary.

The expectations of a young RAF officer aided and abetted by the recruitment process are summarised as follows:

- Their career and advancement will be based on land with majority taking place in the UK.
- They will enjoy a high level of harmony, with very rare occasions of being separated from their family.
- All personnel are there to exclusively support pilots and flying operations.

The expectations of a young Naval officer are:

- Their early career will entail a high proportion of their service being on HM warships.
- FAA aircrews are an integral part of the RN and have career expectations of ship command and moving up to higher ranks. They can also become squadron COs of Naval Air Squadrons.
- They will be separated from their family frequently and for long periods.

Both RN and RAF pilots undergo Basic Flying Training and Advance Flying Training under the sponsorship of the RAF itself. These two stages demand the highest of standards and student's pilots are continuously assessed and graded for their aptitude and ability.

The failure rates are high. Those with the highest aptitude are selected for fast jet training provided they reached a high enough standard. This standard is set by the flying training staff, taking into account many factors:

- Basic flying skills.
- The ability to multi-task, in addition to just flying the aircraft. This covers radar, weapons systems, navigation equipment and the fundamentals of controlling multi-missions and aircraft.
- The aviation safety aspects of piloting to not only themselves, but to other pilots in fast jet environment.

If the student pilot meets these expectations, they move on to Operational Flying Training on the aircraft they have been selected for. Students who fail to meet these expectations but considered safe to operate helicopters, transport and logistics, will with further training be sent to these types. Within the remaining students, only the most highly skilled pilots of any particular course will qualify for fast jet or fighter aircraft.

Those who are perceived to have the highest-flying potential were selected for the RAF's Harrier force. In the FAA, only the highest rated pilots are destined for front line fixed wing squadrons. These pilots are further screened to establish fully their aptitude to deal with embarked, front-line multirole carrier operations.

Those who do not make the grade have the opportunity to transfer to helicopter flying training. With the advent of the F35B, it would be natural to assume that this flying training has merged even further and harmonised between the two services.

One area, which might cause a problem, is in the area of ship's duties. As stated above, FAA aircrew having gone through BRNC Dartmouth, they are naturally familiar with Naval routines, language and its discipline procedures. When in harbour, some aircrew, warrant officers and senior rates quite often have to undertake normal Naval Ship duties. These range from Officer of the Watch, Officer of the Day or taking charge of a shore patrol.

Adding to this plethora of additional work, it has to be understood that the Navy does things by numbers. This ranges from the uniforms being numbered from 1 to 4, with No. 1 being the formal uniform for ceremonial occasions, to No. 4, which is blue shirt and trousers made up of fire retardant material and is the normal working day attire.

Couple this with the award of punishment by 'numbers', with No 9s being the most common, which basically is the withdrawal of leave, privileges and liberty over a number of days. It will be interesting to see who administers and carries out punishment for RAF defaulters whilst at sea.

A Sea Vixen Pilot's Story

To give an idea of the trials and tribulations of a FAA pilot, I approached an old Aircraft Artificer colleague of mine named Paul Bennett, affectionately known during our Navy apprenticeship as 'Wiggy'. Unfortunately, the nickname was a misnomer because it was only during his flying training that he was to lose all his hair due to an incident whilst flying Hunters.

Wiggy was eventually to become a fast jet pilot and was the only one out of a class of 36 to do so. He is living proof of the training given to FAA pilots and the stresses they undergo whilst flying Navy aircraft and supports the descriptions given in earlier paragraphs. Here is his story:

I joined the Royal Navy as an Artificer Apprentice in September 1961. After about seven months of square bashing, kit inspections, assault courses, trekking across Dartmoor and some pretty basic engineering training, I was marched into a room for an interview with a very senior Chief Petty Officer. "Wot do you want to do lad?" he asked in a not too unfriendly voice.

"What do you mean Chief?"

"Wot sort of Artificer do you want to be?"

"Well, I need to know the options."

"Well now, there is Engine Room (we had visited a few ships during our training and crawling around huge engines and boiler rooms, which I did not fancy. Ordnance (didn't fancy working with explosives), Electrical (no interest in electrics), Radar (works by electrics, so of no interest), Shipwright (all sorts of different jobs and skill requirements, so could have been of interest) or finally Aircraft (now, there was something I had no knowledge of or schoolboy interest)."

So because of the mystery, I told the Chief that that was what I wanted to be, and lo and behold, I became an Aircraft Artificer Apprentice. After completing a year of basic training at HMS Fisgard, off I went to HMS Condor at Arbroath in Scotland.

A couple of very important things happened at RNAS Arbroath. I was able to improve my educational standards and gained more 'O' levels and an Ordinary National Certificate (ONC). Also, there was a gliding club that operated on the airfield every weekend-weather permitting. I was always short of cash and a glider tow launch cost half a crown (25p in today's money) so I didn't do too many but did manage to go solo and became fully absorbed in all aspects of the club operating the tow cable return car and the winch.

It was the start of my interest in flying that then shaped the whole of my future career in aviation up until when I retired as a civil aircraft captain at the age of 63. Meanwhile, I progressed with my aircraft engineering training and after 20 months, we were all sent to various Fleet Air Arm operational air stations to do some on-the-job training. I was sent to RNAS Yeovilton, the base of the Sea Vixen.

We were 'farmed out' to various station departments' including-station flight-the spray shop-fuel farm and others, but probably most important to me was my stint on 766 Naval Air Squadron the Sea Vixen, the pilot and observer training squadron and it was on one night in June that my career changed.

The kerosene type aviation fuel of the day had a serious problem, in that, fungus would grow in the fuel and if this was not cleaned out of the fuel tanks regularly, the fungus would block the engine fuel filters and stop the engines. In the worst case, both engines and the aircraft would be lost and sometimes one or both of the crew.

This happened whilst I was at Yeovilton and the pilot and observer died in the crash, just off the airfield and I noted the pilot was just 20 years of age and the observer 19. As an aside, I played in the station brass band and well remember the long march across the airfield to the church on the other side for the burial of the pilot named Eyton-Jones, who was the cousin of another Eyton-Jones (John). He and I became very friendly when flying the Sea Vixen and Phantom. He sadly died flying a Harrier during the Falklands war.

As I said, an aside so how did this so affect my future career?

On that night in June, I was cleaning out the fuel tanks of a Sea Vixen. I was wearing just overalls and plimsolls soaked in aviation fuel that was evaporating and chilling me, so even though it was June I was frozen and also suffering dermatitis rashes all up my arms. After my watch, I showered, had a sleep, got dressed and reported to my Divisional Officer (DO).

In order to make a formal request, you have fill out a request 'chit' and the Divisional Chief would march you into your interview with the DO. Standing to attention, he would read the chit and then looked me in the face and said, "So, you want to be a pilot?"

"Yes Sir, I would rather fly the aircraft than maintain them." My DO said he would look into it, as he had not had such a request before. Well, not only did he 'look into it' but well and truly started the ball rolling for me to become an FAA pilot.

The whole procedure was not rapid, so I will not bore you with the process, except to say that I worked for just six weeks as a freshly qualified Petty Officer Aircraft Artificer, before putting that behind me and starting my pilot career by going to Dartmouth BRNC as an Air Cadet. Of course, the apprenticeship was not totally forgotten and many aspects of it became very useful as I progressed in my new career as a pilot.

Not least, my wariness of not wanting to fly the Sea Vixen and all through my pilot training, I was dead set on becoming a Buccaneer pilot. It was not to be and in the end, I had no regrets. Out of 36 of us on that course at Dartmouth, I was the only fast jet pilot to qualify. Others became Gannet or helicopter pilots while some became air traffic controllers and one even went on to serve on submarines.

When it came close for me to complete my Advanced Flying Training Part 2, i.e. flying the Hunter GA11, the only other trainee was a General List Engineering Officer. He had been an air engineering officer on a Buccaneer Squadron, so he got the only space available on Buccaneers as a Maintenance Test Pilot (MTP). I, therefore, was duly shipped off to my 'old apprentice' days on 766 NAS to train as a Sea Vixen pilot!

In the four years since I had been an apprentice on Sea Vixens, major changes had happened. Most importantly, the boffins had come up with additives to the aviation fuel that prevented fungus from growing and the FAW (fighter all weather) Mk 2 came into service. However, they did not cure the over complicated aircraft that the Sea Vixen was.

For goodness' sake, it had four hydraulic systems, four generators and a fuel system that needed a gang-bar to switch all the main fuel pumps on, which in turn were backed up by a load of auxiliary pumps. The huge intercept radar in the nose, that the observer used to operate, was such a large piece of equipment that when the autopilot was engaged, the aircraft would yaw in opposition to the radar moving from side to side as it scanned.

There were improvements. Extra fuel in the pinion tanks and most importantly, a frangible hatch above the observers 'coal hole' so that he could eject through even if the hatch became jammed. Most importantly though, from a pilot's point of view, it was a 'multi role' aircraft and the huge variety of different tasks that it could perform made it a much more interesting aircraft to fly than the Buccaneer.

As I said, multirole and a very usual sortie would be to do some HLAI/LLAI high/low level aircraft intercept training with at least a couple of the intercepts ending up in a 'dog fight'. This could be followed in the same sortie by some 2" rocket firing, or 28lb practice bomb dropping on a ground controlled firing range or the splash target towed by a ship. Then, on the next sortie we would fly high to low level along a prescribed navigation course to drop more air to surface weapons.

The low level part would be at 250 feet above the ground at 480 knots. Lots of fun but requiring a huge amount of concentration. At other times instead of dropping weapons, we would do photographic reconnaissance and at the end of all of these different exercises finishing with air-to-air refuelling. The Sea Vixen had a refuelling probe attached to the leading edge of the port wing rather, than in line with the pilot's vision, which made it quite tricky and certainly required lots of practice.

Then, having got the hang of it all, there was the added excitement of having to do these exercises at night. On top of all of this excitement/terror came the addition of having to fly from an aircraft carrier day and night and in all weathers; not at all trifling matters when flying and managing the very complicated aircraft like the Sea Vixen.

Let me explain a little, flying from the carrier and tasked with LLAI (low level aircraft intercept), usually under the control of the Gannet AEW (airborne early warning) aircraft and having to be airborne for 1hr 45mins to fit in with the carrier's cycle of operations. From a catapult take-off, we seriously had to conserve our fuel. This was achieved by shutting down one of the engines as soon as we got airborne.

This literally meant as soon as possible and it was usually landing gear up, flaps up and then engine shutdown. We flew at a minimum drag speed of about 240 knots on a single engine. At the halfway stage, we would swap engines to appease the engineers to ensure equal engine running hours. Also during this time, we would manipulate the many fuel switches to enable equal fuel from both port to starboard sides to keep the aircraft laterally balanced and thus, produce less drag, which of course meant less fuel usage.

It was during one of these sorties that the following happened. The observer and I were very engrossed with the LLAI and we failed to notice that our exercise area was drifting further away from the ship. We then realised we needed to return to the ship at maximum speed. It was hugely frowned upon to be late for your landing known as 'Charlie' time. I, therefore, advanced the power on the single engine that we were then flying on and such is the power of the Sea Vixen, we quickly increased speed to 550 knots.

Unfortunately at that speed, too much air was being forced down the intake of the 'dead' engine and that prevented me from starting that engine, which would have allowed me to increase to the speed limit of 630 knots and get back to the ship quicker! So, there I was with an old Navy saying of 'Between the devil and the deep blue sea'.

I dare not decrease speed to allow me to start the engine as I knew I would not make the 'Charlie' time, so I ended up turning down wind and with all the necessary speed reduction and flap and gear selections, I also had to start the engine. I managed and hooked on first attempt but was 45 seconds late and that got me a week of duty officer as punishment.

There are all sorts of experiences I could relate here are but a few. Night flying from Yeovilton as we got to high altitude, (a) it was still light and (b), I noticed my fuel quantity decreasing rather rapidly. I called the other aircraft and he came alongside to visually inspect my aircraft and reported fuel leaking from my port pylon. I hastily returned to Yeovilton and on the instrument approach, a fuel mist filled the cockpit.

I switched the mask over to 100% oxygen and breathing was not a problem but visually my sight was impaired with the fuel stinging my eyes. I managed a landing, opened the canopy, which cleared the mist and proceeded to taxi into dispersal. The ground crew clicked the ladders onto the sides of the fuselage and I then noticed them running away.

Unassisted, the observer and myself got down from the aircraft and went to the line shack to find out why we were not assisted disembarking as usual. Apparently, whilst two of the ground crew had attached the ladders, another had opened a side panel to discover the very hot engines were surrounded by fuel vapour. Luckily, there was no fire.

Flying off HMS Eagle somewhere close to Australia, I was tasked to drop 500-pound bombs on a firing range. These were inert bombs i.e. filled with concrete rather than explosives, so from a flight safety and danger point of view, when there was one 'hung up' (did not release), it was not a problem but a carrier landing was not allowed. I, therefore, had to jettison the bomb.

For the unusual events, we had a checklist known as 'Pilot's Notes'. If anyone is familiar with or seen the inside of a Sea Vixen and seen the positioning of a lot of the little used switches, you can appreciate the cumbersome clothing that the pilots had to wear i.e. immersion suits etc. With this flying gear, one might understand the problem that I had in putting these switches into the 'eye pleasing manner' that would allow the bomb to be jettisoned.

In the end, it was just one switch that I made the error on and that switch was operated in one direction for inner pylons and the other for outer pylons. The bomb that had hung up was on an outer pylon but I operated the switch for inner position and saw a £100,000 Red Top missile gracefully leave the wing and having a low drag profile, it accelerate ahead of the aircraft. Oh dear I thought!

More punishment this time with perhaps loss of leave, which would have been really bad as our next port of call was Wellington, New Zealand. However, as I had arranged to fly up to Auckland to visit some family, the 'Boss' very kindly allowed me to go, so no stoppage of leave and the loss of the missile were soon forgotten.

Incidentally, on the same 'land-on' time that I lost the missile, the squadron's freshly joined Senior Pilot was doing some practice deck landings i.e. bolters (hitting the deck with the hook up) and going around again for another practice deck landing. This time, he hit the deck so hard that the starboard landing gear oleo collapsed. This resulted in him not being able to land normally, so it was decided to land him into the barrier.

This he did, but unfortunately the Sea Vixen had a 'soft' leading edge on the wing and the vertical strands of the barrier cut through the leading edges in several places, which meant the aircraft had to be scrapped. It was stripped of engines and all other useful parts for future maintenance and spares, which resulted in the fuselage shell being bulldozed over the edge of the ship. It now lies on the seabed of the Indian Ocean. Made my loss of a missile seem somewhat insignificant!

Composite image by author of Sea Vixens FAW 2 of 899 NAS

Well, enough is enough with this dissertation as I could bore you with many Sea Vixen stories, but I will finish with a very sad tale. We had just embarked on HMS Eagle. For myself and another pilot, this was our very first time and was very interesting, considering the Sea Vixen simulator was not working and the normal approach practices using a Hunter T8 (dual seat) were not available due to there being no aircraft carrier to practice on.

So, for the first time we saw the deck was on an approach in a Sea Vixen. Again, we were to do a number of approaches and landings but with the hook up (bolters). It should be noted the aircraft has a maximum weight limit for carrier landings along with a minimum fuel load so as to divert ashore should you fail to 'hook on'. The norm was to make 3 or 4 approaches, before diverting.

On my first three approaches, I did not touch the deck as the approaches were not good enough. It was a bit of a surprise when 'Little F' (Lieutenant Commander Flying) ordered me 'hook down'. Well, would you believe on the first time I hit the deck with the hook down, I achieved my first arrested deck landing. Needless to say there was a celebration in the Wardroom that evening to mark the occasion! A hangover was allowed, as the ship then did a transit to the East Coast of Scotland as we had a day without flying.

On the following day, I was launched first, so we were circling over the carrier waiting for the next launch to happen and the deck was being made ready for landings, when my observer said over the intercom "Did you hear that?"

I said I did not and he replied saying, "I'm sure they said eject," As we turned back towards the ship (I was flying in a formation of four from the first launch), I could see a huge circular disturbance in the water. Very shortly afterwards, we were ordered to divert to RNAS Lossiemouth, you have to remember there were no such things as mobile phones in those days, so it was sometime later that the flight leader came into the crew room, after having been waiting in 'Ops' for any news.

He was to inform us that a Sea Vixen had crashed on take-off. The pilot, Bruce Harrison, who I shared a cabin albeit for only for one night, was lost but the observer had survived and was in the hospital ashore. Bruce was on his first catapult launch, as I had been earlier that day and apparently had not stopped the control stick moving backwards during the 3–4g stroke of the catapult. The nose of the aircraft had pitched up and the aircraft stalled causing it to apparently roll to the left and dive into the sea.

The observer afterwards said that he felt things were unusual (remember the observer on the Vixen had no view forward and could only see the flight instruments across the pilot's right thigh). In any case, he decided to eject but due to the altitude of the aircraft, he ejected straight into the sea. Fortunately, the Wessex SAR helicopter diver leapt into the sea from the chopper, managed to get him to the surface and he was winched into the helicopter and flown straight to the hospital ashore.

He had suffered extreme compression of the spine and in fact, permanently lost an inch in height. Sadly, when I got back on board, it was my task to go through Bruce's kit and get it packed and laundered if necessary, so it could be returned to his parents. In the whole of HMS Eagle and 899 NAS deployment during that 2-year period, he was the only aircrew that we lost, which really said a lot to dispel the bad reputation that the Sea Vixen had had up until then.

As a postscript to Wiggy's above anecdotes, it must be remembered the Vixen was coming to the end of its flying life in the FAA and a lot of its idiosyncrasies and bad characteristics were well known, which could be countered. However, despite his final comment, the Sea Vixen was still a difficult aircraft to fly and operate as the following facts reveal:

A total of 145 Sea Vixens built and some 55 were lost in accidents. These included the two DH.110 development prototypes that were also lost, with the tragic break up of WV236 at the 1952 Farnborough Air Show. The loss of 55 Sea Vixens represented a loss rate of almost 38%. Some 30 of these were fatal incidents, which sadly involved the death of both pilot and observer.

During the same time, the German Air Force was flying the Lockheed Starfighter F104, which suffered an accident attrition rate of 32% and this percentage rate was constantly in the press and this was the reason F104 was given the nicknamed the 'Widow Maker'. The Sea Vixen with its higher accident rate never seemed to make the headlines.

Postage Stamp – Personal Anecdote

In 1967, I was the designated Line Petty Officer (glorified petrol station manager) for the day on 766 Naval Air Squadron, which was based temporarily at RNAS Brawdy in Wales. This Sea Vixen training squadron had moved from RNAS Yeovilton, while the runways were being strengthened pending delivery of the Navy's new Phantom aircraft.

Along with the Naval Air Mechanic plane captains, we were there to see off three Sea Vixens from the ramp for a sortie. The three pilots, consisting of two Naval Sub-Lieutenants and a RAF Flying Officer, were about halfway through their Vixen conversion course. The object of the training sortie was to do carrier approaches using the deck landing system on HMS Eagle. These were known in the FAA as dummy-deck landings. HMS Eagle at the time was in the vicinity of St Brides Bay and the idea was to do 2–3 approaches without the deck hook down – 'Bolters' as these approaches were also known.

The aircraft duly departed and the lads wandered back to the crew room for a coffee before the next sortie. Some twenty minutes later, one of the three Vixens sent off earlier, suddenly appeared back on the circuit returning. We rushed out to marshal the aircraft back in. I naturally assumed that the pilot had come back early because of a defect, which had prevented him from doing those deck landing approaches.

When the engines were shut down, I recognised the pilot as the RAF Flying Officer. When he climbed down the cockpit ladder, I immediately noticed his drab olive coloured summer flying suit was stained a dark colour. He was soaking wet with sweat. As he had returned unexpectedly, my natural instinct was to ask if the aircraft was OK i.e. serviceable or otherwise and asked had he been successful on seeing the deck-landing meatball on any of the approaches?

His immediate reply in a somewhat shocked tone was, "See the bloody meatball, I could hardly see the ship! When I flew over at 10,000 feet and looked down, I saw this postage stamp (HMS Eagle) floating on the sea and said to myself, I'm bloody well not landing on that!" I immediately realised the poor lad was severely stressed and somewhat scared.

He had been sweating profusely, hence the reason for his dark flying suit. It was at that point in my Naval career that aircrew went up 200% in my estimation and led to a far better understanding of what they had to go through. It takes guts and courage to land 20 tons of aircraft on to another lump of metal of some 40,000 tons plus tossing and turning on the high seas. Unfortunately, he was withdrawn from that particular Sea Vixen course and we never saw him again.

Hi de Hi!

The following is the lead and direct extract from the RAF's website describing the sovereign base in Cyprus:

"RAF Akrotiri is situated on the Akrotiri Peninsular on the south coast of Cyprus, probably the most sought after posting in the Royal Air Force."

Both the other two branches of the UK's armed services look upon the above with some element of envy. A brief observation of the weather experienced there throughout the year gives a clue. Cyprus has one of the warmest climates and warmest winters in the Mediterranean with average temperatures of 24°C (75°F) whereby thousands of tourists can expect guaranteed sunshine and blue skies. Leisure facilities for personnel at Akrotiri are extremely generous with 11 sporting clubs ranging from angling to a water ski club.

In addition, there 21 further activities on offer, including mountaineering and martial arts etc. Couple this with a 'tropical routine' working environment i.e.

start in the early cooler mornings to finishing around lunchtime. I had the pleasure of participating of these 5 star facilities by playing volleyball for HMS Bulwark and then retiring to the sergeant's mess lunchtime and downing a few duty-free drinks afterwards.

With the surrounding holiday resorts around the island, the idyllic weather, no wonder this was such a sought after post! Those in FAA and Army Air Corps, who have passed through this base, have always looked at their RAF equivalents serving there with a tinge of jealousy. The Red Arrows regularly fly there in late spring to consolidate their winter training. For troops who returned from the combat zones of Iraq and Afghanistan, it was used as an RR (Rest & Recreation) centre for a 'decompression' period prior to them returning home to the UK.

All the above comes at a cost, which RAF Akrotiri imposes on the UK's Treasury. It has a permanent establishment of some 1,600 personnel, many accompanied by their families. Currently based, there is the 903 Expeditionary Air Wing (EAW) consisting of a further 800 plus personnel in support of the operations against IS.

The annual cost for personnel is approximately £840M (at 2018 prices) and does not take into account the huge logistical support chain back in the UK at RAF Brize Norton, which itself has over 7,300 service, contractors and civilians working there. Therefore, some 9,800 are supporting just 14 aircraft of the 903 EAW.

"Cost of British air operations over Iraq and Syria reaches £1.75 billion as of 1st March 2018. The UK has spent £1.75bn on armed air missions against Islamic State in Iraq and Syria since August 2014. Information from responses to Freedom of Information requests was looked over by Drone Wars UK. The full cost of flying the UK's armed aircraft (Tornado, Typhoon and Reaper) for more than 42,000 hours is almost £1.5 billion. The site also reports that, the data shows £268 million in weapons have been fired over the last 3½ years. The full cost of flying the UK's armed aircraft (Tornado, Typhoon and Reaper) for more than 42,000 hours of operations is almost £1.5 billion."

Therefore, with a combined total as detailed above, the conservative estimates are that RAF Akrotiri is costing the British taxpayer somewhere in the region of £2Bn per annum. Remember, this is but one RAF airbase and therefore puts the cost of the aircraft carrier Queen Elizabeth into context.

Sources

htttps://publications.parliament.uk/pa/cm200708/cmselect/cmdfence/424/42405.htm

http://www.rafakrotiri.co.ukource:

https://ukdefencejournal.org.uk/cost-british-air-operations-iraq-syria-reach-1-75-billion

Gabriele Molinelli – The Fleet Air Arm, RAF, the Past and Future 25th April 2011

Chapter 16
Brave Exploits, Service and Sacrifices

This chapter covers a few of the acts of bravery, sacrifices and achievements made by a variety of personnel during their service with the FAA. On the flying side, a whole book would be required to cover all the brave deeds carried out by aircrew, who after all, were always at the forefront of danger and possibility of being killed during any conflict. However, those on the ground, who kept these Naval flying machines going, deserve a mention. A couple of stories of several unassuming and quiet men, who played highly important background roles, are included.

Lt A.L. Tarver RN GM – Heroic attempt to save his Observer – 1966

In 1966, the UK Labour Government under the Prime Minister Harold Wilson's imposed oil blockade, which became known as the 'Beira Patrol' after Ian Smith, the then Prime Minister of Rhodesia, had unilaterally declared independence (UDI). HMS Ark Royal was on blockade patrol in the Indian Ocean just off Beira, Mozambique on the 10th May 1966.

A Sea Vixen FAW 2 of 890 NAS serial number XJ520 with Lt Tarver as the pilot and Lt J Sutchberry as the observer was returning from an operational patrol to HMS Ark Royal, when the gearbox suffered a mechanical failure causing the port engine to shut down. The aircraft was already low on fuel when it began to lose more fuel from the damaged engine.

A Scimitar tanker made an in-flight refuelling attempt from Ark Royal and whilst endeavouring to transfer fuel, the other engine flamed out. The Sea Vixen was now powerless and at a height of 12,000 feet began to fall downwards to the sea. The aircraft had to be abandoned.

For those unfamiliar with the Sea Vixen, it has two aircrew who are strapped into two separate cockpits. The pilot sits on the upper left side of the nose section, whilst the observer sits behind and somewhat lower on the right side of the aircraft. The observer's cockpit was known in the Vixen circuit as the 'coal hole'.

With a very small window to the right side, the cockpit is completely painted black throughout and with the hatch open, it indeed did resemble a coalhole when looking in from the top. There also is no direct visual contact between the two-crew members.

Lt Tarver coolly remained in the cockpit trying to maintain control. With two stopped engines and failed gearbox, there was no hydraulic pressure to the two green and yellow flying control systems. There was just enough hydraulic pressure stored in the accumulators to give the pilot some semblance of very sluggish aerodynamic control.

As the aircraft fell, he instigated a countdown for himself and his observer to eject at a height of 6,000 feet. He was in continuous radio communication with both ship and the pilot of the Scimitar flying above him. Both reported that he relayed the ongoing sequence of events to them in a calm voice.

At 6,000 feet, both crew prepared to eject but the observer's seat cartridge failed to fire and he attempted to bail out manually. The hatch was jettisoned manually (it is fired off via compressed CO_2); the observer then had to manually release himself from the seat. This facility is built on all Vixen ejector seats should a seat malfunction occur. It should be noted that at this stage the seat occupant is still connected to their parachute.

It was clear that every moment, which delayed his own ejection, reduced Lt Tarver's already limited chance of survival. He elected to remain in his cockpit and further the observer's escape as best he could. He then slowly manoeuvred and inverted the Vixen. He did so twice, all to no avail as the observer appeared to be jammed by his harness half in, half out of the coal hole. It is thought at this stage, the observer had lost consciousness.

With all reasonable chance of his own survival gone, Lt Tarver took no action to save his own life and lent back and put his arm through to push the observer's foot (the only part he could see) in the hope of jerking him free before the aircraft hit the sea.

The Scimitar pilot still in the vicinity above the Vixen reported that the aircraft rolled over on its final plunge, the body of Lt Tarver was seen ejecting from the pilot's cockpit, hitting the sea before his parachute had time to deploy within the splash circle. The SAR helicopter from HMS Ark Royal was on route and the only eyewitness i.e. the Scimitar pilot said that there was no chance that Lt Tarver could have survived.

Lt Tarver did indeed survive and was rescued by the SAR helicopter and flown back to the carrier. Subsequently, Lt Tarver was deservedly awarded the George Medal for his brave heroic action in staying with his aircraft to try and save his fellow crewmember. By remaining for several minutes in the crashing aircraft, he forfeited his own chances of escape beyond the point where he could be reasonably expected to live.

Norman Thomas FAA Armourer – Korean Peace Medal
Four years away from home

These were long and arduous commissions where the carriers, aircraft and maintenance crews were subjected to extremes of weather. It is interesting to hear stories of Korean FAA veterans. In particular, we could focus on Norman Thomas, who was awarded the Korean Peace Medal in 2018. He was a FAA armourer throughout this conflict.

All told, he was to spend some $4\frac{1}{2}$ years away from home, broken only by a short leave period in 1952–53 when suddenly he got a posting to go back to the Korean conflict 'on loan' to the Australian Navy's Fleet Air Arm equivalent. One has to wonder how those serving today on assignments and being replaced every 6 weeks to go back home to the UK would cope with this length of separation.

- In 1948, after having already spent 14 months in Malta, he was drafted to HMS Triumph in August 1949, which was sailing to Singapore. She was at the time carrying Seafires and Fireflies. The aircraft disembarked and our man was detailed with a working group off the ship to lay metal tracking (called Sommerfield) to strengthen/extend the runway and taxiing tracks etc. at Changi. Support airstrikes then commenced against the Malaysian terrorists – utilising Seafires.
- Throughout this period, he lived rough under canvas right next to a very large Chinese cemetery, which he claimed at times was very spooky. He re-joined HMS Triumph and then went to join up on exercise with the US fleet.

- On 8th September 1949, the ship sailed northwards. Unfortunately, they hit a Typhoon, which arrived some 12 hours earlier than the weather predicted by the forecasters – they had their 'Michael Fishes' in those days too!
- Here is a précis and summary of what he experienced in that Typhoon verbatim: "It was absolutely frightening. I reckoned that there was more water inside the ship than in the Pacific Ocean! Winds varied from 50 knots to 100 knots 60mph to 120mph to landlubbers the carrier rolling to 20 degrees plus either side. Mess decks flooded to a depth of a foot caused by the ship rolling side to side, creating waves in some passageways. Everything became drenched, clothing, equipment and there were no galleys, which meant no food for 24 hours except for one soggy sandwich. Boats on the weather decks were smashed to pieces, sponsons were twisted but fortunately there was no structural damage and the ship continued sailing."
- I can vouch for these conditions where I too experienced the same on HMS Ark Royal and Bulwark with the forward flight deck dipping into the sea and then looking back and seeing the aft of the flight deck dipping under too. Look out 617 Squadron (Dambusters) on the Queen Elizabeth, you will need to find your sea legs.
- On 25th June 1950, North Korea invades South Korea.
- HMS Triumph joins the US 7th Fleet and becomes part of Task Force 77. This task force provides the air cover for the US landings in South Korea. During this time, our man is taken off to HMS Unicorn as part of a Naval Working Party. His task is to assist in the landing of 1st Battalion of the Middlesex regiment and its equipment in South Korea – all within 24hours. Hours and days of back breaking work. Upon completion, he returns to HMS Triumph, which then has to sail to the west coast of Korea maintaining many months of an extremely high tempo of combat flight operations.
- Norman was an armourer, who spent most of the time on the flight deck loading weapons virtually non-stop. When not at flying stations, he would be involved in the resupply of these munitions i.e. from deeply stored magazines whilst on HMS Unicorn etc. The Seafire, which was based on the Spitfire design and although a splendid aircraft on land, was not sturdy enough for carrier operations. Many undercarriage failures

and wrinkling of the fuselage skin occurred, as it was a very difficult aircraft to land on a carrier.
- They were to be eventually replaced by Sea Furies. Incidentally, a piston engine FAA Sea Fury was to shoot down a MiG 15 jet later on in the war. This was the 1st piston engine aircraft kill against a jet. This type of aircraft still wins air races in RENO in the US having a top speed in excess of 450mph. HMS Triumph is eventually relieved by HMS Theseus, which carried the sturdier Sea Furies.

Author's photograph Sea Fury FB 11 – Oshkosh 2016

- This allowed HMS Triumph to sail back to Pompey via Singapore. Norman had spent 2 years 8 months just on this one commission alone. This commission produced some interesting facts; remember this is for just one British aircraft carrier with two embarked squadrons as there were four other carriers that would produce the same sortie numbers when on station.

    o Some 8,000 flying hours were achieved.
    o Some 3,900 sorties/airstrikes were made.
    o 3,400 rockets were fired.
    o 170,000 20mm rounds were fired.

- It is noteworthy to compare these figures with the statistics of the RAF currently operating from their fixed base Akrotiri in Cyprus from October 2014 to the present date namely:

    o Over 2,200 sorties
    o 900 airstrikes
    o 216 variety of bombs and missiles used

- These figures simply reinforce the potency of an operational fixed wing strike carrier. This is the reason why the Americans are able to position three of them on station around Korea when the situation sometimes demands. They act as a deterrent.
- Norman returned to England 1952–53 but within a few months after being back and very early in 1953, he suddenly got a draft chit to go back to join on a 'on loan' basis with the Royal Australian Fleet Air Arm! He was one of about half a dozen men selected. Consequently, he sailed back to Sydney courtesy of the Oil Product Tanker joining HMAS Albatross (an air station 100 miles South of Sydney) and was assigned to a Sea Fury squadron – NAS 850. His first task was to begin training some very 'gung-ho' Aussie naval air mechanics. He describes their engineering discipline as extremely casual. Norman, by now, was a very senior and experienced armourer and therefore spent most of the time on the flight deck loading weapons virtually non-stop. When not at flying stations, he would be involved in the ongoing workups of Aussie armourers and organising the resupply of these weapons to the flight deck etc. Norman also spent many days doing the same ashore in Korea. Training continued after transferring to HMAS Vengeance at sea and then after 2 months, he was transferred to another carrier, HMAS Sydney.

Once again, he sailed northwards to Korea, there followed months of patrolling under the United Nations flag. During this second tour of duty, he mentions the bitter cold, saying fingertips used to go black with frostbite when working on the flight deck some jobs had to be carried out without gloves such as securing arming plugs on pylons and weapons.

At temperatures of minus 30 degrees, the working day began at 5:30 am with everyone having to chip the ice off the flight deck. When preparing the aircraft ready for take-offs, any work took five times longer at these very low temperatures. It was so cold that even the stokers had to wear overcoats in the boiler rooms! Also other hazards, which he had previously experienced on his first tour on a British carrier, were typhoons.

He briefly described the conditions he and the ship were subjected to one of these typhoons on the second trip, there were 45-foot waves with the carrier rolling side to side. He was often soaked to the skin with conditions being aggravated by having no hot food due to all the galleys being out of action.

The escorting ships were even worse off as some of their engine room boilers were out of commission, suffered numerous electrical fires with most sustaining considerable structural damage to the ship and external fittings, etc.

This was the pattern of life for the next 4–5 months, with a change-over of carriers every two/four week periods or so for replenishment and recuperation. On one break to Japan, he had to escort a wounded Petty Officer across Japan to get him to a hospital in Tokyo.

This saga is worthy of a chapter all on its own, as armed only with a railway warrant, not speaking Japanese and no money for food, they duly set off. He stated that but for American soldiers he met on the long train journeys, he and the injured Petty Officer would have starved.

A ceasefire armistice in Korea was signed in July 1953. The aircraft carriers were slowly stood down and Norman eventually arrived back home in 1954 ready for demob. Therefore, from before 1948 until 1954, he spent some $4^{1}/_{2}$ years away from home. Lived under canvas whilst building runways. Travelled across Japan unaided with no support. He served for long periods on four different (including two Australian) aircraft carriers enduring some really arduous conditions consisting of two typhoons and consistent sub-zero temperatures.

Norman being the modest man he is, never complained saying that those fighting ashore in Korea suffered far worse conditions and were having to fight for their lives on a daily basis. He goes on to say that both the air and ground crews were determined not to let down those who were doing the fighting.

For his unstinting efforts and very arduous conditions during those $4^{1}/_{2}$ long years away from home, he surely thoroughly deserved the South Korean Peace Medal award.

Lt Commander Peter Marshall AFC RN – Saves 'nose-less' Phantom 1969

On the 3rd December 1969, Lt Commander Peter Marshall, was the CO 767 NAS and was flying a virtually brand new Phantom FG 1 just north of Land's End at 18,000 feet. He was on a training combat mission carrying out a mock dogfights sortie, when a heavy thud was felt throughout the Phantom's airframe. Now with both engines flamed out and the airframe vibrating badly, he and his RIO (Observer) Flt Lt Jack Haines were preparing to eject.

The accompanying Phantom for this training exercise flew alongside him and informed him that his nose cone i.e. the radome had somehow opened and was blown away in the slipstream. The missing radome had caused some of the exposed radar equipment and other debris to become detached and ingested by the starboard engine, hence the flameout.

Although, he found the aircraft was still controllable with severe buffeting and virtually no forward visibility due to leaking hydraulic fluid, it would be very difficult to get the aircraft back to RNAS Yeovilton safely some 130 miles away.

He was to say later, "There was hydraulic fluid all over the windscreen, but I could see the motorway (one assumed it was the M5 he sighted) below and I could follow that back to base. So, why should I eject from a serviceable aircraft?" A typical Naval pilot's understatement.

Debris had also punctured the wing's leading edge flaps and ripped the fuselage skin. Assisted by an accompanying aircraft, Marshall decided to attempt a return to Yeovilton, 130 miles away. It proved an extremely hazardous final approach e.g. forward vision, due to the hydraulic fluid on his windscreen, was practically zero, along with pronounced yaw and buffeting, which threatened to throw the aircraft out of control. Nevertheless, Marshall managed to land safely.

By his brave and skilled airmanship, he saved weeks of speculative investigation and the consequent disruption to the Phantom flying programme on 767, the then Phantom training squadron. For this feat, Lt Commander P Marshall RN was awarded the Boyd Trophy in 1969 and the AFC for exceptional skill and personal courage.

Three Phantoms of 767 NAS taking off RNAS Yeovilton Air Day 1969 – Author's photo

Sources

The Daily Telegraph Obituary 5th September 2013
https://www.thefreelibrary.com/
Facebook – My Unofficial FAA History Page

Extracts from Aircraft Artificer 1st Class – Alan 'Al' Slater – Falklands Wartime Diary April/May 1982.

Al was the Senior Maintenance Rating in charge of HMS Alacrity's helicopter flight. HMS Alacrity (F174) was a Type 21 frigate built by Yarrow Shipbuilders. She weighed 3,250 tons. This type of ship was considered to be the 'Ferrari' of the Royal Navy at the time. They had a terrific turn of speed and acceleration, which was due to the power from two Rolls Royce Olympus gas-turbines (same as Concord's engines) along with two RR Tyne gas turbines used for cruising.

She was armed with one 4.5 inch Mk 8 naval gun forward, x4 Exocet missiles, quadruple Sea Cat missiles launcher and a Type 182 towed decoy. Although when originally commissioned, she had a Westland Wasp helicopter embarked but fortuitously, it now had been replaced by the very capable and powerful Westland Lynx Mk 2.

The following are extracts from Alan Slater's private diary, which he kept throughout the time HMS Alacrity was in combat action during that conflict. These are his words:

23rd April – A long hard day, started at 0500. Alert 15 until 1200. Bit of a rest in the afternoon then back to Alert 15 at 2300 until 0800. Slept on hangar floor, ready to launch Lynx helicopter at 15 minutes notice. RAS of fuel for ship and helicopter (Dieso and Avcat). One Sea King lost today whilst on an anti-submarine patrol and returning to HMS Hermes in bad weather. One crewmember did not survive the crash.

24th April – Rough sea today. Swapped Lynx helicopters this afternoon, as our original variant XZ720 was not fitted to carry Sea Skua missiles. We exchanged it for XZ736 from HMS Broadsword, which was able to carry Sea Skuas. We were supplied with four Sea Skua missiles. The hangar was a hell of a mess trying to fit four Sea Skua missiles with the relevant handling frames and the ship's towrope into a space not designed for this purpose.

During rough weather, the ship's main gun turret was turned 180^0 (to point aft) to prevent seawater entering the barrel. The access door at the rear of the turret was now facing forward. Because of the ship's motion and vibration, the turret door opened and the turret was consequently filled with seawater. The Captain was not pleased! Very tired tonight.

1st May – RAF Vulcan from Ascension bombs runway at Stanley. Sea Harriers from the carriers strike at first light. In the afternoon, HMS Glamorgan, HMS Arrow and ourselves sailed around a minefield to carryout Naval Gunfire Support (NGS) against Argentinean troop concentrations encamped on Stanley racecourse. Each ship fired 50 × 4.5" shells to the target area. Ship's Lynx took off with four people on board for spotting. They returned with a bullet hole in pilot's windscreen and a fuel leak.

We found six bullet holes all over the helicopter. Any four of these could have easily downed it. After the helicopter returned, we watched four Argentinean Mirages fly over the island. One was shot down over Stanley by their own troops. The other three turned towards us, strafing HMS Glamorgan and HMS Arrow and planted two bombs either side of our flight deck – this was for real. All three ships returned in the evening for a further NGS, but our main 4.5" gun jammed. Got to bed at 0300am – a day I'll never forget.

17th May – Finished at 0700 after 24 hours non-stop after Special Boat Service (SBS) were airlifted on to ship. Sailed into the Falklands Sound again from the north for the flight to drop off Special Forces, we exited the Sound via the north. The secondary purpose of HMS Alacrity was going into the Falklands Sound to check for mines, prior to the main invasion at San Carlos. Morning in bed, awakened by action stations. Repaired 182 decoy fibreglass dome in the afternoon. Flew late afternoon then Alert 15 – from 2000 until the following morning 0800.

23rd/24th May – The longest day ever. Started at 0345 for three-hour flying stint. Then worked straight through for 31 hours non-stop. Escorted RFA tankers and supply ships during the night to San Carlos in the Falkland Sound, where they were required to provide stores and support to the ground troops that had just landed. Returned to the Carrier Group located 200 nautical miles east before first light.

Eventually, finished at 1045 on the 24th. Four hours sleep then on again. Due to the long hours worked and general fatigue, many mistakes were made last night. Finished at 2200, had first shower for days and a change of clothes. During this period of constant action, everyone slept fully dressed. Anti-flash hoods and gloves were worn during daylight hours. Gas masks, lifejackets and once-only suits carried at all times.

27th/28th May – Another long day. Two periods of flying, transferring the survivors from the Atlantic Conveyor to an RFA, which was heading back to Ascension Island. A moving sight. Late afternoon HMS Alacrity, HMS Glamorgan and HMS Avenger, another Type 21 frigate, heading inshore at maximum speed for the gun line to fire 100 plus 4.5-inch shells into Stanley and surrounding hills.

Before daylight, all three ships headed east at maximum speed to re-join the carrier group. This was followed by RAS of liquids and ammunition. Not much sleep at all as the ship was at action stations with the main gun firing throughout the night. On the 28th after two hours sleep, launched helicopter at 1000 hours.

Hopefully, only one flying period and then a quiet day to enable us to catch up with the helicopter maintenance. Took a short break to go and watch a film in CPO's mess in the evening. Fell over in the hangar walking down a set of steep stairs (weariness?) and ended up with bruised kidneys and very sore back – OK though.

5th/6th June – Day spent alongside Motor Vessel Seaspread to check out ship's defects before heading north. All too good to be true really. Servo jack on the main rotor head, which was part of the helicopter flying controls, was defective. Spent long hours trying to fix it, but no luck.

On 6th June, spent the day undertaking a long 'back' RAS whereby unused stores, food and ammunition for the ships remaining in the south. Started the return journey home back to the UK. HMS Alacrity sailed home on her own. Helicopter still sick, servo jack problems. Left Total Exclusion Zone at 2359 heading north, thank god.

Recollections from an Aircraft Mechanician 1st Class – 'Rob' Shadbolt SMR HMS Antelope – Falklands April/May 1982

It took the author some gentle persuasion to get Rob to write this account, which occurred some forty years ago. He was operating from HMS Antelope under the same conditions and circumstances as described in Al Slater's piece above, except Rob had to endure the dramatic loss of his temporary home, personal belongings during action stations when they had to abandon their sinking ship.

He highlighted the lack of any follow up medical care and whether anyone suffered Post Traumatic Stress Disorder. Also, there was the absurdity of a Navy Board of Inquiry, which in the comfort and safety of a room in the UK, challenged him why he did not carry a large non-essential heavy piece of equipment when he jumped over the side when his ship was sinking! One can imagine Boards of Inquiry making the same sort of comments, following the Battle of Trafalgar some 200 plus years previously.

Here is his story:

Following your query, I've done a bit of digging around with regard to the Lynx damaged by the bomb on Broadsword's flight deck. This helicopter XZ729 was the one, which attacked the submarine Santa Fe in Grytviken harbour in the early days of the conflict. It belonged then to HMS Brilliant but was later loaned to HMS Broadsword, when on 25th April a Skyhawk aircraft attacked the ship, which dropped its bomb, bounced off the sea, striking the hull of the ship and then exiting through the flight deck.

During this trajectory, it took off the nose of the embarked Lynx before flying over the side and into the sea without exploding. The said Lynx subsequently had its tail boom and various parts robbed in order to repair another shrapnel damaged Lynx. What was left of the remaining hulk was airlifted by Sea King to the Atlantic Causeway and whilst there, it was further cannibalised (robbed for further spares) as and when required.

The Causeway sailed back to UK and the Lynx remains were offloaded at Camel's Head near Drake in Devonport and then taken by road to Fleetlands at Gosport in August 82 for a major rebuild. The aircraft did several years of service as a Lynx Mk8 and it is believed to be in storage, possibly at St Athan.

As for my own Lynx helicopter – XZ723, we sailed on HMS Antelope in company with HMS Alacrity very early one April morning. On the 23rd May, our ship was attacked whist we were in San Carlos Water covering the movement of troops ashore. Our Lynx was tasked to attack an Argentine supply ship with Sea Skua missiles. The attack was successful and the two missiles fired made direct hits.

While this was going on, Skyhawks attacked our ship, when two bombs struck and entered the ship neither of which exploded. The Lynx was held off from landing but after the bombs had exploded the ship was on fire, it was to land on HMS Fearless. Later, she transferred to Brilliant replacing XZ729 eventually moving on to Broadsword's and then to HMS Penelope. Here, it stayed until its return to Portland. After the Lynx was retired from service, XZ723 was sold off and sadly is now part of a paintball theme park just north of Bristol.

It is somewhat unbearable to think after all the hours and hours spent preparing her for war along with participating in action in a sinking, she is spending her final days being climbed over and shot at with paint guns for the sake of entertainment.

It is interesting to mention the complement of a typical small ship's flight to keep a sophisticated embarked weapons platform operational. The following is typical of a small ship's flight on the back end of a destroyer/frigate:

1. One pilot (Lieutenant)
2. One Observer (Lieutenant)
3. One Chief Petty Officer (Senior Maintenance Rating)
4. Three Petty Officers (various trades)
5. One Leading Air Engineering Mechanic
6. Two Air Engineering Mechanics

Detailed Account

HMS Antelope sailed from Devonport on the 5th April 1982 in company with Alacrity, destination South Atlantic. On the journey south, the flight were kept busy with continual weapon loading drills, transitioning to wartime maintenance routines, painting out all white lettering and distinguishing marks on the Lynx XZ723, as well as the normal flight activities of deck landing practice, ship integration duties, etc. On 23rd May, we sailed from the main task group together with others and entered San Carlos Water taking up our required position in support of the ground forces.

We had been at 'Action Stations' for some while and in the early afternoon, XZ723 was launched and told to investigate a nearby Argentine supply ship, the Rio Carcarana. This brought a great sense of urgency to the flight as after the continuous weapon loading drills we had gone through on the journey south, we were now doing it for real. Two Sea Skua missiles were loaded and successfully launched from XZ723, where both scored direct hits setting the ship ablaze.

Later in the afternoon, XZ723 was relaunched to assess the supply ships damage and confirm that it was sinking. On the helicopter's return to Antelope it was passed by several Argentine Skyhawk aircraft, which prevented its safe return. It eventually landed ashore safely.

During the air attack by the Skyhawks on the ship, members of the flight and Flight Deck Officer (FDO) took up positions in the forward end of the hangar, which offered the most protection. This protection was somewhat minimal because the ship was made of aluminium. The noise from the attacking Skyhawk aircraft and the gunnery from, not only Antelope but also nearby ships was intense.

However, we kept each other close for reassuring company at this most dangerous of times. Antelope sustained severe damage by one 1,000lb bomb entering the ship on the port side. Another 1,000lb bomb entered on the starboard side. They did not explode. One aircraft flew so low it actually struck the Antelope's FH5 aerial at about 400mph before it disintegrated and flew into the sea.

When the air attack ended, Antelope moved position within San Carlos Water and assessed the damage caused. The flight deck/hangar were undamaged but there was debris everywhere from the attacking aircraft. By leaning over the ship's guardrails, you could visibly see the two entry holes in the ship's side caused by the unexploded bombs.

Although we knew each other well, trying to maintain morale even between my small group of flight members was extremely hard. Our immediate future was uncertain until the bombs could be removed and the damage repaired.

HMS Antelope then embarked two Army bomb disposal experts to work on the bombs. Whilst working on the first using a special tool; the bomb exploded. The noise of the explosion was unlike anything we had experienced before. It literally lifted crewmembers off their feet and a glance over the starboard side of the ship revealed the extent of the damage. It looked to me like, and this is how I remember it, as if someone had taken a tin opener and sliced the hull from water line to the upper superstructure along with the sides being peeled back.

Fires raged and efforts at fire-fighting became increasingly more hazardous and the flight deck became engulfed in black smoke. Despite this, my team worked diligently removing ammunition including torpedoes from the hangar. I took the decision to ditch them overboard rather than let them succumb to the fire because at that time we had not received any order to abandon ship.

The flight deck became a mustering place for some of the ships company including the one member of the bomb disposal team, who was still alive even though he had lost an arm. I remember sitting on a torpedo next to him and giving him my morphine dose as he was in a very bad way.

The order was then given to abandon ship and after a final headcount of my team, saw us jumping over the side from the flight deck. I think I was the last of the flight to leave with one of my Petty Officers, who was next to me, he then placed his arm round my waist and we jumped together. The sky was pitch black made worse by the acrid smoke and we were rescued by Royal Marine landing craft, which made their way to the ship aided by illumination from the searchlights of a Sea King helicopter.

We were taken to three different ships and in my case, I ended up on HMS Fearless where I met up with many junglies I knew from my time at Yeovilton. They were good hosts and it was here I sustained my 'war wound' because after several beers, I managed to fall down a deck ladder from top to bottom slicing a deep gash in my leg!

That evening, our XZ723 helicopter appeared on Fearless and landed safely. Obviously, my team mustered to look after it but we had no equipment, tools or MF700, but it was good to see it after this traumatic day. Next day, I sat with the Aircraft Maintenance Control (AMCO) writer from the junglie squadron and made up a new MF700 for XZ723 from every detail in my head I could remember. This included the important Red/Green page entries, flying hours and flexible operations, etc.

The rest of the day was spent on the tank deck where all the ships in the area had once again come under serious air attack. The second bomb had exploded on Antelope overnight and when we looked at her, she had broken her back and was in a defiant V shape. All Antelopes ship's company from the various ships we had been sent to, were then transferred to MV Norland, a North Sea Roll-on Roll-off (RO-RO) ferry where we were to learn of our future.

We looked a sorry sight as no one had any personal belongings, money, change of clothes or toiletries, etc. All we had was what we left the ship with. In my case, apart from the No 8s (working dress) I stood up in, I just had a Parker pen in my pocket (a good SMR never goes anywhere without his pen!). Three days later, we arrived in Grytviken South Georgia and in that eerie, stunning land, seascape of icebergs and mountains, we transferred to the Cunard liner QE2 for our passage home.

Cunard looked after us extremely well, providing complementary items of clothing and toiletries and we were able to meet up with the ships companies of HMS Ardent and Coventry, who like us were literally in the same boat. It was during our eleven-day trip back to Southampton that daily briefings and meetings between small departmental units took place as we attempted to regain some sort of normality, especially regarding mental stability.

Despite all the training you undergo, nothing can prepare you for the mental and psychological trauma we had all endured and it was extremely hard to try and remain strong for your team. It was especially hard when you retreat to your single cabin and close the door, leaving just you and your thoughts. Of course, those long days at sea were made even longer as we had nothing to occupy our minds and the threat of being shadowed by an Argentine submarine was ever present.

Eventually, we made it back to Southampton and someone decided we should not disembark to meet our families in the tatty No 8s we were wearing when we left Antelope. As we sailed past Falmouth, several Seakings from RNAS Culdrose flew out to us to deliver brand new sets of No 8s, shoes and not forgetting a new beret.

Also, someone from the Culdrose pay office came on board to give everyone a cheque as we had no money and we were all going on ten weeks leave. There was never any mention of trauma or PTSD counselling or medical help upon our return. How very different conditions were then when compared to those serving today.

During those ten weeks, a Board of Enquiry was convened for the ships, which had been lost and the Board interviewed each crewmember. The Board was made up of senior officers (Captains and Commanders etc.), who wanted to know exactly what your job entailed, what you did on the day of the air attack. They also wanted to know about what you didn't do.

When it was my turn, I was asked why I hadn't taken the MF700 (the helicopter's flying log) with me or some ground equipment, such as blade folding poles, as I must have known I would be reunited with XZ723 at some stage. The fact is we were told to abandon Antelope along with leaving Fearless and that XZ723 would remain to be looked after by others. How I was supposed to jump overboard carrying heavy metal ground equipment tucked under my arm and make my way to a landing craft, still baffles me to this day.

After the ten weeks leave, we reassembled back at Portland and all the maintainers stayed together and formed a new flight for a new ship, HMS Nottingham, with the original Pilot and Observer going their separate ways.

All the above seems like only last week, hard to think it was over forty years ago.

XZ723-Lynx HAS Mk2 – History

29/3/82 – Naval Aircraft Support Unit (NASU) Yeovilton
4/4/82 – Transferred to 815 Sqdn Antelope Flight
5/4/82 – Sailed for South Atlantic
23/5/82 – Carried out Sea Skua attack on Rio Carcarana
24/5/82 – Landed on Fearless after Antelope attacked
24/5/82 – Flew to support 3 Cdo Bde, recovering to Fearless
30/5/82 – Transferred to Brilliant Flight
22/6/82 – Transferred to Broadsword Flight
2/7/82 – Transferred to Penelope Flight
23 to 27/5/82 – Loaned to Birmingham Flight then re-embarked Penelope
23/8/82 – Sailed on Penelope back to UK
10/9/82 – Arrived back at RNAS Portland.

Having been sold off by the MoD, XZ723 now resides in a paintball park in Thornbury, Bristol.

Sub-Lieutenant I. W. 'Soapy' Watson RN – Saves a £14M Sea Harrier

What became known as the 'Alraigo Incident', occurred on the 6th June 1983, when 'Subbie' (Sub-Lieutenant) Watson became disorientated and lost while flying a Sea Harrier FRS 1 (number ZA176) then belonging to 800 NAS operating from HMS Illustrious. Watson was launched as part of a pair of aircraft and tasked to locate a French aircraft carrier as part of a NATO exercise. It should be noted that this was Watson's 14th sortie and he was a very junior pilot. Under simulated combat conditions i.e. radio silence and no radar, a search was carried out.

After completing the search, Watson flew to a prearranged rendezvous with his flight leader. When the leader did not appear, he turned towards Illustrious anticipating that it would appear on radar and when he was unable to find the carrier, he made a radio transmission. At this stage, he realised his radio was not working and the NAVHARS (inertial navigation system) had not taken him back to the expected location for landing back on the ship.

Something was amiss and if he didn't rectify the solution as soon as possible, he was more than likely in for a swim in the cold waters below him. Soapy

Watson's training kicked in and he tried all of his available options. With his radar now operating, he didn't observe any blips showing up on the small screen.

Trying the radios, he came to the horrific realisation that they weren't functioning. Transmitting an emergency using his transponder didn't help either. The INS had malfunctioned and he was without the ability to transmit radio messages.

After completing the search, Watson attempted to return to HMS Illustrious but was unable to locate it. Unfortunately, running low on fuel and with his radio not working, he headed for a nearby shipping lane. Here, he made visual contact with a container ship, the Alraigo and his first instinct was to eject in sight of the vessel. Watson did a slow flypast of the ship and noticed it was carrying a number of flat-topped shipping containers roughly in size to a practice landing pad similar to one based back at Yeovilton, except this one was moving!

Making another approach, he landed the Sea Harrier on the first container forward but as he was landing, felt the aircraft slipping back. In order to stop this backward movement, he tried to lower the undercarriage but this failed, so the aircraft slipped further back until the fuselage embedded itself on to a roof of a van, which was parked directly in front of the container.

Subsequently some four days later, the ship docked in Santa Cruz, Tenerife amid a large media presence with the Sea Harrier still wedged with the front fuselage on the container and the remaining section on the van at an angle of 45 degrees. When asked by reporters about the amount of fuel he had left once he had landed on Alraigo, he said "About a minute's worth."

The aircraft was salvageable and the crew of Alraigo were able to claim £570,000 in salvage rights. As for Soapy Watson, when he returned to HMS Illustrious the Board of Inquiry did not pursue the matter. When the ship returned to port, he was subjected to another inquiry, which was made public by the National Archives when released in 2007. It should be noted that Sub-Lt Watson had only completed 75% of his Harrier training before being sent to sea.

The Board blamed his inexperience and commanders for allowing him to fly an aircraft 'not fully prepared for the sortie'. The polite way of saying the Sea Harrier was not fully serviceable for the search exercise. He was grounded for a while, but went on to do a further 2,000+ hours in the Sea Harrier and over 900 hours on exchange with the USN before resigning in 1996. He remained very stoic over his treatment stating that the Admirals were embarrassed by all the media coverage, but refused any criticism of them saying, "It was me, I was there and that's where it should stop."

Without doubt and in the circumstances, it was a fine piece of airmanship to save a valuable aircraft and to have the courage for a pilot with so little experience and to land on such a miniscule area i.e. on top of a shipping container. This incident once again highlights the stresses and strains placed on Navy pilots over their land based contemporaries.

Ashore, they simply would have diverted to one or other diversionary airfields. What started out as a fairly innocuous exercise suddenly became very critical and dangerous in a short space of time. Soapy Watson having no diversionary airfield or flight deck had to make instant decisions for which he should have been commended. He could have ejected and nobody would have been the wiser.

Lt Commander Eugene Kingsmill Esmonde DSO VC – Mission Impossible 1941

What was to become known as the 'Channel Dash', took place on 11th–13th February 1942. Three of Germany's largest warships, two battlecruisers, the Scharnhorst and Gneisenau along with the heavy cruiser Prinz Eugen broke out of Brest and attempted to return to their home bases at Kiel and Wilhelmshaven. This operation was to be called by the Germans 'Operation Cerberus' – in Greek mythology, this was the name of the three-headed dog, guarding the entrance to Hades.

On the British side, the answer by the RN and the RAF was the pre-planned 'Operation Fuller', which was to consist of a series of combined attacks in order to destroy or cripple these large warships. A part of the operation, slow, obsolete and fabric covered Fairey Swordfish torpedo-carrying aircraft of the FAA would be ordered to attack from the airfield at RAF Manston in Kent. Operation Fuller had been devised back in April 1941 as a plan for combined operations by the RN and RAF.

It was assumed that radar with air patrols; any dash from Brest would be quickly discovered. The Operation would combine 32 Motor Torpedo Boats (MTB) based at Dover to attack the ships with torpedoes. Swordfish torpedo bombers would follow up with a fighter escort, plus Beaufort torpedo bombers along with coastal guns at Dover whilst the ships were within range. Bomber

Command would then attack any German ship that had been damaged or slowed down.

On 4th February 1942, six Fairey Swordfish biplanes (nicknamed Stringbags) from 825 NAS, commanded by Lt Cdr Eugene Esmonde RN were moved from Lee-on-Solent to RAF Manston near Ramsgate in Kent. Over the next few days, the aircraft were maintained in a state of readiness with their ground crews working tirelessly in the snow to ensure that the engines remained warm and torpedoes serviced.

On 11th February, the Squadron was stood down, as there was no real threat. Lt Cdr Esmonde had an appointment in London in order to receive his DSO from King George VI at Buckingham Palace. This award was for his part in the sinking of the Bismarck in May 1941.

With the breaking of the Enigma code, the Admiralty were aware that departure of these three warships was imminent. These three German ships with a strong escort of smaller ships entered the Straits of Dover. They were protected by an all-embracing air cover consisting of 250 Luftwaffe aircraft. Esmonde received his orders to attack the German ships and circled Ramsgate waiting for five squadrons of Spitfires to act as escorts.

Unfortunately, only ten Spitfires of No 72 Squadron RAF rendezvoused with his Swordfish squadron. As part of the German's Operation Donnerkeil (Thunderbolt) to provide air superiority for the breakout from Brest, the two squadrons were attacked by Jagdgeschwader 2 and 26 flying mainly Messerschmitt 109s and Focke-Wulf Fw 190s. This attack left all of Esmonde's squadron damaged and resulted in the fighter escort becoming separated from the Swordfish torpedo bombers.

They continued their attack despite the damage and protection. The German warships put up a wall of heavy anti-aircraft flak and Esmonde's aircraft was believed to have been hit, which badly damaged the port wing. He continued to lead his flight weaving through a protective screen of destroyers and smaller ships. He was some 2,500 feet from his target when he was hit by shells from a Fock-Wulf 190, which caused his aircraft to burst into flames resulting in it crashing into the sea. The remaining squadron aircraft were all shot down whilst continuing their attacks.

Of the 18 aircrew involved in the six aircraft that set off, only five survived. The courage of these FAA aircrews was commented upon and noted by both sides for the courage shown against all odds and way beyond the call of duty.

Admiral Ramsay RN was to say that this gallant sortie by these six Swordfish aircraft constituted one of the finest exhibitions of self-sacrifice and devotion to duty the war had ever witnessed.

Scharnhorst's Captain Hoffmann was to say, "The poor fellows, they were so very slow, it was nothing but suicide for them to fly against these big ships." Lt Cdr Eugene Esmonde RN was posthumously awarded the Victoria Cross, four surviving officers received the Distinguished Service Order, and the rating aircrew survivor was awarded the Conspicuous Gallantry Medal.

Captain Eric 'Winkle' Brown CBE DSC AFC RN – Pilot Extraordinaire

No book on the Navy's air force would be complete without an entry on his remarkable career. A former FAA pilot. He was nicknamed 'Winkle' by colleagues, short for 'Periwinkle' (a small mollusc) because of his height. He was only 1.70 m (5ft 7in) tall. However, he was to state that this height disadvantage was to save him from serious injuries by curling up in the cockpit whenever disasters threaten or when an aircraft mishap occurred.

For example, on one occasion while flying a De Havilland 108 ('Swallow') in a dive from 40,000 feet and approaching Mach 0.88, the aircraft went into uncontrolled high g-pitch oscillation. By gently pulling back the control column and throttle, this severe undulation stopped as quickly as it started. He believed because he was shorter, he survived a potential broken neck from these oscillations.

Geoffrey de Havilland had possibly suffered such a neck fracture and crashed following a test flight on another DH 108 earlier carrying out similar high Mach number dives. All three De Havilland 108 test aircraft were lost in crashes. Winkle Brown was to describe the aircraft "A killer. It has nasty stall tendencies with vicious longitudinal oscillations at speed."

He is credited with a world record of carrying out the most aircraft carrier take-off and landings, namely 2,407 take offs and 2,271 landings. In his flying career, he flew 487 types of aircraft, more than anyone else, which in the modern era is unlikely to be surpassed. As well as these achievements, he also had many naval aviation 'firsts'. These include the first landing on a carrier of a twin-engine aircraft, the first of an aircraft with tricycle undercarriage and the first jet aircraft.

He had studied German at Edinburgh University and learned to fly in Germany and was in the country prior to WWII under sponsorship of the Foreign Office. Winkle Brown joined the Royal Naval Volunteer Reserve as a FAA pilot where he was subsequently posted to 802 NAS flying Martlets. Whilst on HMS Audacity, he is credited with having shot down two Focke-Wulf 200 Condor long-range maritime German aircraft.

He exploited the blind spot in their defensive armament by attacking them head-on. From here, after a short spell with the Royal Canadian Air Force, he was sent to the Royal Aircraft Establishment (RAE) at Farnborough and was sent to Southern Italy in 1943 to evaluate captured Luftwaffe and Regia Aeronautica aircraft. He subsequently moved back to RAE and in the first month on the Aerodynamics Flight department, he flew thirteen types including the powerful and capable Focke-Wulf 190 fighter.

His deck landings experience was sought and he began to perform testing on the naval versions of the Seafire and Sea Hurricane. His expertise led to posting for the testing of carriers' landing configurations and arrangements. During 1943, he carried out some 1,500 deck landings on 22 different carriers.

Also, whilst at Farnborough he became the chief naval test pilot and was involved in deck landing trials for the Sea Mosquito (for more details see You Tube). The reason for selecting the Mosquito was for 'Operation Highball' utilising a spherical bouncing bomb on the same principle as the cylindrical one used by the Dambusters.

Some 22 aircraft were to be embarked on two aircraft carriers with the intention of sinking Japanese capital ships in their home harbours. The operation was never carried out as the atom bomb ended the war against Japan in August 1945.

The end of WWII was in sight; RAE Farnborough geared itself to get its hands on German aeronautical technology and the latest aircraft. As he spoke German, he was made the Commanding Officer of 'Operation Enemy Flight'. Of interest to the Allies, particularly the US, was a jet bomber known as the Arado Ar 240. This was a German twin-engine, multi-role heavy fighter aircraft, developed for the Luftwaffe, to replace the Messerschmitt 110.

Its first flight was in 1940 but problems with the design hampered development. What was of interest to Farnborough and the Allies was the design work around pressurised cockpits to reduce pilot fatigue and optical range finding and targeting for its guns. A number of these aircraft were located in Denmark.

With assistance from members from the aerodynamic flight, plus a friendly German pilot, they managed to ferry twelve of these 234s back to Farnborough across the sea. During this period, he was to test fly some 53 different German aircraft including the rocket powered Messerschmitt Me 163 fighter.

In March 1949, he was given a permanent commission in the FAA as Lieutenant, becoming a Lt. Cdr in April 1952, Commander December 1953 (becoming Cdr Air of RNAS Brawdy in 1954) and then promoted to Captain in December 1960. His last appointment was as a Captain of HMS Fulmar then RNAS Lossiemouth, now occupied by the RAF. He retired from the Navy in late 1970.

Winkle Brown flew aircraft from Britain, Germany, United States and Russia. He holds the Guinness book of records for flying the most types of aircraft. This officially stands at 487 but it should be noted this number refers to the basic mark/model of any particular aircraft. He flew some 14 different versions of the Spitfire and Seafire and the record does not include the aircraft he flew in as the co-pilot.

Due to the period of history he flew in and the circumstance of war, the world record of the number of carrier landings, some 2,407 on 20 aircraft carriers to be precise, will never be achieved again.

It seems his Commanding Officer at RAE Farnborough summed up Winkle Brown's flying abilities aptly in his annual assessment for 1944, rating him as an exceptional pilot. He also goes on to make the following comment:

"A flawless pilot in every respect. An acute analytical mind makes him one of the country's finest test pilots. A brilliant aerobatic flyer."

Sources

https://www.greentigergroup.com/downloads/truck-names/lieutenant-commander-eugene-kingsmill-esmonde-vc/
https://en.wikipedia.org/wiki/Eric_Brown_%28pilot%29
https://en.wikipedia.org/wiki/Channel_Dash
https://en.wikipedia.org/wiki/Operation_Donnerkeil
https://en.wikipedia.org/wiki/Eugene_Esmonde

Chapter 17
Fleet Air Arm Squadrons – Numbering

It would probably surprise the general public that there has been well over 200 Naval Air Squadrons during the FAA's existence since its inception in 1933, 207 to be precise. Obviously, they did not operate all at the same time. However, at the onset of the Second World War, the Fleet Air Arm consisted of 20 squadrons with only 232 aircraft but by the end of the war the strength of the FAA was 9 aircraft carriers, 3,700 aircraft, 72,000 officers and men and 56 air stations. It had taken five years during the WWII for the FAA to recover the lost years of the 1920s–30s and regain its fighting strength, which it had in 1918.

Unlike the RAF squadron numbering, from 1933, FAA units were to be numbered in two blocks: 800–899 for first-line (front-line normally meaning aircraft carrier embarked based squadrons). The second block was 700–799 representing second-line units (normally shore-based). For example, the frontline embarked Sea Vixen squadrons were 899, 890, 892, and 893 respectively.

Each one would be part of a Carrier Air Group (CAG), although the squadrons allocated these CAGs would vary depending upon which aircraft carrier was in commission at the time. The training squadron for the Vixen was 766, which trained both aircrew and maintainers prior to going to a frontline outfit. All the Vixens were based on RNAS Yeovilton, with only the former 800 series earmarked for frontline service at sea.

Once these numbers had been exhausted, the '1' was added in front of the 700 and 800 squadron numbers i.e. 1700 and 1800 series of numbers respectively. For example, 1850 squadron was formed in 1944 with Corsairs IV serving on HMS Vengeance as part of the Pacific Fleet. To be even more specific Naval Air Squadron numbers were further divided into blocks, organised by type and function as follows:

First Line Squadrons

800 to 809 Single-seat fighter squadrons in carriers.

810 to 819 Torpedo bomber squadrons in carriers, later torpedo spotter reconnaissance and torpedo bomber reconnaissance squadrons.

820 to 859 Spotter reconnaissance squadrons, later torpedo spotter reconnaissance and torpedo bomber reconnaissance squadrons.

860 to 869 Torpedo bomber reconnaissance squadrons. These numbers were later reserved for Dutch-manned and then Dutch Navy squadrons.

870 to 879 Single-seat fighter squadrons. These numbers were later reserved for Royal Canadian Navy use.

880 to 89 Single-seat fighter squadrons in carriers.

Table of the FAA's Front Line Squadrons

Squadron	Motto	Battle Honours
800	Nun quam Non paratus (Never unprepared)	Norway 1940–44; Mediterranean 1940–41; Spartivento 1940; Malta Convoys 1941–42; 'Bismarck' 1941; Diego Suarez 1942; North Africa 1942; South France 1944; Aegean 1944; Normandy 1944; East Indies 1945; Burma 1945; Malaya 1945; Korea 1950; Falkland Islands 1982.
801	On les aura (We'll get them)	Battle Honours: Norway 1940–44; Mediterranean 1940–41; Spartivento 1940; Malta Convoys 1941–42; 'Bismarck' 1941; Diego Suarez 1942; North Africa 1942; South France 1944; Aegean 1944; Normandy 1944; East Indies 1945; Burma 1945; Malaya 1945; Korea 1950; Falkland Islands 1982.
802	Primus ferire (First to strike)	Norway 1940; Atlantic 1941; North Africa 1942; Arctic 1942; Korea 1952.
803	Cave punctum (Beware of the sting)	North Sea 1939, Norway 1940, Libya 1940–1, Matapan 1941, Crete 1941, Mediterranean 1941
804	Swift to kill	Norway 1940–44; Atlantic 1941–42; North Africa 1942; Normandy 1944; East Indies 1945; Burma 1945; Korea 1951–52.
805	Over sea and sand	Crete 1941, Libya 1941–2, Korea 1951–2
806	Sursum in pugnam (Up! And into the fight)	Norway 1940; Dunkirk 1940; Mediterranean 1940–41; Libya 1940–41; Matapan 1941; Crete 1941; Malta Convoys 1941–42; Diego Suarez 1942

807	Quoquo versus (Ready to strike in all directions)	Atlantic 1940, Malta Convoys 1941–2, North Africa 1942–3, Sicily 1943, Salerno 1943, South France 1944, Aegean 1944, Burma 1945, Malaya 1945, Korea 1950–3
808	Strength in unity	Spartivento 1940; 'Bismarck' 1941; Malta Convoys 1941; Mediterranean 1940–41; Atlantic 1943; Salerno 1943; Normandy 1944; Burma 1945; East Indies 1945; Korea 1951–52.
809*	Immortal	Bismarck, North Africa, Italy, Suez, Falklands 1982 **To be re-commissioned in 2023 with the F35B**
810	Ut fulmina de caelo (Like a thunderbolt from heaven)	Norway 1940; Mediterranean 1940–41; Spartivento 1940; Atlantic 1941; 'Bismarck' 1941; Diego Suarez 1942; Salerno 1943; East Indies 1944; Korea 1950–53.
811	Ventre a mer (Full speed)	English Channel 1942, North Sea 1942, Atlantic 1943–4, Arctic 1944
812	Dex aie (God aid)	North Sea 1940, English Channel 1940–2, Mediterranean 1941, Malta Convoys 1941, Korea 1951–2
813	Full sails	Calabria 1940; Mediterranean 1940–41; Taranto 1940; Libya 1940–41; East Indies 1941; North Africa 1942–43; Malta Convoys 1942; Atlantic 1944; Arctic 1944–45.
814*		Atlantic 1940 **Merlin**
815*	Strike deep	Battle Honours: Taranto 1940; Mediterranean 1940–42; Libya 1940–41; Matapan 1941; Malta Convoys 1941; East Indies 1944; Falkland Islands 1982; Kuwait 1991. **Wildcat**

816	Initiate the action of the tiger	Battle Honours: Taranto 1940; Mediterranean 1940–42, Libya 1940–41; Matapan 1941; Malta Convoys 1941; East Indies 1944, Falkland Islands 1982; Kuwait 1991.
817	Facere animo (To act with spirit or courage)	Norway 1941; North Africa 1942; Atlantic 1942, Sicily 1943; East Indies 1944; Korea 1951–52.
818	Sin mora (Without delay)	Norway 1940, Narvic 1940, English Channel 1940, Spartivento 1940, Mediterranean 1940–1, 'Bismarck' 1941
819	Partem infirmizzinam pettio (Strike at the weakest point-post 1991)	Mediterranean 1940–41; Libya 1940; Taranto 1940; Atlantic 1941; Malta Convoys 1941; North Sea 1944–45; Arctic 1944; Normandy 1944.
820*	Tutamen el ultor (Protect the avenger) i	Norway 1940–44; Spartivento 1940; Mediterranean 1940; 'Bismarck' 1941; Atlantic 1941; Malta Convoys 1941; North Africa 1942–43; Sicily 1943; Salerno 1943; East Indies 1945; Palembang 1945; Okinawa 1945; Japan 1945; Falkland Islands 1982. **Merlin**
821	A coup sûr (With a sure or certain blow)	Norway 1940; Libya 1942; Mediterranean 1942–43; Korea 1952–53.
822		Norway 1940; Libya 1942; Mediterranean 1942–43; Korea 1952–53.
823	Vigueur de dessus (Strength from above)	Norway 1940
824*	Spectat ubique spiirtus (The wind everywhere looks on)	Norway 1940; Libya 1942; Mediterranean 1942–43; Korea 1952–53. **Merlin**

825*	Nihil obstat (Nothing stops us)	Operation Fuller (known as the Channel Dash); participation in the attack on the Bismarck, 1982 Falkland's War. **Wildcat**
826	Latet anguls in aqua (A snake lies in the water)	Dunkirk 1940; North Sea 1940–44; Atlantic 1940; East Indies 1941, Matapan 1941; Crete 1941; Mediterranean 1941–43; Libya 1941–42; Falkland Islands 1982; Kuwait 1991.
827	Ya-mansuramit (Conqueror fight desperately)	Diego Suarez 1942, Malta Convoys 1942, Norway 1944, Korea 1950
828		Mediterranean 1941–3, Norway 1944, Japan 1945
829	Non effugient (They shall not escape)	Battle Honours: East Indies 1941; Matapan 1941; Crete 1941; Mediterranean 1941; Diego Suarez 1942; Norway 1944; Falkland Islands 1982; Kuwait 1991
830	In via gloria (In the way of glory)	Mediterranean 1940–42, Norway 1944
831	Aquil non capit muscas (Eagles do not catch flies)	Diego Suarez 1942; Malta Convoys 1942; Norway 1944; Sabang 1944; East Indies 1944
832		Malta Convoys 1942; North Africa 1942; Arctic 1942; East Indies 1944.
833		North Africa 1942, Atlantic 1944, Arctic 1944
834	Una feriendo dilemus By striking together we destroy)	Salerno 1943; East Indies 1944
835	Semper miseri sumus (Always in trouble)	Atlantic 1943–4, Arctic 1944–5

836	Mari coeel (By sea and sky)	Atlantic 1943–45
837		Atlantic 1943
838		Atlantic 1943, Normandy 1944
840		Atlantic 1943
841	Lucemus nocte (We shine by night)	English Channel 1943, Norway 1944
842	Tantivy (At full speed)	Atlantic 1943–4, Norway 1944, Arctic 1944
845*	Audio hostem (I hear the enemy)	East Indies 1944–45; Burma 1945; Falkland Islands 1982; Kuwait 1991; Al Faw 2003 **Merlin**
846*	Semper instans (Always threatening)	Atlantic 1944, Arctic 1944–5, Norway 1944–5, Normandy 1944–5, Falkland Islands 1982, Kuwait 1991 **Merlin**
847*	El alto concutimus (We shake them from on high)	East Indies 1944, Falkland Islands 1982, Al Faw 2003. **Wildcat**
848	Accipe hoc (Take that)	Normandy 1944, Okinawa 1945, Japan 1945, Falkland Islands 1982, Kuwait 1991
849*	Primus video (The first to see)	Battle Honours: Normandy 1944; East Indies 1945; Palembang 1945; Okinawa 1945, Japan 1945. **Merlin**
850	Vincit omnia virtus (Courage conquers all)	Normandy 1944, Atlantic 1944
851	Be forthright	East Indies 1944; Malaya 1944; Burma 1945.
852		Norway 1944
853	Defend, avenge	Arctic 1944–5, Norway 1945

854	Audentes fortuna juvat (Fortune helps the daring)	English Channel 1944; Normandy 1944; Palembang 1945; Okinawa 1945.
855	Delere ut protegemu (Annihilate in order to protect)	English Channel 1944; North Sea 1944; Normandy 1944.
857	Animis opibusque parati (Prepared in mind and resources)	East Indies 1945; Palembang 1945; Okinawa 1945.
860	Arcens affigo (Warding off, I afflict)	Atlantic 1944–45
870	Intercedimus el delemus (To intercept and destroy)	
871	Pugnandum surgimus (We rise to fight)	
878	Feles non pusilla (A cat, but no weakling)	Salerno 1943
879	Si vis defendere oppugna (Attack is the best defence)	East Indies 1945; Palembang 1945; Okinawa 1945.
880	Repérer et détruire (To seek out and destroy)	Diego Suarez 1942; Malta Convoys 1942; North Africa 1942; Sicily 1943; Salerno 1943; Norway 1944; Japan 1945.
881	Ense constanter alato (Steadfastly with winged sword)	Diego Suarez 1942; Norway 1944; Aegean 1944; Normandy 1944; South France 1944; Atlantic 1944.
882		Diego Suarez 1942; North Africa 1942; Atlantic 1943–44; South France 1944; Aegean 1944; Norway 1944–45; Arctic 1945.

883		North Africa, Arctic 1942
884		Malta Convoys 1942, North Africa 1942
885	Celerrime (Very quickly)	Arctic 1942; Malta Convoys 1942; North Africa 1942–43; Sicily 1943; Salerno 1943; Normandy 1944; Okinawa 1945.
886	Vires acquirit eundo (It gains strength as it goes)	Salerno 1943, Normandy 1944
887	Believe none	Salerno 1943, Norway 1944, English Channel 1944; Palembang 1945, East Indies 1945; Okinawa 1945; Japan 1945.
888	Sine Missione (No quarter)	North Africa 1942–43; Sicily 1943; Salerno 1943; East Indies 1945.
890	Caelum verrimus (We sweep the sky)	Salerno 1943
891	Venamur ut necemus (We search in order to kill)	North Africa 1942
892	Strike unseen	Atlantic 1943
893	Saepe feriendum (Strike often)	North Africa 1942–43; Sicily 1943; Salerno 194
894	Omnium capax ubique (Capable of anything anywhere)	English Channel 1944; Salerno 1943; Norway 1944; East Indies 1945; Okinawa 1945; Palembang 1945; Japan 1945.
895	Sicut falco expeditus (Ready like the hawk)	
896		Norway 1944; Atlantic 1944; Normandy 1944; Burma 1945; East Indies 1945
897	Quam possumus optime (The very best we can)	Salerno 1943, Normandy 1944
898	Far and Wide	Norway 1944, Atlantic 1944

		Strike and Defend	Sicily 1943, Salerno 1943, South France 1944, Aegean 1944, Falkland Islands 1982
	899		

*Current Front line FAA Squadrons are highlighted in bold asterisk ***

Second Line and Reserve Squadrons

700 to 749 – initially for catapult flights, later becoming catapult squadrons. When these ceased to exist, the range became available for training and ancillary squadrons.

700 to 710 – were earmarked for use by amphibian and floatplane squadrons in 1943 but this later lapsed.

750 to 799 – Training and ancillary squadrons.

1700 to 1749 – Torpedo bomber reconnaissance squadrons, reallocated to amphibian bomber reconnaissance squadrons.

1750 to 1769 – Single-seat fighter squadrons (not taken up).

1770 to 1799 – Two-seat fighter squadrons.

1800 to 1809 – Torpedo bomber reconnaissance squadrons (not taken up)

1810 to 1829 – Dive-bomber squadrons.

1830 to 1899 – Single-seat fighter squadrons.

1830 to 1844 – Used for Royal Naval Volunteer Reserve squadrons and latterly Royal Naval Reserve squadrons.

To illustrate the diversity and numbers of naval squadrons, the following pages show tables and few selected mottos. Some early squadrons show that whilst they were formed, they operated only for a short period and therefore, no emblems/badges were allocated. Even those outfits that had badges sometimes did not even have mottos. Heraldic designs and approval take time, especially during wartime. Full details of aircraft types, numbers and former Commanding Officers of these naval squadrons are contained in the excellent researched book listed below under Sources.

Naval Air Squadrons numbered 800 upwards to 899 were Front Line squadrons i.e. operational and carrier based.

Naval Air Squadrons numbered 700 upwards to 799, were generally experimental or training squadrons with the object of producing trained aircrew for the 800 numbered squadrons. For example, 700P was the Intensive Flying

Trials Unit for the FAA's Phantom in 1968, which in turn became 892 NAS in 1969.

1700 and 1800 numbered Naval Air Squadrons were used when the 700 and 800 series ran out. 1800–1899 were used for mainly for RNVR squadrons and then RNR squadrons. They mainly flew single seat fighters.

700 numbered Naval Air Squadrons			
700X	726	751	777
701	**727**	752	778
702	728	753	779
703	728B	754	780
704	729	755	781
705	730	756	782
706	731	757	783
707	732	758	784
708	733	759	785
709	734	760	786
710	735	761	787
711	**736**	762	788
712	737	763	789
713	738	764	790
714	739	765	792
715	740	766	793
716	741	767	794
717	742	768	795
718	743	769	796
719	**744**	770	797
720	745	771	798
721	746	772	799
722	747	773	
723	748	747	
724	749	775	
725	**750**	776	

1700 numbered Naval Air Squadrons	1800 numbered Naval Air Squadrons	
1700	1820	1842
1701	1830	1843
1702	1831	1844
1703	1832	1845
1710	1833	1846
1770	1834	1847
1771	1835	1848
1772	1836	1849
1790	1837	1850
1791	1838	1851
1792	1839	1852
	1840	1853
	1841	

Current FAA Squadrons are highlighted in bold text

Sources

The Squadrons of the Fleet Air Arm by Ray Sturtivant and Theo Balance ISBN 0 85130 223 8

http://www.royalnavyresearcharchive.org.uk/SQUADRONS

https://www.fleetairarmoa.org/fleet-air-arm-squadrons

https://en.wikipedia.org/wiki/List_of_Fleet_Air_Arm_aircraft_squadrons

https://www.1000flags.co.uk/royal-navy-fleet-air-arm-faa-including-fly-navy--3621-c.asp

Chapter 18
Fleet Air Arm's Timeline of Actions Since 1945

It is remarkable to observe that the following listing gives a simple illustration and reflects the decline of Royal Navy and its activities since the World War Two.

1945	On the completion of hostilities, the Fleet Air Arm consisted of 59 aircraft carriers, 3,700 aircraft and 7,200 officers with men posted at 56 air stations around the world. 9th August, Lt R H Gray RN leading a strike of Corsairs from 1841 and 1842 NAS awarded a posthumous VC whilst attacking a destroyer. 15th August – Sub Lt F Hockey RN flying a Seafire with 894 NAS was shot down near Higashimura, Japan and was executed by three senior Japanese officers; some nine hours after Japan surrendered. November – A FAA Sikorsky R-5 makes first FAA air/sea rescue. November – FAA fly six Lancaster bombers as part of 734 NAS Engine Handling Unit. They operated from RNAS Hintstock Shropshire at a satellite airfield known as RNAS Peplow, which had long runways in order to accommodate them. The first jet landing to land on an aircraft carrier was made by Lt Cdr Eric 'Winkle' Brown RN in December.
1946	Mediterranean-Corfu Channel. Operation Retail led by the carrier HMS Ocean and mine sweepers clear the channel after the mining of two RN destroyers. The carrier HMS Eagle launched. Aircraft carriers used extensively for trooping duties and repatriations. Landing trials of jets to commence.
1947	HMS Triumph visits Russian port of KRONSTADT St Petersburg, which was to be the last of such visits before the onset of the Cold War.

	First helicopter squadron namely, 705 NAS formed at RNAS Gosport-HMS Siskin.
1948	HMS Ocean and Triumph aircraft covered the British forces withdrawal from Palestine in May 1948. RAF aircraft and personnel had been evacuated earlier, so therefore only carrier-borne aircraft could provide the necessary air cover protection. Carrier HMS Centaur launched. Carrier HMS Vengeance carried out Arctic cold weather trials with commercial helicopters embarked. During the Malayan emergency until 1950, RN forces provided gunfire support and also carrier strikes against guerrilla targets. These were carried out either independently or in direct support of land forces. Carriers were used to transport forces with FAA helicopters lifting them into remote locations.
1949	Due to rising tensions with the Communists during the Chinese Civil War, the carrier HMS Triumph was sent to reinforce the Far East Squadron. Carrier HMS Implacable became the Home Fleet Flagship taking over from the battleship HMS Howe. Carrier HMS Bulwark launched. Escort carrier HMS Campania to be used as a mobile exhibition during the Festival Britain under the Red Ensign. January – 809 NAS commissioned at RNAS Culdrose-HMS Seahawk with the de Havilland Sea Hornet NF.21. A derivative of the Mosquito. The Sea Hornet an all-weather strike fighter, had flown deck-landing trials on board HMS Ocean in August 1945. A total of 79 aircraft were built and operated from HMS Vengeance, Indomitable and Eagle before retiring from front-line service in 1954. A liberty boat carrying sailors ashore from the carrier HMS Illustrious into Portland harbour sank in Weymouth Bay with the loss of 29 either dead or missing. The majority are buried in Portland Harbour cemetery.
1950	In June of this year following the invasion of South Korea by North Korea, the British response was immediate by the positioning and deployment of the carrier HMS Triumph. She joined the single US carrier that was initially available in support and it was to show of unity with the Americans and the United Nations. Triumph actually carried out the first carrier strikes of the war. None of the airbases in South Korea could operate American tactical jet fighters and many airbases were overrun by the Communist's invasion. US jets operating out of Japan could only loiter over South Korea for 15 minutes and because of engine technology at that time, they could only operate at an attitude of around 15,000 feet.

	There was therefore, a heavy reliance of naval air power throughout the war, which was to provide over a third of the total air war effort. Throughout the time of the conflict, Britain provided in rotation, some four aircraft carriers, with nearly 50 support warships including ships of the Royal Fleet Auxiliary. RAF involvement was a minor one and consisted of just patrols and transport. No offensive operations were carried out by them.
	The contribution of naval air power prevented both China and the USSR from escalating the war by widening the conflict and the transfer of large quantities of aircraft and materials to North Korea. This carrier force provided close air support and air cover during the major amphibious landing at Inchon and the diversionary raids along the enemy coast.
	The carrier HMS Perseus was re-commissioned in 1950 to serve as a trials ship and used in the development of steam catapults.
	The carrier HMS Ark Royal launched.
	The carrier HMS Victorious to be modernised.
	The carrier HMS Indefatigable to be brought out of reserve.
	The carrier HMS Majestic – construction work to be resumed and then transferred to the Royal Australian Navy and to be renamed HMAS Melbourne.
	Airborne anti-submarine warfare requirements recognised by 5th Sea Lord.
	Flight decks to be strengthened to enable use of new aircraft along with the future use of steam catapults and vertical take-off aircraft.
1951	First operation FAA jet squadron, 800 NAS, equipped with Supermarine Attackers formed at RNAS Ford.
	Escort carrier HMS Campania begins Festival of Britain cruise.
	Royal Naval Air Station – RNAS Simbang commissioned at HMS Sembawang.
	RN helicopter trials carried out on Royal Fleet Auxiliary Fort Dusquesne.
	Future use of helicopters in antisubmarine warfare recognised.
	The carrier HMS Eagle commissioned.
	The carrier HMS Triumph brought forward out of reserve.
	The carrier HMS Indomitable replaced the battleship HMS Vanguard as Home Fleet Flagship.
	Royal Navy Volunteer Reserve air squadrons re-equipped with Sea Furies and Firefly Mk VI aircraft.
1952	The 17th Carrier Air Group on board HMS Theseus flew a record sixty-six sorties in a single day over Korea.
	Four Sea Furies of 802 NAS from HMS Ocean led by Lieutenant 'Hoagy' Carmichael attacked by eight MiG 15s whilst over Korea. Carmicahel was credited to having shot one down and two others damaged.

	Steam Catapult trials completed on HMS Perseus. She sailed to the US to give demonstrations of the new launch system. HMS Perseus earlier embarked the first operational helicopter squadron, namely 848 NAS. The carrier HMS Illustrious carries out the first trials of the new prototype Mirror Deck Landing Sight. Setbacks on the refit of the carrier HMS Victorious were further exacerbated by the need to fit an angled flight deck and steam catapults. The Malaysian emergency continued through 1952 with the FAA carrying out carrier airstrikes. 848 NAS formed as the first helicopter squadron embarks on HMS Perseus in December, with first operational sorties taking place in January 1953.
1953	On 3rd February on the carrier HMS Indomitable, AVGAS (petrol) fuel vapour ignited below the island on the hangar deck, followed by an explosion. Ten gallantry medals including two George Medals awarded for rescue operations. Also in February, following the great North Sea tidal surge and flooding, all FAA helicopters were put on standby to help in either England or Holland. Some went to Kent for use over the flooded areas of England. Nine helicopters of 705 NAS with aircrew and mechanics from their base at the RNAS Gosport – HMS Siskin were sent to Gilze-Rijen in Holland. These aircraft worked at full pitch for four days from the 4th to 7th February inclusive, during which period the nine pilots flew a total of 237 hours and rescued 752 people. Two FAA pilots between them saved 257 people in one day. From 8th February onwards, the 705 NAS squadron was held at immediate readiness to deal with the effects of any further flooding that might occur during the next series of spring tides and was, in fact, used then mainly for supply dropping. In a week, the pilots flew a further 185 hours and rescued 58 people. In total, 422 hours were flown and 810 people saved (80 of whom were hoisted into the helicopter by winch). *Extracted from Hansard 18th March 1953 vol 513 cc1f-6W.* 806 NAS with Hawker Sea Hawk enters service in March at RNAS Brawdy. First fit of a British angled flight deck to a US Navy aircraft carrier. Aircraft and helicopters from carrier HMS Theseus used to provide relief in the Greek islands following an earthquake. After four years of development, the turboprop Wyvern S.4 (following on from the piston engine version Mk 1s in 1946) entered service in 1953 with

	813 NAS at RNAS Ford – HMS Peregine. Followed by 827 NAS, which embarked on board HMS Eagle in May 1955. 830 and 831 NAS also operated Wyverns, and the former saw operational service during the Suez Crisis in October 1956. A total of 127 Wyverns were built by Westlands. The carrier HMS Eagle commissioned. 806 NAS formed at RNAS Brawdy equipped with the Sea Hawk. The carrier HMS Vengeance loaned to RAN pending completion of HMAS Melbourne. RN helicopter trials continued on Royal Fleet Auxiliary Fort Dusquesne. Korean armistice signed 27th July 1953. In August, following earthquakes on the Greek islands, FAA helicopters carried out extensive relief operations. Fighters from the carrier HMS Theseus carried out photographic reconnaissance and survey of the damage in Cyprus. The ship stayed on station to provide disaster relief. During the Malaysian emergency, the FAA helicopter lifts troops into combat for the first time.
1954	1954–59 EOKA insurgency emergency in Cyprus. UK Aircraft carrier's foreign commissions to be of 2 years duration. The first possibilities and references to the use of nuclear weapons by naval aircraft were raised. 845 NAS, began service as the Royal Navy's first operational antisubmarine helicopter squadron. 890 NAS formed at RNAS Yeovilton with the first all-weather, day and night jet fighter. The Sea Venom was the forerunner on what was to become known as a multi-role aircraft. Mirror Deck Landing Sight introduced into service. HMS Hermes to be fitted with angled flight deck. First angle flight deck trials carried out on the carrier HMS Albion. In September, the carrier HMS Warrior used to evacuate fleeing refugees from Haiphong North Vietnam. The carrier HMS Centaur evacuated the last of the British Forces from Trieste, Yugoslavia. A hydraulic catapult exploded aboard the U.S. Navy attack aircraft carrier USS Bennington (CVA-20) while she was steaming in Narragansett Bay off Naval Air Station Quonset Point, Rhode Island, killing 104 men and injuring 201. October – FAA pilot Lieutenant B. D. Macfarlane RN successfully ejected from underwater after his Westland Wyvern flamed out and ditched in the Mediterranean from the aircraft carrier HMS Albion. He suffered only minor injuries.

	Westland Whirlwind entered service with 848 NAS. Admiralty promulgates official battle honours in a Fleet Order, which included FAA squadrons as well as ships.
1955	During January, the carrier HMS Glory provided fuel for FAA and RAF helicopters during Scottish blizzards. The carrier HMS Ark Royal, the fourth to bear the name, commissioned fitted with steam catapults and an angled flight deck. Mirror landing sight demonstrated to US Navy's 6th Fleet in Mediterranean during exercises. Plans to replace the Wyvern with the Blackburn Buccaneer. The carriers HMS Ocean and HMS Theseus ferried stores for 3rd Commando Brigade in Cyprus. Build-up of RN forces in Falklands after Argentina seizes Peruvian whalers. Orders announced Wessex MK 3 Anti-submarine helicopters. Orders announced for the De-Havilland Sea Vixen and the Supermarine Scimitar aircraft. Filmed landings on embarked aircraft become standard practice following a crash landing on the carrier HMS Eagle. Minesweeping trails commenced using helicopters.
1956	802 NAS reformed at RNAS Lossiemouth – HMS Fulmar with Sea Hawk FB 3s. Squadron was to be embarked on HMS Albion for the Suez crisis. 3rd February-SAR Helicopter Flight from RNAS Lossiemouth flew to the Pentland Firth and rescued thirty-two Norwegian seamen from MV Dovrefjell. Suez crisis, canal nationalised – Operation Musketeer – 26th July. The operation depended heavily upon carrier-borne airpower from the carriers HMS Eagle, Albion and Bulwark and provided the majority of sorties. The statistics showed that nearly 70% of these sorties were carried out by only one third of the aircraft utilised in this operation i.e. the embarked Naval squadrons. RAF Hunters could only loiter for ten minutes over the Suez Canal area from their bases in Cyprus. Not only were FAA Squadrons able to provide close air support rapidly and flexibly, they were able to also give air defence for the Hunters but also protect the offshore fleet. The 'Musketeer' operation was the first use of a helicopter borne assault from the sea from aircraft carriers. Using Whirlwinds and Belvederes, three Royal Marine Commando units were involved in the vanguard and were disembarked and airlifted from the carriers HMS Ocean and Theseus. The carrier HMS Centaur was to be fitted with steam catapults and updated radar fit.

1957

9th January – The twelve squadrons of the Royal Naval Reserve Air Divisions ceased flying and were to be disbanded in March.

11th January-First production Supermarine Scimitar F.1 (XD212) flies. The single seat jet had a top speed of 640kts at sea level, and an operational range of over 1,200 nautical miles. A total of 76 aircraft were built, serving with 736, 800, 803, 804 and 807 NAS finishing is service with FRADU.

Operation Grapple during March–June – the carrier HMS Warrior assisted in the British testing of thermo-nuclear weapons testing on Malden Island in the Pacific.

Operation Steadfast, HM the Queen's review of the Fleet, included the aircraft carriers Ark Royal, Albion and Ocean in the Cromarty Firth on 2nd–9th May 1957.

The 'Duncan Sands' (the then Defence Minister) Defence White Paper forecasted the end of the manned fighter concept. It went on to look at creating a strategic reserve for intervention overseas. Additionally, it stated that air transport was problematic because of the limited equipment that could be carried. It also highlighted the requirements needed by land-based aircraft to obtain over-flight rights, lack of fighter cover, the lack of overseas runways and finally, the difficulties of maintaining aircraft over such distances. The White Paper therefore, made a limited war and peacekeeping east of Suez, the main role for aircraft carriers and amphibious forces.

"On account of its mobility, the Royal Navy, together with the Royal Marines, provides another effective means of bringing power rapidly to bear in peacetime emergencies or limited hostilities. In modern conditions, the role of the aircraft carrier, which in effect is a mobile air station, become increasing significant."
Defence 'Outline of Future Policy' Cmnd 124 paras 37–38

A carrier task force led by HMS Albion and Centaur exercise with the Far East Fleet. HMS Albion visits the HQs of the Indian Navy, whilst Centaur visited the Pakistani Navy in Karachi conducting carrier borne flying demonstration. Task force continued via Ceylon on to Singapore and Hong Kong.

The carrier HMS Ark Royal visited New York as part of the US Navy's International Fleet Review 350th anniversary of the founding of Virginia. It was seen as a diplomatic effort to rebuild political and military relations post 'Suez'. Afterwards, HMS Ark Royal conducted joint exercise with the carrier USS Saratoga. Six USN aircraft types cross-operate with the British carrier, whilst Ark Royal's aircraft of Sea Hawks, Sea Venoms, Wyvern and Gannets landed on the Saratoga.

	The carrier HMS Ocean visited Helsinki. The RNVR (Air Branch) disbanded.
1958	Refit of the carrier HMS Victorious with angle deck and the new Comprehensive Display System (CDS) Air Warning Radar system completed. The carriers HMS Eagle and Hermes to be fitted with new CDS Air Warning Radar system. The on-going Cyprus campaign against EOKA continued with support of aircraft from the carriers HMS Ark Royal, Eagle, Bulwark and Victorious. The carrier HMS Ark Royal, with Albion and Bulwark, prepared to evacuate British nationals from Lebanon. Ark Royal remained until relieved by the carrier HMS Eagle. March – HMS Eagle whilst operating in the western Mediterranean was ordered to sail southwards in order to search for two French Navy pilots following a mid-air collision. Only one pilot was recovered. A small task group led by the carrier HMS Bulwark carried out a major salvage operation and a tow after two tankers collided, which caught fire, in the Indian Ocean just off Qatar. Pilot of a Scimitar landing on the carrier HMS Victorious and ditched into the sea, was trapped in the cockpit, where unfortunately he lost his life when he was unable to escape. This led to the consideration of developing underwater ejection systems. July-October-Jordan appeals to Britain for military assistance. The carrier HMS Eagle provided air cover for trooping flights into Amman. HMS Bulwark brings in troops and heavy equipment followed by HMS Albion bringing in another 1,000 plus their transport. The Sea Venom and Scimitar aircraft join the FAA. First flight of the Westland Wasp, specifically designed as a small ship's helicopter.
1959	The RN took delivery of its first nuclear weapons in 1959. Designated as Red Beard, it was a free-fall tactical nuclear bomb to be carried by the FAA's Scimitar and later, the Buccaneer. RNAS Portland – HMS Osprey, opened for the support of sea training. First military helicopter station in UK. Details of a new underwater ejector seat announced. First front line De-Havilland Sea Vixen squadron formed at RNAS Yeovilton. The carrier HMS Bulwark as a Commando Carrier commissioned with 848 NAS in December. Fairey Gannet AEW 3 to replace Skyraiders.

	HMS Ark Royal commissioned in December. HMS Eagle enters Devonport for an extensive four year refit and modernisation.

Contingency plans continued for a potential operation to defend Kuwait. Problems of moving troops, equipment and aircraft across the Middle Eastern, Mediterranean and North Africa area also continued to cause planning dilemmas. The usual problem of getting over flights, permissions and availability of suitable airfields were a major hindrance to Britain's military planners.

The carrier HMS Victorious deployed to the western Atlantic for exercises with four US Navy carriers. The carrier visits New York. |
| **1960** | Order placed for the gas turbine powered Westland Wasp helicopter based on the Saunders Roe Skeeter – a piston engine helicopter.

Agreement reached with the RAF over the operational control of maritime aircraft.

The carrier HMS Albion to be converted as a Commando Carrier.

The carrier HMS Bulwark re-commissioned as a Commando Carrier.

HMS Ark Royal carried trials on new Deck Landing equipment to replace mirror landing system.

US designed catapult recovery strop to be installed on the carrier HMS Victorious.

The Blackburn NA39 (Buccaneer) aircraft deck landing trials carried out on the carrier HMS Victorious.

Sea Vixens embark on the carrier HMS Ark Royal.

Westland Wasp trials carried out for use on anti-submarine frigates.

Wessex replaces the Whirlwind. |
| **1961** | HMS Bulwark carries out amphibious exercise with US forces in North Borneo in support of the new Malaysian Federation as a show of British determination of intent in Indonesia.

Buccaneer Trials Unit 700Z NAS formed at RNAS Lossiemouth – HMS Fulmar.

In July, first ASW helicopter squadron of 815 NAS commissioned and equipped with the Westland Wessex at RNAS Culdrose.

Naval hovercraft unit established at RNAS Lee-on-Solent – HMS Daedalus for exploring ASW.

Deck Landing Projector Sight (DPLS) and Height Indicator (HILO) to replace Mirror Sight. HILO trails carried out on the carrier HMS Albion for 10 months.

HMS Eagle to be fitted with Action Data System.

Kuwait came under explicit threat from Iraq and formally requested British assistance. Under Operation Vantage, Royal Marines landed from the |

	Commando Carrier HMS Bulwark to secure airfield. The carrier HMS Victorious arrived to establish a full air defence with her fighters. She also provided air direction control for her own FAA aircraft but also for the RAF. A second carrier HMS Centaur was deployed off Aden in case she was required. This successful deployment ensured there was no requirement to send a much larger force at greater cost in order to deter Iraq. In November, the carrier HMS Victorious, later replaced by HMS Centaur, and using helicopters with Royal Marines carried out humanitarian work after severe flooding in Kenya. HMS Victorious spent 222 days at sea out of 333 having steamed some 62,000 miles.
1962	January-the carrier HMS Centaur with RFA Tidesurge went to the aid of a Greek tanker the Stanvek Sumatra, which had broken in half in the South China Sea. HMS Centaur deployed in response to further threats to Kuwait by Iraq. January saw the beginning of the Malaysian Confrontation where Indonesia commenced a guerrilla campaign to prevent the creation of Malaysia and take over Borneo. In Brunei, a revolt encouraged by Indonesia, was thwarted by a joint British operation. Some 1,500 troops (half being airlifted in) the other half being deployed from a cruiser, destroyers, amphibious craft and importantly, helicopters. The Commando Carrier HMS Albion became a platform for both FAA and RAF helicopters, providing troops, supplies, transport and a base in which to carryout maintenance/repairs for these helicopters. HMS Bulwark lifted a company of Royal Marines of 42 Commando from Singapore across to Brunei, where it arrived on 10th December. This company went on the rescue British hostages held in Limbang. In the spring during a NATO exercise named 'Dawn Breeze', aircraft from HMS Victorious cross-operated from the French carrier Clemenceau and vice versa. This was the first cross-operation carried with an ally other than the US. A task force consisting of HMS Ark Royal and Bulwark exercised with the US Navy under the guise of the South East Asia Treaty Organisation (SEATO). This task force conducted a show of force in the South China Sea. HMS Ark Royal on route home, transported 34th Artillery Regiment and their equipment from Singapore to Aden. Announcement forecasting the requirement for new Fleet Aircraft Carrier(s). Wessex HAS 3 (an anti-submarine version) to be used on carriers and guided missile cruisers.

	845 and 846 NAS along with 40 RM Commando were on board HMS Albion sailed on the 5th December from Mombasa. She arrived at Singapore, loaded on stores, ammunition and additional troops and quickly sailed to Kuching in Sarawak arriving on the 14th December. In less than 10 days of being off East Africa, the Royal Marines and their equipment were landed in Sarawak. Queen's Commendation for Brave Conduct awarded to Lt N Tristam RN for safely landing a Scimitar on the carrier HMS Hermes following a major bird-strike to the aircraft's windscreen and canopy at 3,000 feet. The new Wessex helicopter to be used on the Commando Carriers. The future long-term nuclear defence of the United Kingdom was to be handed over to RN via its Polaris submarines. The RAF's V-bombers were to be stood down.
1963	HMS Albion assisted in flood relief in Borneo. She was rapidly re-tasked to transport troops to Borneo in light of the rising tensions with Indonesia, where they were landed by helicopters. The second phase of the Malaysian Confrontation was to commence, whereby Indonesia began to infiltrate forces in to both east and west Malaysia by sea and one by air. The Command Carriers HMS Albion and Bulwark ferried, troops, supplies, vehicles and helicopters into theatre. Their main role was transport troops and logistic into inaccessible jungle areas, it was where the nickname term 'Junglies' and thereafter were always referred by the pilots, crews and helicopters of the FAA squadrons involved in these operations. The carrier HMS Victorious provided in the form of AEW aircraft and fighters for incursions either by sea or air. Support air strikes were carried out for the forces ashore from the carriers, HMS Ark Royal, Victorious, Hermes and Centaur. These carriers were considered to be key in an attempt by Britain to act as a deterrent and prevent an escalation in the conflict. This deterrent was essential as many potential Indonesian targets were outside the range of bombers based in Singapore or Australia. Replacement of Fleet Aircraft Carrier, designated CVA01 was announced. Admiralty formally authorises the uses of 'Sonar' as opposed the 'Asdic'. February first VSTOL P1127 prototype aircraft deck landed on HMS Ark Royal. Phantom aircraft selected in-lieu of the cancelled P1154. British troops landed by FAA and RAF helicopters from the carrier HMS Centaur following insurrection in the Radfan, South Arabian Federation – Aden. On the 24th December, the carrier HMS Centaur on passage to the Far East, co-ordinate the rescue operations for the Greek cruise liner SS Lakonia, which had caught fire off Madeira in the Azores. Damage control parties

	from Centaur were first on board to fight the fires. Lakonia taken under-tow but sank. A total of 128 people perished with Centaur, eventually having to land some 88 bodies in Gibraltar two days later.
1964	50th Anniversary of the Royal Naval Air Service celebrated at HMS Heron, Yeovilton. Attended by HRH Duke of Edinburgh, who opened the FAA Museum at Yeovilton.

HMS Victorious recommissioned in Singapore.

The updated Sea Vixen FAW2 introduced to Naval Air Squadrons replacing the FAW1 model. The Mk 2s were eventually to serve on 766, 890, 892, 893 and 899 NAS. Many went on to also see service on the Fleet Requirement and Direction Unit (FRADU) and Boscombe Down trials unit.

28th May – FAA museum opened by HRH Duke of Edinburgh.

The carriers HMS Ark Royal and Centaur sent to the Far East to reinforce the carrier HMS Hermes, all in support of the Confrontation conflict. Ark Royal took part in the exercise FORTEX held off the coast of Malaysia but unfortunately suffered a main engine failure requiring dockyard assistance. It was decided to send HMS Victorious to relieve her.

Helicopter training/support ship HMS Endgadine ordered.

Between January and March, the combined fixed wing and helicopter assets of the carrier HMS Centaur along with 45 Commando RM, quelled the Tanyanyika and East African Mutinies. Apart from the normal air group, Centaur also carried two RAF Belvedere helicopters. Six Sea Vixens of 892 NAS from Centaur armed with 2 inch rockets flew fully fuelled to the garrison at Tabora. Fast low-level noisy runs were made, which disorientated the rebels and enabled them to be quickly overpowered by the Royal Marines.

The carrier HMS Victorious arrived at the end of January to relieve Centaur, whilst 41 Commando, which had been flown in to prevent an uprising in Uganda. They took over the policing of the main towns from 45 Commando RM.

In May, the carrier HMS Centaur embarked a Royal Artillery battery with 5.5 inch field guns whilst in Singapore. She sailed across the Indian Ocean arriving off the coast of Aden. The guns were landed along with 815 NAS and commenced flying operations with the forces deployed ashore. Over a period of eleven days, 560 sorties were flown transporting supplies, men and ammunition in support of operations by the army. Centaur continued to conduct flying operations off the coast of Aden and in June her Sea Vixen aircraft of 892 NAS carried out strikes against various Yemen rebel positions and forts in the Radfan area. |

	HMS Victorious with Royal Marines deployed to Kenya on the 15th November to provide assistance following major flooding. 825 NAS helicopters landed and provided emergency supplies. Helicopters from 824 NAS from HMS Centaur relieved them on the 3rd December.
1965	The carrier HMS Triumph commissioned for use as a maintenance ship in Singapore. First Buccaneer squadron 801 NAS formed at RNAS Lossiemouth. FAA Buccaneer S2 from Naval Test Squadron at Boscombe Down flew non-stop from Newfoundland to RNAS Lossiemouth, HMS Fulmar without refuelling. First FAA aircraft to cross Atlantic in one hop. First Wessex HU5s taken to Far East on HMS Albion. FAA Phantom F4K order for RN confirmed. RNAS Halfar in Malta handed over to RAF. HMS Albion diverted to pick up Russian seaman from tanker and taken to Seychelles. Following the announcement of Unilateral Declaration of Independence (UDI) in November by Southern Rhodesia and a request for assistance by Zambia, HMS Eagle provided air cover over this land locked country. RAF fighters were unable to be deployed immediately because overflights were denied. Eagle remained on station for five weeks. With the Confrontation still continuing, between April 1965 and July 1965, HMS Albion's eighteen Wessex and two Whirlwind helicopters of 848 NAS flew 5,000 hours transporting 12,000 men and 5,000,000 pounds of freight in Sarawak. Two Royal Navy SR.N5s hovercraft arrived in Borneo, where they operated in the rivers and swamps. They carried out valuable work over a period of six months, demonstrating the reliability of such craft. Large numbers of these Air Cushion Vehicles were to be used by the USN in Vietnam.
1966	27th January – The Admiralty Board formally approved the design for CVA01 super-carrier. Less than one month later, on 22nd February, a Defence White Paper announced the cancelation of the project. Admiral David Luce resigns as 1st Sea Lord over the cancellation of the new carrier CVA01 and the phasing out of aircraft carriers. Christopher Mayhew MP, then Minister of Defence for the Royal Navy also resigned. HMS Ark Royal to operate Phantoms and Buccaneers after a refit. Crashed Buccaneer from HMS Victorious recovered from English Channel from a depth of 360 feet. Following gearbox failure and engine flame out, Sea Vixen Pilot of 890 NAS awarded the George Medal trying to release his Observer before the aircraft hit the sea.

9th April – 700B Flight the Buccaneer S Mk2 Intensive Flying Trials Unit (IFTU) formed. 801 NAS with Buccaneers S Mk2s formed in October, followed by 809 NAS in October and 803 NAS in July 1967.

Buccaneer S2 extends its range and endurance by the use of in-flight refuelling.

VSTOL Harrier trials carried out on HMS Bulwark.

March–December Following the Unilateral Declaration of Independence by Southern Rhodesia the Beira Patrol was set up to intercept oil tankers reaching the port of Beira. This followed a UN Resolution calling for economic sanctions against Rhodesia. Maritime surveillance was carried out by Gannet AEW 3s aircraft operating from HMS Ark Royal and later by HMS Eagle. Eagle carried out the longest peacetime patrol by an aircraft carrier for a total of 71 days involving flying 1,000 fixed wing sorties and 800 helicopter sorties.

December 1965, the Commando Carrier HMS Albion was going back to Singapore when an Indonesian patrol boat attacked her. The gunboat opened fire with 40mm guns at close range. The Captain of HMS Albion promptly rammed and sank the gunboat.

RNAS Facility at Naga Ket in Borneo given name of RNAS Tauari (name of local bird),

1967

HMS Bulwark provided humanitarian aid following flooding in eastern Malaysia.

During the run up to the Six Day War, Egypt blockaded the Strait of Tiran. The carriers HMS Victorious sent to Malta and Hermes to the Red Sea respectively to provide air cover for possible international action on the right of passage in the Straits.

HMS Ark Royal's £34M refit and modernisation starts to enable the Phantom to embark and to extend her operational life carry until the mid to late 1970s. HMS Eagle to also remain until the mid-70s.

HMS Albion with 41 RM Commando deployed off coast of Africa as a precaution during Nigerian civil war for evacuating British nationals.

30th March – FAA Buccaneers of 800/809 NAS from RNAS Lossiemouth bombed the oil tanker Torrey Canyon, which ran aground on rocks in Cornwall. Sea Vixens of 890 and 899 NAS from RNAS Yeovilton also dropped napalm in an attempt to burn the leaking crude oil.

Following the Chinese 'Cultural Revolution' border incidents and riots occurred in Hong Kong, the carrier HMS Bulwark and 40 RM Commando deployed to support garrison. In late summer after further riots, HMS Hermes deployed to support anti-communist raids. FAA of 845 NAS helicopters supported troops and police helicopters.

	First radar equipped ASW helicopter the Wessex HAS 1 of 814 NAS is formed in August.
Evacuation of Aden: Operation Magister Oct 67 – Jan 68. The British Government decides to withdraw from Aden. Following the removal of RAF fighters in the November, air cover/support was provided by the two carriers HMS Eagle and Hermes. The Commando carrier's HMS Albion and Bulwark supported by the amphibious assault ships HMS Fearless and Intrepid supported the evacuation. The RM of 42 and 45 Commandos were landed to protect the final evacuation.
HMS Victorious to be scrapped following a fire in Portsmouth dockyard.
First VTOL on HMS Bulwark by the Harrier.
1968	The Commando Carrier HMS Bulwark returned from the Far East and was rapidly deployed to Norway in Polar Express for the first time in June 1968 with twenty Wessex HU5 helicopters of 845 NAS and 650 Royal Marines of 45 Commando embarked.
HMS Eagle and Albion deployed off Aden during diplomatic talks over its post-colonial government.
Demonstrating the FAA's air mobility capability, twelve Sea Vixens FAW2s of 893 few 2,200 miles from RNAS Yeovilton to RAF Akrotiri in Cyprus refuelling from Victor tankers. It was the first time a Naval squadron had been deployed in such a way. The Vixens then took part in 10 days air defence exercise operating from a shore based airfield before returning to the UK.
29th May – first Phantom F4K delivered to HMS Heron, RNAS Yeovilton. Intensive Flying Trials Unit (IFTU) – 700P NAS flying the new Phantom FG 1 formed at RNAS Yeovilton.
HMS Bulwark with RM 45 Commando with her helicopters of 845 NAS, deployed to Norway.
HMS Hermes, Albion and Intrepid sailed through territorial waters near the Philippines to demonstrate right of 'innocent' passage.
HMS Lion to be converted to carry helicopters.
In August four Buccaneers flew direct to the Far East without the need for large shore establishments. The S 2S of 803 NAS flew from Lossiemouth in Scotland to join HMS Hermes in the Far East.
Harrier carries out operating trials on HMS Ark Royal and Bulwark.
Wasp helicopter to be replaced by the Lynx in the mid-1970s.
Plans to replace the Gannet AEW3 cancelled.
Sea King helicopter to enter service in 1969.
Also in 1968, HMS Eagle demonstrated her value by acting as a mobile airbase for a major a NATO exercise coded 'Silver Tower'. It was the first

Year	
	time such an exercise had been carried out without an American attack carrier
1969	700P Phantom Intensive Trials Units (IFTU) disbanded. In January, 767 NAS formed in order to train Phantom aircrews. First frontline Phantom squadron 892 NAS formed at RNAS Yeovilton on 5th March.

In May, the RN enters a Phantom of 892 NAS in the Daily Mail Trans-Atlantic Air Race flying the west to east leg. With the aid of RAF tankers, the Navy won the trophy for the fastest flight eastwards. The winning time for the FAA competitor, i.e. the Phantom's Observer from the top of the Empire State Building, New York to the top of the Post Office Tower in London was 5 hours 11 minutes.

41 Commando RM conduct an assault landing from HMS Bulwark at Gibraltar following Spanish political pressure and military movements.

Later in September, HMS Eagle deployed to Gibraltar following continued Spanish diplomatic and military pressure.

The concept of 'Through Deck Cruisers' was announced – to eventually to become the Invincible Class of carrier.

First Westland Sea Kings delivered.

892 NAS deploy six Phantoms for deck landing and launches on the USN carrier USS Saratoga in the Mediterranean. HMS Ark Royal was overdue its refit.

RNAS Arbroath HMS Condor, the FAA technical training school for Aircraft Artificers and mechanics transferred to HMS Daedalus, Lee-on-Solent. The air station an establishment was to be used by 45 Commando RM (future Arctic Warfare Commando).

RNAS Lossiemouth – HMS Fulmar to be handed over to RAF.

RNAS Brawdy-HMS Goldcrest Pembrokeshire to close.

Helicopter refuelling trials whilst hovering carried out with HMS Rothesay. |
| 1970 | HMS Ark Royal recommissioned by the Queen Mother.

HMS Eagle completed refit.

HMS Hermes to be converted to Commando Carrier.

The front-line aircraft operated by the Fleet Air Arm includes: twenty-four F-4K Phantoms and same number of Buccaneer S.2s Some Sea Vixen interceptors and Gannet AEWs. On the rotary wing front, there were sixty Sea King ASW helicopters, 150 Wessex helicopters and ninety Wasp general-purpose helicopters.

Lt Cdr P Marshall RN awarded AFC for returning a crippled Phantom of 767 NAS to RNAS Yeovilton following the loss of its radome.

15 Feb RN-Hovercraft BH 7 Mk2 begins trials at HMS Daedalus RNAS Lee-on-Solent. |

	Royal Naval Aircraft Yard (RNAY) Fleetlands for the Services repairs of hovercraft. Sea King helicopter enters service. RNAS Prestwick – HMS Gannet established at the civilian airport in Ayr. RN Sea King Search and Rescue to be based there. Anti-submarine Sea Kings to operate from there. Sea King XV649 of 824 NAS flown by Lt Cdr V Sirret RN flew non-stop from Lands Ed to John O'Groats, a distance of just under 700 miles in 4 hours 19 minutes. WG 13 (Lynx) helicopter began manufacturer's trials. HMS Ark Royal visited Oslo. HMS Bulwark left after the initial phase of Exercise Bersatu Padu to visit Japan to part in EXPO 70. HMS Hermes assists in repair work off Malta to the Panamanian ship EARNER. November – The carrier HMS Ark Royal was participating in the exercise Lime Jug 70, when a Soviet Kotlin class destroyer, the Bravyy attempted to cut across the bows of Ark Royal. The carrier, which was at flying stations, sent emergency warning signals and went full astern in an attempt to avoid hitting the Russian ship. The ships collided and the bows of Ark Royal struck the destroyer's stern, rolling it over and wrecking the whole after section. The destroyer righted itself but seven Russian sailors were washed over the side. HMS Yarmouth carried out a search and managed to rescue four Soviet sailors. November – HMS Intrepid was the command and control ship for a major disaster relief operation. The Bhola cyclone was a devastating tropical cyclone that struck East Pakistan (present-day Bangladesh) and India's West Bengal. HMS Intrepid with the carrier HMS Triumph left Singapore to assist with the relief efforts. The Force controlled twenty Wessex HU 5 helicopters, eight landing craft, 650 troops, and assisted international and civilian rescue teams distributing supplies. At least 500,000 people lost their lives in the storm. Sailors and soldiers had to help bury the dead, for which Navy rum (which was traditional given carrying out this far from envious task), had recently been stopped. It had to be re-instated temporarily.
1971	HMS Eagle exercised in the Malacca Straits, deployed then to the Persian Gulf and joined up with HMS Albion with 40 Commando RM for Operation Bracken covering the evacuations from bases in the Persian Gulf. November – Third Indo-Pakistani War began. A state of emergency was declared and a task force was despatched for the evacuation of British Nationals. HMS Albion with escorts and 826 NAS equipped with Sea Kings,

	which been previously embarked on HMS Eagle, sailed to the Bay of Bengal. The new state of Bangladesh came into being on the 16th December. December – Dom Mintoff, the then Prime Minister of Malta, issued an ultimatum for the withdrawal of all British Forces from the island. The Commando carrier HMS Bulwark and the helicopter cruiser HMS Blake formed up off the coast whilst 41 Commando RM were deployed ashore to guard key points. This task force remained off Malta during the winter until the following March when the situation had eased.
1972	28th January – Following threats to British Honduras (Belize) from neighbouring Guatemala, two 809 NAS Buccaneer S.2s launched from HMS Ark Royal in the Atlantic. After in-flight refuelling from two further squadron aircraft, they flew on to Belize. They flew over the city at 1,000 feet and then did a low level run over the airfield at 400 feet. They then backtracked to HMS Ark Royal refuelling once again on the return leg by their own squadron aircraft. This journey was a 2,600 mile round trip, lasting 5 hrs 50 minutes. It was a total FAA 'organic' operation with no other external assets utilised. 23rd January – The last Sea Vixen squadron at sea disembarked when aircraft of 899 NAS flew from HMS Eagle to RNAS Yeovilton.
1974	HRH Prince of Wales learns to fly Wessex HU 5 in commando role. A flight with two helicopters was formed. It operated under the code name – 'Red Dragon II' to carryout training with 707 NAS at RNAS Yeovilton. Cyprus Emergency 15th July – 30th September. Following the overthrow of Archbishop Makarios and his rescue by British Forces, Turkey invaded Cyprus. A task force was assembled in the eastern Mediterranean, which included the carrier HMS Hermes after embarking 41 Commando RM in Malta. Arriving off the coast of Malta, 41 Command RM were landed on the sovereign base reinforcing 41 Commando RM. British forces rescued and evacuated refugees and British nationals. 1st April – Air crewman Branch formed. From 15th May – 'Junglies' (Commando) squadrons of 707, 845 and 848 with Wessex 5s move to RNAS Yeovilton from HMS Seahawk, RNAS Culdrose. 1st August – Phantoms of 767 NAS disbanded. Phantom training undertaken by the Phantom Operational Conversion Unit at RAF Leuchars.
1975	Red Dragon embark on HMS Hermes with 845 NAS and 45 RM Commando to the western Atlantic, which included exercises in the Caribbean and New Brunswick, Canada. 10th–11th March – Operation Faldage. The helicopter cruiser HMS Blake steamed across the Gulf Siam to the coast of Cambodia at the port of

	Sihnoukville. Her task was rescue British nationals and Commonwealth personnel following the outbreak of civil war and reign of terror by the Khmer Rouge. HMS Blake's Sea Kings of 820 NAS were able assist in protecting the nationals, who were eventually taken out by RAF C130 Hercules. May – Brazex 75 HMS Ark Royal's group, following live firings on the US Atlantic Fleet weapons range, join up for a joint exercise with the Brazilian Navy.
1976	HMS Bulwark and 40 Commando RM deployed for exercise Rum Punch on the island of Vieques, Puerto Rico. They were followed by HMS Ark Royal and HMS Blake for a major NATO exercise Safe Passage taking part with the USS Nimitz, America and Franklin D. Roosevelt using the Rodman bombing ranges. Following her return home to the UK, HMS Bulwark was paid off and placed in the Reserve Squadron. September–October. Exercise Display Determination took place in the Mediterranean with HMS Ark Royal and HMS Tiger.
1977	3rd May – HMS Invincible launched.
1978	On the evening of 1st February 1978, at the height of a Force 10 storm, the oil-drilling rig Orion with a maintenance crew of thirty-three men on board broke away from its tow and began to drift towards Guernsey. It was being towed to Brazil on a barge, when it subsequently grounded on the rocks off the west coast of the island. 706 NAS personnel at RNAS Culdrose were called in and briefed with two Sea Kings being brought to an immediate readiness state. The first Sea King was launched at 2255 with the second shortly afterwards. 24 crew members were rescued by Sea Kings (2 had already been saved by lifeboat) from the rig. The remaining 7 were rescued early on the 3rd in perilous conditions. 13th November – first Sea Harrier decking landing on a carrier, with deck trials on HMS Hermes. 14th December HMS Illustrious launched. 27th November – Last catapult launch for the RN/FAA when a F4K Phantom was finally launched from HMS Ark Royal. December – 892 NAS decommissioned at RAF Leuchars. Last conventional fixed wing squadron in the FAA.
1979	Last 'Cats and Traps' conventional carrier, the Ark Royal, paid off at Plymouth. First operational Sea Harrier delivered to RNAS Yeovilton. August – Fastnet Race Disaster. Over 300 yachts took part in this 605 miles race from Cowes to the Fastnet Rock and then to Plymouth. Storm forces

	winds with devastating speeds of 60mph were unleashed on the yachtsmen, on the night of 11 August 1979, there unfolded the UK's largest peacetime rescue, which centred around RNAS Culdrose – HMS Seahawk. 303 yachts had set off and over the 11-12th August, some 75 boats capsized with five sinking. Tragically, 19 sailors died, which included four spectators, who were in a yacht following the race from a distance. A total of 140 people were rescued with the FAA helicopters directly rescuing 75 of those survivors. The remainder being picked up by RNLI lifeboats and shipping. Fifteen helicopters made up of Wessex's, Sea Kings and Lynxes flew over 200 hours on rescue sorties working out of RNAS Culdrose. On the 14th, HMS Broadsword, which was on sea-trials was tasked as the Scene of Search Coordinator in the area. Additional FAA aircrew with search and rescue experience were called in from both. RNAS Yeovilton and Prestwick.
1980	January – The formation of the RNR Air Branch was announced. The FAA had not had a reserve since the disbanding of the RNVR Air Divisions in 1957. The Air Branch was formed in April, but originally comprised only aircrew. In 1985, it was opened up to other officers and then ratings from all FAA trades. July – HMS Invincible, the first 'through deck cruiser' was commissioned.
1981	The Nott Defence White Paper, reinforced the doctrine of land based power. Subsequently, the amphibious assaults ships would be scrapped and a cut to the aircraft carrier force.
1982	April – Argentina invades the Falkland Islands. A task force was formed led by the carriers HMS Hermes as the flagship and Invincible under 'Operation Corporate'. Some 149 FAA aircraft and helicopters, from 14 Naval Air Squadrons were used. Sea Harriers amassed 1,435 sorties with 20 kills for the loss of six aircraft. Unfortunately, some 17 FAA personnel lost their lives in the conflict, which was fought nearly 8,000 miles away. At the end of the conflict until August, HMS Invincible provided air cover remained off the Falkland Islands until HMS Illustrious relieved her. This cover was as a precaution whilst the runway at Port Stanley was lengthened and strengthened FAA helicopters operated off two RFAs, namely Diligence and Reliant.
1983	February – 737 NAS Wessex HAS 3 disbanded at RNAS Portland – HMS Osprey. A task group led by HMS Invincible took part in exercise 'Caribbean 83' with Portuguese, US, Bahamas and Belize. RAF Harriers were also involved. September – Saw the task force 'Orient Express' led by HMS Invincible to visit the Far East. On route, the ship deployed off Lebanon during the civil war until she was relieved by HMS Illustrious and Hermes. The task force

	sailed through the Red Sea and visited India, which resulted in the Sea Harrier being purchased for their own carriers. On the return trip home, FAA helicopters of 820 NAS carried out a clandestine surveillance on a Soviet naval base in Egypt.
1984	February – 846 NAS with three Sea King HC4s embark on the RFA Reliant, evacuated over 5,000 civilians including British Nationals from Beirut in a four-week period during the civil war in Lebanon.
1985	October – The cruise ship Achille Lauro was seized by Palestinian terrorists. HMS Invincible deployed to eastern Mediterranean in readiness to for an assault by Royal Marines. Later, an Egyptian airline carrying terrorists was forced to land by embarked aircraft from the USS Saratoga.
1986	April – December. During the 'Global 86' deployment, HMS Illustrious led a task force on a global deployment, the first for 10 years. In eight months, the ship sailed some 42,000 miles and visited 21 countries taking part in several exercises on route. November – HMS Intrepid with 40 Commando RM joined the 'Global 86' task force for exercises with the Omani forces.
1987	HMS Ark Royal leads exercise 'Caribtan' for live firings and bombings with the US Navy. November – HMS Ark Royal, Illustrious and Intrepid conduct an amphibious exercise with 39 warships to test the lessons of the Falkland War.
1988	June – December. During the 'Outback 86' deployment, HMS Ark Royal exercise with the French, Italian and US Navies in the Mediterranean. She then travelled to the Far East exercising again with the US Navy off the Philippines carrying out visits to Hong Kong, Malaysia, Singapore and demonstrations for the Indonesian Navy. Visits to Australia and India followed.
1990	March – Annual NATO amphibious exercise off Norway consisted of HMS Invincible and Intrepid with landing craft Sir Bedivere, Percivale and Tristram. 42 and 45 Commando RM took part. Post of Flag Officer Naval Aviation (FONA) formed. Iraq forces invade Kuwait. Embarked FAA Lynxes utilising Sea Skua missiles sink and destroy vessels of the Iraqi Navy.
1991	January – The Navy Board agreed to the employment of WRNS as aircrew.
1993	January – British carrier group deployed to the Adriatic under NATO command to support British land forces in Yugoslavia. The RN was to be present in the area for nearly ten years.

1995	December – British carrier group deployed to the Adriatic under NATO command to support for operations against the Bosnian Serbs and take part in Operation Deny Flight. Operations reverts to UK Command in February 1996.
1997	HMS Invincible deployed to the Mediterranean in support of diplomatic efforts following Iraq's refusal to allow access to suspicious sites. Invincible enters the Adriatic twice between December 1997 and January 1998 for sorties under Operation Deliberate over former Yugoslavia to support NATO ground forces. Sea Kings from 814 and 849 NAS and Sea Harriers from 800 NAS were on board.
1998	February – 810 NAS, embarked in RFA ARGUS for operational training, rescued eleven survivors from MV Delfin del Mediterranean 248 miles off Cape St Vincent, Portugal. February – HMS Ocean – purpose built helicopter carrier named by HM Queen at Barrow-in-Furness. She was to be commissioned in September.
1999	30th January 1999 Operation BOLTON II: Carrier Task Group (HMS Invincible, 800 and 814 NAS and 849A Flight) deployed into the Gulf for Maritime interdiction operations and air surveillance operations over the Iraqi 'no-fly' zone. March – FAA squadrons 800, 814 and 849 embarked on HMS Invincible used to support NATO operations against Serbian ethnic cleansing in Kosovo. In November, Sea Kings from HMS Ocean provide humanitarian relief around Duzce in Turkey following a major earthquake.
2000	Flag Officer Maritime Command (FOMC) formed with Air Officer Commanding 3 Group RAF at High Wycombe. Joint Harrier Force formed with Sea Harriers and RAF Harriers. May – HMS Illustrious, escorts and RFA deployed to Sierra Leone supporting HMS Ocean on NATO duties for Operation Palliser giving aid to the government against rebel forces. 42 Commando landed by Sea Kings HC4s on beaches in the same operations.
2001	January – After eight years continuous support of UN and NATO operations in former Yugoslavia, two Sea Kings HC 4s of 845 NAS return home to RNAS Yeovilton. After flying a total of 13,500 hours, 845 carried out 620 emergency evacuations, often under hostile fire.
2003	In March, Britain joins with the US in what became known as Operation Telic for the invasion of Iraq. It was the largest amphibious landings by British Forces for nearly fifty years (Suez). The Battle of Al Faw was one of the first battles of the Iraq War; it took place March 20–24, 2003.

	HMS Ark Royal and Ocean were involved utilising some seven FAA squadrons i.e. 814, 815, 820, 845, 847 and 849.
2006	With both the Royal Marines and 800 NAS with Harrier Gr7s, the total number of RN personnel in Afghanistan totalled over 3,000. This included logistics, medical support, language, intelligence and engineers amounted to more than half of the total British forces in Afghanistan. Aquila 06 Task Group with HMS Illustrious carrying 800 NAS Harrier GR7s, 814 with Merlins 'A' Flight 849 NAS deploy to the Indian Ocean and Arabian Sea. July – Operation Highbrow-Naval Task Force with RFAs led by HMS Illustrious and Bulwark evacuate over 4,400 foreign nationals from Lebanon. FAA Sea Kings from 846, 848 and 849 NAS took part.
2007	The FAA consisted of Harrier GR7s and GR9s subsumed in to the Naval Strike Wing of the Joint Harrier Force. Operation Herrick V – GR7 Harriers of 800 NAS support 3 Commando Brigade against Taliban in Helmand River valley. Becky Frater, who has served in both the Fleet Air Arm and Army Air Corps, obtained her naval wings in 2007. She was the first female to lead the 'Black Cat's' helicopter display team, the first female Qualified Helicopter Instructor (QHI) and the first woman to command a Naval Air Squadron (she also played hockey at International level). March–July Caribbean deployment of HMS Ocean with Sea King Mk 7s of 845NAS and Merlins MH1 of 700M (the Operational Unit for the Merlin). Autumn – build-up of RN personnel in Afghanistan under Operation Herrick VII involved 40 RM Commando, Harrier GR7s and 9s of the Naval Strike Wing and Sea King HC4s of 846 NAS were involved. End of November, the Sea Kings 845 NAS, the longest serving helicopter squadron on Operation Telic returned to the UK after serving there for three and a half years.
2008	Task Group 08 with HMS Illustrious deployed in January to the Middle East with Merlin helicopters from 814 and 849 NAS embarked. 3rd July, the Defence Minister Baroness Taylor signs contract for the two new 64,000-ton aircraft carriers the Queen Elizabeth II and the Prince of Wales. July – Decision made to purchase the first batch of 48 F35Bs. 1st October – Naval Strike Wing (NSW) with Harriers GR9s deployed Afghanistan. Joint Force Harrier operations ended there in June 2009.
2010	October – Strategic Defence Review and Security Review. Harrier Force to be scrapped. HMS Ark Royal to be decommissioned. One of the Queen

	Elizabeth class carriers would have catapults and arrestor wires to enable the F-35C carrier variant to be operated. 24th November – Naval Strike Wing reverts to 800 NAS flying the Harrier GR9 and 9A versions. Last Harrier GR9 flight from a RN aircraft carrier.
2011	11th March – HMS Ark Royal decommissioned.
2012	February – First deck landing trials of the Wildcat helicopter. 19th July – first F35B delivered for trials work in the US. RN provides Command and Control facilities during London 2012 Olympics based on HMS Ocean located on the Thames. HMS Bulwark is stationed off Weymouth. 815 Sea NAS Kings ASaC, 815 NAS Mk 8 Lynx and 814 NAS Merlin Mk1 helicopters were embarked.
2013	10th April – First FAA pilot flies F-35B. Lt Cdr Tidball RN flew a sortie at Elgin Air Force Base. 23rd July – First Merlin Mk 2 handover to 824 NAS. The FAA will eventually be equipped with some 30 Mk 2s.
2014	Queen Elizabeth aircraft carrier launched on 17th July. She was commissioned just over two years later on 7th December 2017. 1st August – 702 and 700W merge to become 725 NAS operating the Lynx Wildcat HMS Mk 2 helicopter. 30th September – formal handover of the Merlin Mk 3 helicopters from the RAF took place at RAF Benson. RN accepts the Merlin and 846 NAS stands up and will move to RNAS Yeovilton in the Spring of 2015.
2017	Prince of Wales aircraft carrier launched on 21st December. She was commissioned some two years later on 10th December 2019.
2019	F35B first operational missions made over Syria and Iraq in support of Operation Shader.
2021	Spring – Task Force led by the carrier HMS Queen Elizabeth leads deployment to the Far East. On board are x8 UK and x10 USMC F35Bs along with x14 helicopters. 30th November F35Bs operating off HMS Queen Elizabeth in the Mediterranean is lost. Pilot safe. 9th December QE returns to Portsmouth from Indo-Pacific tour.

Chapter 19
Summary

Hopefully, some rarely known facts about the Fleet Air Arm have been highlighted in this book. There are many more, but to recap, here are a few of them:

- The Royal Naval Air Service (RNAS) produced many air aces during World War 1 from 1914 – 1918. Pilots such as Raymond Collishaw (60 kills), Robert A Little (47 kills) and Roderick Stanley Dallas (39 kills) were rated amongst the most successful fighter pilots in the British Commonwealth.
- The RNAS and FAA have been in existence longer that the RAF.
- Admiral Beatty devised a plan in 1918 with the intention of using naval torpedo bombers to attack the German High Seas Fleet in Wilhemshaven harbour using one of the first aircraft carriers, HMS Argus. It was rejected by the Admiralty Board. The basic idea was sound as it was used successfully on the raid at Taranto some 22 years later in 1940 made by the FAA. The concept of utilising naval air power was to be copied by the Japanese at Pearl Harbour in 1941.
- Over 50 FAA pilots and two Naval Air Squadrons served directly in the Battle of Britain.
- The FAA was able to cripple the Italian Fleet at Taranto in 1940. This attack becoming the first template and pivotal example of how British naval airpower spelt the beginning of the end of the battleship era.
- On 15 August 1945, a FAA pilot flying a Seafire was the last serviceman to be killed in WWII. He was executed even though Japan had surrendered.

- The Royal Navy's Pacific Fleet in early 1945 assembled the Royal Navy's largest fleet, since the time of Nelson in 1805 and was able to protect the US Navy's carrier fleets' flanks off Okinawa against some of the numerous Japanese Kamikazi attacks. Britain's aircraft carriers with their armoured flight decks were to figure prominently with their greater survivability compared to the wooden decks of the US carriers. Most of the battle damaged US carriers had to return to America for lengthy repairs. Britain's carriers were back in action within a few hours.
- The FAA actually flew Lancasters during the post-war period albeit in an engine test-bed environment.
- Throughout the Korean War in 1950–53, the FAA of the Royal Navy was Britain's sole contributor and provider of tactical airpower throughout the whole of the conflict. The Royal Navy kept an aircraft carrier on station off the Korean peninsula continuously for three years.
- During the devastating North Sea floods of 1953, over 800 people were rescued by FAA helicopters. The Navy's Search and Rescue units were duly formed at this time.
- The FAA introduced the concept of landing marines/troops from the sea by 'Commando Carriers' using helicopters for the first time during the Suez crisis of 1956. It was also able to provide direct air cover from its strike carriers during these landings. The concept was to be further developed and refined during the following decades. This modus operandi by helicopter was also to be replicated by the US Marines in their Marine Expeditionary forces.
- During the post WWII period particularly in the 1960s and despite the new carrier cancellations, it was able to support Britain's policy of withdrawing from the Middle and Far East. FAA fixed wing and helicopters squadrons based on aircraft carriers provided the necessary air cover protection when these overseas bases were finally closed.
- The use of helicopters in jungle warfare was further refined by Naval Air Squadrons in the Indonesia/Malaysian emergency and the Borneo confrontation from 1963–66.
- The operational experiences and expertise of FAA Pilots and Observers flying Sea Vixens were instrumental in the revision of the McDonnell Douglas Phantom tactical manual. The experiences learnt from flying the dual seated Sea Vixen coupled with the air warfare instructing

techniques used by 764 NAS. Many were adopted by the US Navy and to some extent utilised in the formation of the Top Gun School based at the Naval Air Station Miramar, California in 1969.

- The FAA with the Royal Navy was heavily involved in the trials, testing and implementation of four major British inventions. These were to result in quantum leaps in safety and operational improvements on aircraft carriers i.e. steam catapults, angled flight deck, and mirror deck landing system and the concept and use of a ski-jump ramp on an aircraft carrier.
- It is widely accepted that without the embarked Sea Harriers squadrons and operated by the FAA, Britain would never have had the ability to gain air superiority during the Falkland Islands conflict in 1982. Once this was achieved, British Forces had the advantage of being able to retake the Falkland Islands in 1982.
- The FAA has been the UK's only service to have shot down aircraft in air-to-air combats since World War II.
- The FAA pioneered the use and development of helicopters in anti-submarine, anti-ship roles and airborne early warning roles. Coupled with a multitude of other roles, the embarked flight has all but become the most flexible main offensive/defensive weapons system available to a destroyer/frigate ship's captain.
- FAA Lynx helicopters during the first Gulf War of 1991 single handily destroyed the Iraqi Navy with their Sea Skua missiles.

Throughout its relative short history, the RAF has rightly or wrongly dominated military thinking with respect to aviation in the UK. As well as the FAA, this dominance has also extended to the Army Air Corps, whose heavy lift assets i.e. the Chinooks along with the Puma are owned and controlled by the junior service. The British Army finds itself in a most unusual state of affairs, as no other army air force in the world replicates this setup.

It looks as if this anomaly will continue as the current replacement for the UK's new medium lift replacement helicopter will again be in RAF hands. Most of the previous chapters are self-explanatory and contain many examples of this apparent dominance over the Fleet Air Arm. There are absolutely no issues with the pilots, aircrew, maintainers and their support teams of the RAF. They are highly trained and motivated.

The issues lie with the higher echelons of the RAF with their thinking and influence over many decades on Britain's Government defence policies with regard to the use of the UK's airpower. This air force thinking has also swayed many generations of defence ministers and politicians whatever their political colour. This attitude is still being reflected in their current use of terminology being reflected in several recent policy papers, when the RAF hierarchy have referred, rather dismissively, to the new QE type aircraft carriers as 'alternative airfields'.

The backbone of Naval Aviation was broken in 1918, when the RAF was formed. This shift of emphasis was to have far reaching consequences and caused the Royal Naval Air Service to virtually disappear by the transfer (consisting of over 30,000 personnel, squadrons and many hundreds of aircraft) to this new force. Thereafter, naval aviation was to wander in the wilderness for nearly 20 years until 1937, when under the Inskip Report, the Navy got back control of its own organic air force with the eventual title of 'Fleet Air Aim' being fully restored in 1946.

However, the damage had been done to the Royal Naval Air Service and it would take decades to recover. Through no fault of its own, the FAA was ill-equipped at the beginning of WWII, not only in aircraft types but also by the lack of naval aviation expertise in positions of command and influence within the Admiralty.

Whilst in the wilderness years from 1918 until 1937 and continuing through the early years of WWII, this transfer caused it to lose overnight most of its senior experienced pilots to this new fledgling land based air force. Amongst this group that had been transferred, there were several Naval air 'Aces' resulting from actions seen in WWI. These pilots along with many officers, who would have been marked out as future commanding officers of Naval Air Squadrons and even captains of aircraft carriers, (and by default future naval air minded Admirals), were simply lost.

Similarly, the natural progression and experience of having naval aviation expertise earmarked for the Admiralty Board dried up. Except for one or two Admirals, this caused the Admiralty Board to have a real lack of knowledge of naval aviation operations and its impact. This lack of experience and leadership at the high levels of command was to dog the FAA right up until WWII and possibly beyond. No wonder Britain fell so far behind the US in the 1930s after having paved the way in the early years on the practicalities of how to utilise aircraft at sea.

Throughout the early part of the 20th century, the Admiralty were somewhat slow to recognise that naval aircraft were becoming the main weapons system for attack and defence of the fleet. The Lords of the Admiralty watched blindsided by the unfolding use of naval airpower gaining prominence over the battleship's big guns. The size of any ship's armament still prevailed. The burgeoning use of Naval airpower was to manifest itself in virtually crippling part of the Italian feet at Taranto in 1940. From that moment, the Italian Fleet was a spent force nor was it a real threat again in the Mediterranean.

History shows that this attack by the FAA was unfortunately observed and copied by the Japanese Navy. There followed further examples of the aircraft carrier becoming the new capital ship of the world's navies, by the sinking and loss by the Japanese of both the battleship HMS Prince of Wales and the battle cruiser HMS Repulse by air attacks in December 1941. These two battlewagons were transiting to the Far East without any organic air cover.

The Japanese had cleverly observed and learnt from the Italian Taranto raid and realised the importance of the utilisation of embarked naval airpower. What they observed was put into practice by the devastating attack at Pearl Harbour just one year later in 1942. The shock of Pearl Harbour subsequently led to the clawing back of Japanese-held territory by US naval airpower from numerous carrier fleets across the Pacific in the following years.

Since the Second World War, RAF policies have to some extent relied on some of the exploits created by the 'Battle of Britain' and 'Dambuster' operations. These were unquestionable successes and to a large extent since the 1950s, the RAF based their continued existence as an air force on those two operations. The V-bomber force was to be Britain's nuclear deterrent for over two decades.

Coming up to the present date, it is interesting to observe that following the Iraq and Afghanistan conflicts and the questioning of its existence, the RAF started paying attention to the emerging 'Strike Carrier' concept. This interest was aided and abetted by budget restraints and loss of numerous squadrons, which led the total number of their aircraft held on their books to rapidly diminish.

Following the bitter inter-service rivalry of the 1960s when the RAF's island hopping strategy won the day, which was to result in the cancellation of the building of two new large aircraft carriers. It is ironical to see such keenness and support for the Queen Elizabeth class of aircraft carriers following the shenanigans some 40 years earlier.

This enthusiasm is such, that the first squadron to embark on HMS Queen Elizabeth operationally, is going to be 617 Squadron the Dambusters and not by a FAA squadron as tradition normally dictates. The UK is the only country that has allowed a land based air force with no previous sea going operational history, on to its new aircraft carriers to act as the RN's principal embarked strike and fleet defence capability.

Another point to note with regard to 617 Squadron RAF flying the F35B, the question of who has operational control of the aircraft whilst embarked? Is it the Royal Navy or the RAF? This aspect will be followed with much interest. Also, with such mixed personnel from both the FAA and RAF, there are the questions of harmony and separation rules regarding families.

The two services have historically had totally different family separation rules and conditions of service. It is assumed that they will duly become aligned and harmonised, so as to avoid disruption to fleet deployments of the Queen Elizabeth class of carrier.

Perhaps the contents of this book may have enlightened some readers, that although the FAA is relatively small, it has a long history and tradition of being a cost effective 'can do' air force. It has always carried out its duties for the country with the minimum of fuss and publicity. It simply gets the job done as directed by its political masters.

There are many examples of this flexibility of the FAA's operations ranging from the Battle of Taranto, Korea, Suez and the Falklands. Without the FAA's fighter/strike version of the Harrier, the islands of the latter would never have been retaken. This flexibility is demonstrated further in the rotary wing side, as the FAA pioneered the use of helicopters at sea resulting in the development of the Commando Carrier concept after its initial use at Suez.

Its use of helicopters, has resulted in spectacular rescues in parallel with the clever tactical use of them for special-forces insertions and recoveries. It is interesting to note that the carrier QE carrier is referred to with a lot of emphasis on the resurrected term, 'Carrier Strike'. Until the advent of the 'Commando

Carrier', all the aircraft carriers throughout the 1950s, 1960s and into the 1970s were by default, all strike carriers.

The RAF unquestionably, has been able to mobilise a slicker public relations organisation throughout its existence and therefore enabled it to be more astute in dealing with politicians, the MOD, the public and of course the Treasury. This has led them having greater influence in shaping their own future and maintaining a generally larger share of the Defence Vote.

However, in fairness perhaps one should consider whether the Admiralty lacked the guile, or resources in the past to get the Fleet Air Arm's message across? One major factor that has to be built into this equation is the disadvantages the FAA has had to face over its lifetime. It is after all, only but one branch of the Royal Navy.

One of these other branches is, of course, the submarine service, where the Polaris and Trident has concentrated a lot of Naval minds and energy for many years. The 'Silent Service' i.e. submarines have absorbed a large chunk of the Naval Vote in order to maintain Britain's nuclear deterrent. Once the large aircraft carriers were scrapped in the late 1960s, the Naval Staff were resolute in obtaining the nation's nuclear deterrent via Polaris and then operating and keeping one nuclear submarine at sea 365 days of the year.

Therefore, the Navy Admiral's minds were fixated on ensuring they got the share of this part of the Navy's budget for the submarines, while the FAA had to struggle to make its case. There have been several occasions in the last twenty years where the political wind has changed because of costs and the influence of the nuclear disarmament lobby.

As a result of this pressure, a cheaper alternative nuclear deterrent was seriously considered whereby it was muted that it could be achieved via standoff weapons, i.e. the use of RAF aircraft launching second-generation cruise missiles. These potential changes of policy made the Admiralty fight even harder to keep the nuclear deterrent, so the FAA's requirements were pushed even further down the agenda.

For the last 60 years, both the RAF and FAA have had virtually the same specifications requirements, so why develop two completely different aircraft for each air arm over the years? A definite weakness in the UK's aircraft procurement procedures, has been the lack of cohesion between the services. One early post war example being the Sea Vixen/Javelin purchase and to some degree the same could be applied to the FAA's Buccaneer.

The latter was initially rejected by the RAF but ended up in their inventory and paradoxically became a well thought of and capable aircraft. The US seems to have avoided this pitfall with the advent of their McDonnell-Douglas Phantom II and LTC A-7 Corsair. The former was built for the USAF, Navy and the Marines, whilst the latter was procured for the US Navy and Marines.

Meanwhile here in the UK, there was also muddled thinking and political interference of the Phantom purchase of the 1960s. According to the McDonnell representative based at Yeovilton in 1969, under the same purchase contract, Britain could have bought with very little modifications some 300 Phantoms for the same price. Throughout this period, the FAA was anticipating that some 120 Navalised Phantoms would be procured for the FAA.

Following all the shenanigans of this procurement, it should be noted that George Brown, the then Labour Deputy Prime Minister, was also the MP for Derby where Rolls Royce (RR) was based. Lo and behold for political reasons, the American Phantom was re-designed with RR engines, leading to vastly reduced aircraft numbers and a lesser performing aircraft.

It should be stated here that the then Labour Government was reluctant to purchase equipment from the US, so 'offsets' on British built elements was to be expected. Eventually, only 50 F4Ks were built with some 29 eventually earmarked for Naval squadrons i.e. 892 and 767 NAS. Because of the low numbers for the RN's version, it was to be the priciest Phantom version to be built.

Obtaining employment for RR's workers was to be applauded but it did come at a cost resulting in an engine, which did not quite live up to expectations. It was also ironical that for the defence of the Falkland Islands after the war in 1982, the RAF then purchased a further 15 Phantom F-4Js models with the J79 engines and spares, all based on the original US version back in the mid-1960s!

Why this was approved with so many surplus Phantoms and spares available at the time was difficult to comprehend. The French have learnt from this previous lack of 'joined up' thinking and went ahead in producing the Dassault Rafale for both their Navy and Air Force. This French aircraft built for two services has led to many overseas exports and therefore, saved separate development costs for the French government.

On the new carrier front, it was with the insistence and backing of then Prime Minster Gordon Brown, the go-ahead was given for the construction of two new large aircraft carriers. This was to ensure employment at Rosyth dockyard that was within his Scottish Constituency. However, with the RAF under pressure for a reduction in aircraft numbers and questions over its existence, it became very 'Navy' minded.

Perhaps, this was due to the fact that a completely new aircraft type (a 5th generation stealth fighter) would be embarking on these new ships. Following the initial purchase of 48 F35Bs because of the ski-jump fit, there are predictably whisperings that the remaining 100 F35s of the UK's order might be the land based A version. As of the winter of 2022, this decision is in abeyance. (Dependent upon the cost of the next RAF aircraft project the Tempest perhaps?).

With the introduction of F35B, there are sceptics, who think that history will be or is being repeated following what occurred during the 1930s e.g. where during this period there were clashes between the FAA and RAF on who had strategic/tactical command over the aircraft? Likewise with the Harrier Force of the 2000s, who owned what, probably led to the inefficient use of the Sea Harrier and its early removal from service use.

Coming up to date, F35B RAF squadrons will be managed by RAF Commanding Officers when ashore at RAF Marham getting their orders from Strike Command at High Wycombe. However, who will have command and control when operating aboard one of the two QE II class aircraft carriers and who will have ownership and tasking control over frontline operations at sea? It should not be forgotten that the QE class aircraft carriers themselves would be under the command of a RN Captain (or Commodore), responsible directly to the Admiralty and MOD (Navy).

What can be learnt? All the chapters and topics covered earlier have as always, been dependent upon costs and budgets. If we include the fact that since WWII, Britain has been a declining power and if ministers and politicians had acknowledged this, the UK could have saved millions if not billions since 1945 by integrating the designs of many of its aircraft.

The same goes for operations, has Britain used its air force in the most effective way i.e. getting the most 'bang for your buck'? Based on some of the historical contents in this book, it must be asked, to what level is the RN and its the Naval Air Staff involved with the new Tempest project – a 6th generation aircraft with potential wingman drones?

More importantly, when these second and third generation drones become more widely introduced and utilised, the QE class carriers are going to be excellent mobile platforms for such weapons. Perhaps, the Navy should skip this

6th generation manned aircraft and concentrate wholly on reconnaissance, surface/sub-surface attack drones, including Airborne Early Warning ones?

The future must surely lie in the integration and utilisation of airpower across all three of the UK's armed services. Additionally, the cost effectiveness of every equipment purchase and operation should be carefully monitored and justified by an independent body even enshrined by an Act of Parliament perhaps? We as a nation cannot continually avoid such unchallenged expenditure.

The FAA has an underlying 'can do' attitude and perhaps the RAF could absorb some of the 'dark blue uniform' virtues on how to operate aircraft from the sea. This not only includes such areas as flying operations but behind the scene activities like the amalgamation of maintenance and servicing procedures, along with the better budget control of aircraft modification and upgrade programs.

Historically, the FAA has operated a far more effective aircraft servicing procedures along with a much disciplined management system of aircraft servicing/modifications. Both these could offer large savings but also enable a greater number of aircraft to be available for operations. Equally, there are things, which the FAA could learn from the RAF.

Another matter, which needs studying, is the realigning of the trade structure of the RAF in order to reduce manpower to cost-effective levels. At the moment, the RAF has only been exposed to the trade structure of the FAA's fixed wing engineering element for its crewing of F35B squadrons. It therefore would be interesting to see how the junior service would cope with the manning levels based on those of a small ship's flight.

These flights are made up of a single FAA helicopter like the Merlin or the Wildcat embarked on frigates of destroyers. They also operate from Royal Fleet Auxiliaries and consist a maintenance crew of around seven and operate autonomously for long periods on their own.

Further integration could be made of the aircrew side, ranging from training to flying operations. Perhaps one of the most important factors would be the Defence Minister imposing on the RAF, a clear career and promotional path to those, who choose to stay, fly and operate with the Navy's FAA.

Previously, any connection with the Navy has not been seen as a conduit to a two star rank i.e. Air Vice-Marshall. A balanced consensus must be reached whereby the virtues of land-based airpower are merged with the flexible virtues of carrier-based air power, which is the tip of the UK's out of area defence and its offensive spear.

Throughout its life, the Fleet Air Arm has been treated a bit like a Cinderella brought about by three distinct periods resulting in a major curtailing of its effectiveness, based on some of the following:

1. From 1918 onwards, the formation of the Royal Air Force denuded the Royal Naval Air Service of both men and materials. This was to set back British naval aviation development of the Fleet Air Arm by some 20 years or more. Those policies instigated in the Trenchard era and still linger to this day.
2. The 1966 Defence Review where the RAF persuaded politicians, defence experts and the Treasury, that they could provide air cover anywhere in the world. This was under their policy strategy of 'island hopping'. An allegedly false map was presented for that review, whereby the Australia continent and adjacent countries were 400 miles nearer the Asian mainland. The problems of over-flight permissions, local political approvals and the sheer logistical support required, were brushed aside. There was also the fact that at the time, the RAF did not have the aircraft to implement their 'island policy'. Because of this very clever and shrewd lobbying, the two carriers CVA01 and CVA02 were cancelled, which in effect meant the ending of the FAA's strike capability when the likes of the Phantom and Buccaneer were retired. Crucially, it also resulted in the loss of the RN's fixed wing Airborne Electronic Warfare in the shape of the Gannet, which was to be sorely missed during the Falklands war. The FAA was able to survive as a maritime force with the advent of the 'Through Deck Carriers' via the Invincible class of mini-carriers, albeit in much reduced circumstances. However, fortuitously another 'all British built' aircraft appeared on the scene at the right time and place in the shape of the Sea Harrier. Flown by superb and highly trained pilots, the FAA with its carrier borne aircraft was once again to become a saviour during Operation Corporate (Falklands War 1982). Without the Sea Harrier, the Falklands would have been occupied by the Argentineans for a long period.
3. In the 2000 decade, post – Afghanistan and Iraq, the RAF unfortunately found itself somewhat exposed and questions asked about its very

existence. The RAF Staff after decades of denial on the advantages of aircraft carriers and their uses suddenly became advocates. This conversion was so strong that they were able manoeuvre themselves into a position where they had a major influence on what type of carrier the UK was going to get and what version of the new 5th generation aircraft i.e. the F35 that was going to be procured.

Finally, a radical rethink is required. Faced with an ever-reducing defence budget, now further stretched by the financial repercussions of COVID, the UK should pursue an utterly ruthless policy of value for money. The following are some possible solutions:

- There is an urgent need for a fully independent Value for Money (VFM) task force to assess, evaluate, monitor and audit ongoing military operations. Whilst there are checks on VFM for MOD equipment contracts covered by the National Audit Office, there appears to be no organisation dealing with the VFM covering actual operations. For example, was the bombing of the main airfield during the Falklands war in 1982 by the Vulcan using thousands of gallons of fuel and the entire refuelling capacity of the RAF, only one bomb was dropped on the runway. Was this a cost effective operation for so little return? The Vulcan's cost was over £4.6M per single operation, whilst the Sea Harrier's cost was £400[1] per operation. The same 'value for money' question could be asked of the recent Poseidon aircraft purchase. Could not this UK based maritime capability have been fulfilled by a far cheaper airframe? Lastly, is the use of the expensive Typhoons and now the F35Bs in Operation Shader, really required in the suppression of the relatively low tech armed ISIS/Daesh threat? The RAF bases in Cyprus, backed up by an even larger air base at RAF Brize Norton, are very expensive pieces of real estate to maintain.
- The Navy i.e. the Fleet Air Arm given the responsibility for all the global strike requirements for the UK. For the future, the QE carriers will also provide an excellent mobile platform for strike drones as this form of warfare matures over the next 40 years. The FAA needs to optimise and make full use of the two new aircraft carriers HMS Queen Elizabeth and Prince of Wales. Evidence since 2020, despite technical issues to both

ships especially the latter, shows gross underutilisation of these capital ships.
- All future UK's defence policies and requirements regarding the deployment of airpower should be integrated irrespective of the service branch that operates them. In particular, the FAA should be closely involved and play a major part in the development of the Tempest project and drones operating from aircraft carriers. The Navy's platforms are going to be most flexible and sovereign based assets in which to utilise drones around the globe.
- Air defence of the UK to remain the responsibility of the RAF. It has historical experience in that role.
- The RAF to form a new command organisation along lines similar to the Unites States Air Mobility Command. Under this command, its core operations would be centred on airlift capabilities and logistics of both troops/materials, air-to-air flight refuelling and air medical evacuation.
- The Navy to form a new command to be entitled Maritime Command with the integration all of the UK's anti-submarine assets i.e. surface ships, hunter killer submarine, helicopters, satellites, drones and the newly acquired Poseidon aircraft. This new command to be under control of the Royal Navy of at least a two-star rank level.

To conclude, it would be worthy to note two extracts from a regular defence commentator and journalist, Gabriele Molinelli. He wrote an in-depth and thought provoking article entitled 'Fleet Air Arm, RAF the past and future' dated 25 April 2011[2].

Quote 1 – "The FAA is a service that, by its nature, is at war every day, even in peace time."
Quote 2 – "The Fleet Air Arm is required to do a lot with few personnel and few airframes."

Sources

[1] *Ward 'Sharkey' – Annex H of 'Her Majesty's TOP GUN' – Mill City Press, 2020*

[2] *By permission of Gabriele Molinelli, 2021*

https://firstworldwar.com/airwar/navalwarfare.htm-Beatty

Wilson, Ben – 'Empire of the Deep' – Weidenfield and Nicolson-2014

Bibliography

Adlam, Henry 'Hank',	The Disastrous Fall and Triumph of the Fleet Air Arm 1912 to 1945	Pen & Sword, Barnsley, 2014
Allison, George	Myths surroundings the Queen Elizabeth class aircraft carriers	UK Defence Journal (UKDJ), 19th July 2020
Benbow, Tim	British Naval Aviation, the first 100 years	Routledge, Abingdon, paperback 2016
Bond, Steve	The Fleet Air Arm Boy's Volume 1	Grub Street, London 2020
Brown Eric, 'Winkle'	Wings on my sleeve	Revised edition Weidenfeld & Nicolson, 2006
Defence Committee	F-35 and carrier strikes -HC 775	House of Commons, 13th November 2020
HM Government	Defence Review- Statement of Estimates Feb 1966	MOD
House of Commons Public Accounts Committee	Delivering Carrier Strike – 23rd Report of Session 2019–21	House of Commons, 13th November 2020
Insinna, Valerie	Pentagon cuts the number of flaws in half	Defence News, 16th June 2021
Insinna, Valerie	Number of major F35 flaws is shrinking	Defence News, 16th June 2021

Author	Title	Publisher
Insinna, Valerie	The Pentagon will have to live with limits on F-35's supersonic flights	Defence News, 24th April 2020
MOD (UK)	Carrier Strike: the 2012 reversion decision	HM Stationary Office, May 2013
Newdick, Thomas	Storm clouds gather over F-35B as UK prepares Defence Review	The War Zone, the Drive, September 2020
Parliamentary Debate	Carrier Strikes Strategy and its contribution to UK's Defence	House of Commons library, 25th February 2019
Peterson, JE	Defending Arabia Chapter 3- post war policy	St-Martins press, 1986
Roberts, John	The story of the modern Royal Navy	Seaforth Publishing 2009
Rogoway, Tyler	F35B Pilots will make rolling landings on RN Carriers	The War Zone, The Drive, August 2017
Sands, E Duncan	Minster of Defence – Defence outline of future policy	HM Stationary Office, 1957
Secretary of State of Defence	Defence in a competitive age	HM Stationary Office, March 2021
Shaw, Jason	RAF wasting money on already outdated F35 aircraft	Air101, 19th July 2020
Sturvant, Ray & Theo Balance	The squadrons of the Fleet Air Arm	Air Briton (Historians) Ltd, Tonbridge
Trenchard, HM	Secretary of State for Air, Permanent Organisation on the RAF	HM stationary Office, 1919
Various Authors	The Falklands War – the day-by-day record	Marshal Cavendish Ltd, London 1983

	from invasion to victory	
Ward, 'Sharkey'	Her Majesty's TOP GUN and decline of the Royal Navy	Mill City Press Inc Maitland, Florida, 2020
Woodward, Sir John GBE, KCB	Defence, written evidence to Common Select Committee	Publications, Parliament, March 2013
Wragg, David	The century of British Naval Aviation 1909-2009	Pen & sword, Barnsley, 2009

Glossary

AA	Anti-aircraft
AEO	Air Engineering Officer
AEW	Airborne Early Warning
AFB	Air Force Base-US
Airey Fairey	Colloquial (some say derogatory) name given by the General Service Navy for Fleet Air Arm personnel. It is thought to have originated around WWII, when the majority of aircraft were manufactured by Fairey Aviation i.e. Swordfish.
AMMARG	Aerospace Maintenance and Regeneration Group
AMRAAM	Advance Medium Range Air-to-Air Missile
AS	Anti-submarine
AWACS	Airborne Early Warning and Control System
BPF	British Pacific Fleet
BRNC	Britannia Royal Naval College – located at Dartmouth, Devon
CAP	Combat Air Patrol
CATOBAR	Catapult Assisted Take-Off But Arrested Recovery
Chief 'Tiff'	Chief Artificer
CO	Commanding Officer
Crabs	Original nickname for a member of the Royal Air Force. The name was attributed to the colour of the uniform, which was worn on the RAF's formation on 1st April 1916. The light blue uniform came about by the cancellation of a huge order, but abandoned, to the Russian Tsar's Imperial Guard. This light blue colour was also identical to the greasy mercury oxide jelly used

	in the early 20th century for the treatment of body lice – 'crabs'.
CTOL	Conventional Take-offs and Landings
CVA	Attack Aircraft Carrier
Daily Orders	These are published daily by command of a ship, establishment or squadron. It details the daily routines and other matters that personnel should be made aware of.
DSC	Distinguished Service Cross
DSM	Distinguished Service Medal
DSO	Distinguished Service Order
FAA	Fleet Air Arm – the Royal Navy's air force
FAW	Fighter All Weather
FG	Fighter, Ground Attack
FGR	Fighter, Ground Attack and Reconnaissance
FOMC	Flag Officer Maritime Command
FONA	Flag Officer Naval Aviation
FONAC	Flag Officer Naval Air Command – former headquarters of the FAA
FR	Fighter, Reconnaissance
GA	Ground Attack
HAS	Helicopter Anti-Submarine
HLAI	High Level Aircraft Intercept
HMAS	Her (or his) Majesty's Australian Ship
HMS	Her (or His) Majesty's Ship, Her (or His) Majesty's Service.
HU	Helicopter Utility
Humphrey	The nickname given to the Wessex 3 Helicopter Flight of HMS Antrim
IFTU	Intensive Flying Trials Unit
IMF	International Monetary Fund
JHF	Joint Harrier Force
Junglies	Affectionate name given to all the FAA helicopter squadrons which operated in the 'Commando' role during the Borneo; the nickname bestowed by the

	troops, who were supported during the Jungle campaign of Malaysia and Borneo in the 1960s.
EOKA	Ethniki Organosis Kypiron Agoniston (National Organisation of Cypriot Fighters. A Greek Cypriot nationalist guerrilla organisation that fought a campaign for the end of British rule in Cyprus from April 1955.
Junior Service	By default, the Royal Air Force (RAF) is historically the youngest of the three UK Armed Forces. Likewise, the Royal Navy is (RN) known as the 'Senior Service'.
JSF	Joint Strike Fighter
LTC	Ling-Temco-Vought-the Corsair II manufacturer consortium
LLAI	Low Level Aircraft Intercept
MAC	Merchant Aircraft Carriers
Meatball	Is the 'ball' on the optical landing system giving glide-path information to pilots during an aircraft carrier landing.
MiG	A member of the family of Soviet military fighter aircraft produced by the design bureau founded in 1939 by Artem Mikoyan (M) and Mikhail Gurevich (G)
MOD	Ministry of Defence
NAS	Naval Air Squadron
NATO	North Atlantic Treaty Organisation
NBCD	Nuclear Biological and Chemical Defence
NSW	Naval Strike Wing
OOW	Officer of the Watch
PTSD	Post Traumatic Stress Disorder
R and D	Research and Development
RFC	Royal Flying Corps
PR	Public Relations
QE	Queen Elizabeth class carriers
RAE	Royal Aircraft Establishment
R and D	Research and Development
RFC	Royal Fleet Auxiliary
RFC	Royal Flying Corp
RN	Royal Navy

RNAS	Royal Naval Air Service or Royal Naval Air Station
RNFS	Royal Navy Fighter School
RNVR	Royal Navy Volunteer Reserve
R and R	Rest and Recreation
ROK	Republic Of Korea
SAR	Search and Rescue
SAS	Special Air Service
SBS	Special Boat Service
SDR	Strategic Defence Review
SHRIKE	A US developed anti-radiation missile
SMR	Senior Maintenance Rating
SRVL	Shipborne Rolling and Vertical Landings
STOVL	Short Take Off Vertical Landing
TAG	Tail Air Gunner
Tiffy	Artificer
TSR 1	Torpedo, Strike and Reconnaissance 1 nomenclature for the Fairey Swordfish.
TSR 1	Torpedo, Strike and Reconnaissance Mark 1
UN	United Nations
USAAF	United States Army Air Force
USMC	United States Marine Corp
USN	United States Navy
USSR	United Socialist Soviet Republic
VE	Victory in Europe
VSTOL	Vertical or Short Take Off and Landing
WT	Wireless Telegraphy
WWII	World War Two